PSYCHIC BREAKTHROUGHS TODAY

Fascinating Encounters with
Parapsychology's Latest Discoveries

PSYCHIC BREAKTHROUGHS TODAY

Fascinating Encounters with Parapsychology's Latest Discoveries

D. Scott Rogo

THE AQUARIAN PRESS

Wellingborough, Northamptonshire

First Published 1987

© D. SCOTT ROGO 1987

British Library Cataloguing in Publication Data

Rogo, D. Scott
Psychic breakthroughs today.
1. Psychical research
I. Title
133'.072   BF1031

ISBN 0-85030-570-5

*The Aquarian Press is part of the
Thorsons Publishing Group*

Printed and bound in Great Britain.

Contents

For Jay Keenan,
in gratitude for his friendship

Preface

Psychic Breakthroughs Today represents an up-to-date examination of parapsychology and its newest discoveries. Research into the byways of extrasensory perception and psychokinesis (the 'mind over matter' effect) is taking place around the world. This research is becoming more and more diversified; so much so that it is becoming progressively more difficult to keep abreast of the latest findings. This volume is designed to take a look at over a dozen of the field's newest, most provocative (and fruitful) horizons. Topics such as whether the weather can disturb or enhance psychic functioning, whether psychic powers can be tapped, whether there exists a seat for psychic phenomena within the structure of the brain — these are the subjects with which contemporary researchers are grappling more seriously than ever, though the results of their search have too often been buried in technical journals or scientific publications. This research will be summarized — some of it for the first time — and presented in popular form for the reader.

To keep this book as contemporary as possible, I have tried to limit my coverage to research conducted within the field from roughly 1970 to the present. For some chapters, however, I have had to offer considerable historical background in order to keep the more current research in proper perspective. (In fact, chapter three is *more* historical than current, since the reports included in that chapter help to set the stage for the exciting research chronicled in chapter four. But this is an exception that is not repeated anywhere else in the book.)

The fact that parapsychology *is* such a burgeoning field is the primary reason for writing this volume. By focusing on selected topics currently being studied by those most actively engaged in the field, the reader will be able to get a bird's eye view of the exciting new directions in which the field is moving. He/she will also be getting a crash course in the new technology the field is developing in order to isolate the sixth sense, and share in the adventure as researchers around the world collect even more fascinating proof of the reality of psychic phenomena. What is even more exciting is that researchers within more conventional disciplines are currently studying the paranormal. This is especially true of medicine.

The voices of the sceptics have been just as active and prominent, however. So to keep this book somewhat balanced, the thinking and writings of some of parapsychology's most vocal critics will also be cited . . . and answered from my own perspective as a researcher working regularly in the field.

Some of these chapters have been adapted from articles that originally appeared in *Fate* magazine. They have been expanded, revised, and substantially rewritten for the purposes of this volume. Thanks are extended to the editors of *Fate* for allowing the use of this material in the present and revised form. Chapter nine was co-authored with Mr Rodger Anderson, a writer on philosophical topics with an expertise in parapsychology. It originally appeared in *Fate* magazine under Mr Anderson's name, but it has been totally revised, edited and rewritten for the purposes of this book. This chapter evolved from a correspondence between us on the nature of the survival controversy, but the views expressed herewithin are solely my own.

D. Scott Rogo

Northridge, California
May, 1986

1.

The Case for Parapsychology

Parapsychology is a young science, but it isn't a new discipline. Its roots go back to the end of the Victorian Age, when the Society for Psychical Research was founded in England. Back then psychical research was predominantly concerned with the survival issue, the study of whether we can psychically communicate with the souls of the dead. The field began to change radically during the years separating the two world wars, when psychical research finally entered the psychology laboratory to study extrasensory perception. There it found its roosting place, changed its name to parapsychology, and never left the cosiness of behavioural science. While science and conventional psychology tended to shun psychical research, the experimental science of parapsychology slowly began winning the interest of the scientific establishment. When the consciousness explosion of the 1960s and 1970s revolutionized Western culture, parapsychology finally came of age.

Parapsychology today has been firmly recognized by the scientific establishment. This doesn't mean that every scientist believes in the existence of psychic phenomena, only that the field is generally recognized as a legitimate field of study. Within recent years, for example, symposia on parapsychology have been arranged at the annual meetings of the American Association for the Advancement of Science. Over ten years ago, in 1975, Dr J. B. Rhine — the father of experimental parapsychology — was invited to give a keynote address to the American Psychological Association. Papers on extrasensory perception and psychokinesis are likewise finding their place in such normally reserved publications as *Nature*, the *Journal of Communications, Omega — The Journal of Death and Dying,* and *Perceptual and Motor Skills.* These journals represent the voice-boxes of the scientific community, and the fact that their pages are opening up to parapsychology is more than revealing.

Parapsychology, however, has always had its critics and debunkers. Despite a century of solid research, these critics still complain that parapsychology is a slipshod science at best, and a pseudo-science at its worst. Parapsychologists have not been immune from personal attacks either. They have been accused of everything from engaging in a fruitless search for proof of the 'supernatural' to downright fraud.

So who can make the better case, the parapsychologist or the debunker? Before turning to the subject of today's psychic breakthroughs, this issue cannot be ignored.

The Sceptic's Position

What are the chief criticisms of the sceptics? They break down into several categories, and oddly, they haven't changed very much over the decades. For instance, Champe Ransom — then a research associate working at the University of Virginia's parapsychology division — surveyed several contemporary criticisms of the field in 1971. He found that these criticisms could be grouped into nine major categories:

1. Parapsychology has no repeatable experimental findings.
2. Many so-called 'conclusive' experiments 'proving' the existence of extrasensory perception and psychokinesis were contaminated by fraud — either by the subjects or by the experimenters.
3. Parapsychologists use improper statistical procedures when they evaluate their data.
4. Extrasensory perception and psychokinesis are *a priori* (i.e., scientifically) impossible.
5. Parapsychologists consistently misinterpret their evidence.
6. The existence of psi (a collective term for ESP and PK) has no relevance to the organized body of knowledge collected by conventional science.
7. Parapsychologists make use of inadequate experimental designs.
8. They disagree about their own evidence.
9. They are biased in favour of the existence of psychic phenomena.

It is interesting to note that J. Fraser Nicol, a scholar of the field from Lexington, Massachusetts, conducted a similar survey in 1955. During a presentation he made to a Ciba Foundation symposium on parapsychology, he listed some of the same basic criticisms. So while parapsychology has grown increasingly sophisticated during the last three decades, its critics have not!

Readers with a strong sense of scientific objectivity should be able to see that some of these criticisms are not really cogent, since they represent simple value judgements. The fact that parapsychologists believe in psi is no more damning than the fact that physicists believe in sub-atomic particles. Similarly, whether or not the field's findings will eventually be relevant to the rest of science bears very little on the experimental case for extrasensory perception and psychokinesis. Nor does contemporary science know enough about the universe to declare that *anything* is *a priori* impossible or not. Some of the other criticisms the sceptics still like to raise were invalidated years ago. This is certainly true of their claim that parapsychologists rely on improper statistical procedures while evaluating the results of their experiments. As far back as 1937, the American Institute of Mathematics certified that the statistics used by parapsychologists were totally valid. It should also be stressed that the methodology and statistics used in parapsychology were not invented by parapsychologists, but were borrowed from those widely used in experimental psychology. The sceptic who believes that parapsychologists rely on faulty experimental methods and statistics is thereby condemning experimental psychology as well. If parapsychology fails on these counts, then all experimental science falls with it.

There are really only three criticisms of parapsychology which are fundamentally valid: that fraud can explain the positive results we see in the laboratory; that parapsychologists constantly misinterpret their findings; and that the field lacks repeatability.

Frankly though, none of these criticisms can begin to explain the strong and impressive results reported from the world's top parapsychology centres every year. The establishment of sophisticated parapsychology laboratories — such as those within Princeton University's engineering department and the Psychophysical Research Laboratories in New Jersey — has finally given research workers both the technology and the personnel to protect against experimenter error and fraud. Fraud has certainly been uncovered from time to time within the field, but experimenter and subject fraud is a problem to which every science is prone.* But let's look at these three criticisms in more depth anyway, since considerable recent research has gone far to answer them.

The Case Against Fraud

The case against fraud has been growing ever since the field began developing its own special technology. The sheer complexity of many sophisticated parapsychology experiments virtually excludes the problem of fraud on the part of the subject. The use of totally automated equipment has likewise eliminated experimenter fraud and recording error. The extensive research of Dr Helmut Schmidt is typical of this technological study of psi.

Dr Schmidt is German by birth and education, but came to the United

States after receiving his Phd in physics. While working at the Boeing Research Laboratories in Seattle, Washington, in the 1960s, he became the first parapsychologist to appreciate fully the importance of relying on automated ESP and PK experiments. So he began building his own equipment. For one of his first crucial experiments, he built a random generator run by a piece of strontium-90. It is well known that the decay of a radioactive particle is a totally random process, since it is impossible to predict the exact time an electron will shoot off from any particular atom. They shoot off at random intervals, and travel in random directions. This principle became the cornerstone of Dr Schmidt's apparatus, which also contained a high-speed oscillator. This oscillator continually switched rapidly between four possible positions. When the machine was activated by the subject or experimenter, it would stop randomly in any one of the positions. This position was determined as soon as the *next* electron was emitted by the strontium-90 and registered by a Geiger-Muller tube built into the apparatus. Each subject for this ESP (in this case precognition) test sat before a panel of four lights, each corresponding to one of the four positions. He or she was simply instructed to guess which light would be illuminated by the next decaying electron. The subject made his/her choice by pushing a button, and the machine stopped within milli-seconds of being signalled by the Geiger-Muller tube. The guess and the corresponding target were then simultaneously recorded by the machine. The subject received immediate feedback whether he/she was right or wrong, since the correct light would go on when the guess was made. By chance, Dr Schmidt's experimental subjects should have been successful 25 per cent of the time, but that wasn't what happened.

During his first tests in Seattle, Dr Schmidt ran across some subjects capable of scoring considerably beyond chance expectation, which showed that these subjects were *precognizing* either the rate of the radioactive decay, or seeing which light would illuminate next. For example, one of the physicist's subjects completed 7600 trials with the machine, and succeeded in making 165 more hits than chance could account for. The odds against such a success rate occurring by chance are about 100,000 to 1. Dr Schmidt then worked with three additional gifted subjects. Their combined scores were even better. Their results would have only occurred by chance once every 500,000,000 times the experiment was conducted! To be even more certain of his results, Dr Schmidt ran a 'control' series with the machine after the experiment was completed. This control test was conducted by pushing the guess buttons randomly, with no reliance on the sixth sense. These results were right at chance level, so we can reasonably assume that the machine was not malfunctioning during the previous experiments.

Dr Schmidt later reworked his generator so that it could be used for testing psychokinesis. For these new tests, the subject tried to *make* the apparatus stop in a certain position or positions. These experiments introduced a phenomenon generically called *micro-PK* to the parapsychological world — i.e., the direct influence of the mind to modify events transacting at a sub-atomic (quantum) level. For one of his first experiments into the byways of psychokinesis, Dr Schmidt built a simpler version of his random number generator (or RNG). This machine incorporated two outputs instead of the four used in his original equipment, though this RNG was linked to a display panel consisting of nine light bulbs set in a circular formation. When the RNG was activated, the machine oscillated randomly between the two (+1 and −1) positions before stopping at the target for the individual trial. Each experiment entailed, of course, a considerable number of such choices. When a succession of +1 positions were chosen by the RNG, the bulbs would light progressively and sequentially around the circle. But the display would backstep itself each time a −1 was chosen. Of course, under controlled conditions, the lights would produce a random walk around the circle, going backward and forward erratically and unreliably. So the subject's job was to will the lights to move consistently in the *forward* direction. The only way the subject could perform this feat was by interacting with the generator. He or she had to use psychokinesis to force the RNG to lose randomness, thereby biasing it to produce more +1s than −1s.

Dr Schmidt employed the services of eighteen subjects for his first experiment, but they tended to score in the *negative* direction. (In other words, the lights tended to go in the reverse direction from the subject's conscious choice — but sometimes to a statistically significant degree.) Some of the physicist's subjects succeeded more forthrightly, but Dr Schmidt wisely decided to see if his subjects could produce this curious 'psi-missing' effect deliberately. These later tests were highly successful.

The use of RGNs — which are impervious to subject fraud — soon became common to most parapsychology laboratories. Replication of the small-scale precognition and micro-PK effect were soon being reported by several other parapsychologists. Dr Schmidt later extended his research to see if animals could use psychokinesis to influence his generators, but that story will be told in a later chapter of this book.

Even after fifteen years, Dr Schmidt's findings represent some of the best parapsychology can offer. Few sceptics have successfully challenged his findings or experimental designs, and today, twenty years later, dozens of similar experiments proving the existence of the micro-PK effect have been reported.

The Case Against Misinterpretation

Do parapsychologists misinterpret their experimental results? This is extremely doubtful. To begin with, the (statistical) results for some psi experiments are simply extraordinary. The scores are so far beyond chance that only ESP can successfully explain them. Some research recently undertaken by Dr Charles Tart of the University of California at Davis, represents a strong case in point.

Dr Tart designed his experiments to determine whether some people can learn to *improve* their ESP scoring with practice. The psychologist implemented his research by using ESP 'teaching' machines. The first of these is commercially available to the general public and consists of a box complete with a front panel showing four geometric shapes. A corresponding push-button is placed next to each of them. When the machine is activated by the subject or the experimenter, its internal circuitry randomly selects one of the shapes, which becomes the target for the trial. (This information is stored within the device.) The subject

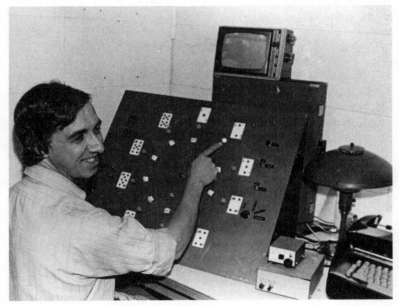

Dr Charles Tart with his ten-choice ESP training machine. (Dr Charles Tart)

guesses which target has been chosen by pushing the corresponding button, although he can pass should he prefer. (The target can then be re-selected.) If the subject guesses correctly, the target will illuminate and a pleasant chime will ring. The machine also keeps constant track of the subject's progressive scoring. If the subject consistently succeeds while making his/her guesses, special panels set in the console will begin to light up — flashing such encouraging signs as 'good beginning' or 'useful in Las Vegas' or 'outstanding ESP ability'. Dr Tart constructed his second machine himself. The main console for this training device consists of a circular configuration of ten playing-card faces. Each has a pilot light and push-button by it. Since this machine is especially designed for experiments in telepathy, a duplicate console is placed in a separate room for the experimenter's convenience and the two devices are electrically linked. When the experimenter randomly chooses a target from his room, he signals the subject, who merely presses the button on his own console which he feels corresponds to the card that is being sent to him. The experimenter or 'sender' can also monitor the subject by closed-circuit television, so that he or she can watch the subject while he/she is making the guesses.

The idea behind these experiments was to provide the subject with constant and immediate feedback. Dr Tart hoped that this procedure would help each of them to get the 'feel' for when they were genuinely responding through extrasensory perception, and not merely guessing at the target choices. Dr Tart screened dozens of students with the machine, hoping to find subjects who could score significantly with it. Several weeks of testing went by before he found these promising subjects. He then set about working with them, in hopes of finding their ESP scores steadily improving the more they practised.

He eventually published his first set of findings in 1975, where he reported that most of his subjects found their ESP scores stabilizing and not progressively declining — which often happens when subjects are tested too much. But some of his subjects did gradually improve with time and practice. Those who steadily improved racked up cumulative scores too extraordinary to be coincidental. Some of the best subjects scored against chance at rates of millions-to-one. With results this astonishing, there is little chance that Dr Tart was misinterpreting his findings.

Of course, not every sceptic will be impressed with data such as these. They want to see more obvious evidence for the sixth sense. They argue that the laws of probability are complicated by flukes, upon which parapsychologists have been capitalizing for years. Luckily though, not every parapsychology experiment relies solely on guessing strategies. Starting in the 1960s, researchers began to focus away from such 'forced-choice' tests to pursue 'free-response' experiments. These are experiments during which the subject is asked to respond to a pictorial target, usually sent to him/her by telepathy. Some parapsychologists prefer this type of experiment because the results can be dramatic, and sometimes the process by which the sixth sense works becomes obvious by studying the way the target is received and described by the subject. Precognition can also be tested by way of free-response strategies. For these tests the subject tries to describe a picture to be chosen by the experimenters in the future. Successful free-response precognition tests are especially impressive since subject fraud cannot serve as a factor during them. Since the target isn't chosen when the experiment is run, he can't peek!

An excellent example of a free-response precognition test was conducted in Brooklyn in 1970. Researchers at the Maimonides Medical Center were interested in whether dreams could foretell the future, so they decided to explore the possibility that summer. A single subject was recruited for the experiments — Malcolm Bessent, a young British psychic known for his many successful predictions.

The experiment the researchers subsequently designed took over two weeks to complete. The subject slept at the Brooklyn laboratory for sixteen nights, during which his brainwaves were constantly monitored. Every *other* night he was requested to dream about a picture to be chosen the following day. The EEG tracings from Bessent's brain were watched throughout the night by a research assistant, who woke him up periodically when they showed that he was dreaming. The groggy subject would then report (via an intercom system) the contents of his dreams before going back to sleep. Twelve hours after this procedure had been completed, early the next morning, another experimenter — who remained totally ignorant of Bessent's reports — randomly selected a target packet from a pool of them kept at the centre. These packets contained thematically-linked slides and tapes of related music. When the target selection was finally made, the subject watched the slides while listening to the tapes.

The results of these tests were simply amazing. For example, the target packet for one of the experiments was entitled 'police'. The night before this packet was chosen, Bessent reported dreaming about people in uniform, confrontations between students and armed guards, a police state, and so on:

> It's like getting the armed guard or something, because if they arrive half an hour later and contribute nothing except silence and a kind of menacing

silence . . . I forget what you call them in the States, kind of young policemen, but a particular kind to do with campus disorders . . . I wish I could remember the name — National Guard, perhaps . . .

For another night's experiment, the target chosen the next day was entitled 'birds'. This seemed to be a success, for Bessent had reported dreaming the night before about a parapsychologist well known for his psychological research on birds! He was also able to focus more clearly on the target. 'I remember seeing various different kinds of doves,' he had reported the night before concerning another of his dreams, 'Ringtailed doves, ordinary doves, Canadian geese. There were many, many different kinds of varieties.'

Even Bessent realized that the forthcoming target would concern birds, and told his experimenters so!

In order to demonstrate that these correspondences were genuinely due to precognition, the researchers in charge of the experiments took things a step further by statistically evaluating the results. They took the transcripts for each night's dreams and randomized them. They then gave these sets of (randomized) transcripts to a blind (i.e., independent) judge, who was provided with the target slides. His job was to read through the transcripts and try to correctly match each set to the corresponding slides. He had little difficulty. So for this experiment, we have statistical proof (by way of the judge's rankings) for extrasensory perception as well as strong descriptive evidence.[†]

The Problem of Repeatability
Probably the most serious charge the sceptics like to make is that parapsychology has no repeatable experiment. Even for promising lines of research, the field's findings rarely seem consistent. The sceptics charge that findings that can't be replicated can't be called findings; and a science without findings can't be considered a science. There is some truth to this position. But the fact remains that there is some replicability within parapsychology, and some of it is downright impressive.

The fact that certain experimental patterns often recur during the course of many ESP experiments is a form of replication. In fact, these repeating trends tend to be every bit as convincing, when evaluated retrospectively, as the results procured from so-called 'conclusive' experiments. For if the existence of extrasensory perception were a delusion, why would so many researchers — working totally independently of each other — constantly discover the same patterns in their results? A good example of this phenomenon occurred during the first years after experimental parapsychology's birth. When Dr J.B. Rhine began working with his ESP card-guessing experiments at Duke University in the 1930s, he discovered that his best subjects uniformly scored better during the beginning of a session than toward the end. This frequently-observed pattern soon became known as the 'decline' effect. But Rhine was not the first researcher to notice this curious pattern in his data. Several years earlier, Dr George Estabrooks had discovered the same phenomenon while conducting some telepathy tests at Harvard University. Researchers working with statistical card-guessing experiments in England found the same declines in *their* data.

Parapsychology's critics think they know the explanation for the decline effect, though. They claim that these experimenters merely elicited some spurious extra-chance scoring during the first runs of their tests, which they mistakenly took for ESP.[§] They then discontinued their experiments when their subjects' scores regressed back to chance. This explanation certainly sounds reasonable, but these early decline effects even occurred during experiments for which the specific number of card-guessing runs was determined in advance.

The next repeatable effect discovered by parapsychologists was the so-called sheep/goat effect. The roots of this fascinating finding go back to 1958, when Dr Gertrude Schmeidler — then a psychologist at City College in New York — revealed the pattern in her book *ESP and Personality Patterns*. This slim volume represented the results of a series of experiments comparing the ESP scores for people who believed in ESP with the scores for a similar group of sceptical subjects. Dr Schmeidler tested her subjects with standard ESP cards (printed randomly with either a star, square, cross, circle or wavy lines), and her findings were repeatedly consistent. The combined scores of the sheep (the believers) were slightly above chance, while the corresponding scores for the goats (the disbelievers) constantly fell below. The difference between the subject populations was often statistically significant. Dr Schmeidler publicly reported her findings only after replicating her discovery several times.

Very few sceptics have dared to tackle the phenomenon of the sheep/goat effect. The usual explanation they give is that these experiments were probably biased to favour the believers. But how? Dr Schmeidler used the exact same experimental procedures while testing both sets of subjects. So either her results represent some sort of fluke, or they represent a genuine finding about the psi process. The only way to resolve this issue was through replication, so several *other* parapsychologists began replicating Dr Schmeidler's sheep/goat research when her book was published. The results of their explorations were fascinating. Sometimes the replications never reached statistical significance, but the goats *never* seemed capable of scoring better than the sheep. So let's take a more detailed look at these studies. What are they revealing?

The best answer I know of comes from Dr John Palmer, who offered it when he was a research associate at the division of parapsychology at the University of Virginia. In 1971 he published a critical examination of all reported sheep/goat experiments run between 1958 and 1968. This body of research consisted of seventeen series of experiments carried out by twelve experimenters (or experimenter teams) working independently. Six of these projects, close to a third, upheld the sheep/goat effect. For some of the other experiments, the sheep failed to outscore the goats to a significant degree, but no experiments were reported for which the goats *ever* significantly outscored the sheep. In other words, no significant *reversal* of the sheep/goat effect has ever been reported, while the replication rate stands at an impressive 30 per cent. Even today, fifteen years after Dr Palmer's important survey, the sheep/goat effect is still holding up, sound and healthy. Dr Palmer returned to the sheep/goat effect in 1978 and re-evaluated his earlier findings in the light of even more studies. His general conclusions remained the same, and he was still able to report that 'all the significant sheep/goat differences have been in the predicted direction; none of the reversals has even approached significance.'

The sheep/goat effect is only a single instance of parapsychology's replicability record, for several other personality factors seem consistently linked to extrasensory perception as well.

A Final Evaluation

I hope this chapter has shown that parapsychologists are serious and critical scientists occupied with a very important — perhaps crucially important — field of study. Parapsychology is a descriptive science in that it collects, analyses, and seeks to corroborate the psychic experiences of people like you and me. But the field is also an experimental science, since it is hoping to explore the secrets of ESP and psychokinesis by testing theories about them in the laboratory. To do so, it has been forced to borrow its methodology from experimental psychology and, more recently, physics. So as a science, it has nothing for which it should apologize. In fact, the field represents the Western scientific ethic at its best.

Dr D.J. West is a British psychiatrist who left parapsychology in the 1960s to pursue a career in behavioural research. Returning to the subject of his first love in 1970, he summed up this point concisely and forcefully while speaking before an international conference on parapsychology which convened in St Paul de Vence, France. He stated that:

> ... having had my first taste of research in the field of parapsychology, and then gone on to work in other branches of behavioral research, I am continually struck by the contrast in standards. Research workers in conventional fields of social and psychological inquiry are content with much lower standards. They are prepared to base conclusions upon observations known to be subject to a certain amount of bias and inaccuracy, and they are prepared to accept statistical evidence that falls short of certainty. If they tried to emulate the perfectionism advocated by some parapsychologists, the quality of their investigations might be improved.

I hope every reader of this book will ponder these words deeply as they read the experiments and case reports that fill the following chapters.

End-Notes for Chapter One

* For an in-depth look at the widespread problem of fraud in science, please refer to William Broad and Nicholas Wade, *Betrayers of the Truth.* (New York: Simon & Schuster, 1982.)

† This experiment evolved from a lengthy exploration into the psychic world of dreams carried out in Brooklyn, NY during the 1960s and early '70s. The story behind this research will be told in greater detail in the next chapter.

§ A run is a series of twenty-five card-guesses. Several runs constitute an experimental series.

2.

Isolating the Sixth Sense

Parapsychologists generally believe that everyone possesses some power of extrasensory perception. We know this from our experience in the laboratory, from the fact that so many people come in and do well on our tests — even if they have never had a conscious psychic experience before. Given the correct instructions and expectations, it seems that any of us can use the sixth sense.

But if ESP is such a common talent, why is it such a capricious ability? Why are psychic experiences so rare during our daily lives?

This is contemporary parapsychology's primary dilemma. We know that ESP is a widespread capability, but we often find it difficult to flush out of our subjects. Some of the problem lies with the nature of the sixth sense itself, which is a primarily unconscious process. So in this chapter, we will be taking a look at some of the ways researchers are learning to tap into our psychic potentials.

The Nature of the ESP Process

When you or I have a conscious ESP experience — such as a precognitive dream or telepathic flash — we are actually witnessing the end result of a two-stage process. During the first stage, the unconscious mind receives an ESP message and then, if the message has been urgent enough, the unconscious mind transfers this information into the conscious mind. It is during this second stage that the problem arises. ESP impressions virtually have to 'fight' their way into our conscious minds. That's why vivid and conscious ESP experiences are apparently so rare. The idea that the reception of an ESP impression is a two-stage process is not idle speculation either, for there is a considerable amount of laboratory research that has proved the basically unconscious nature of ESP.

For example, some years ago, E. Douglas Dean (then a professor of electrical engineering at Newark College) designed an ingenious test to demonstrate that ESP can function at a totally unconscious level. He split up a pair of experimental subjects and placed them in separate rooms. One subject, called the 'receiver', was settled in a comfortable sitting-room and told to lie or sit there and relax while one of his fingers was hooked up to a plethysmograph. (A plethysmograph is an apparatus which gauges blood flow to various parts of the body. Any emotional upset or sudden stimulus disrupts this flow.) Dean knew that if his ESP subject were disturbed in any way, the plethysmograph would record it by printing out a 'dip' on a read-out chart. The other subject was placed in a room totally isolated from the receiver, and was given a group of cards to look at sequentially. Some were printed with names randomly drawn from a telephone book, others were blank, and some were printed with the names of persons emotionally linked to either the sender or the receiver. The sender was asked to look at each card for several seconds and then go on to the next. Each sender went through a series of several cards before the test was concluded.

The results of this test were amazing. Dean discovered that whenever the sender concentrated on names that were emotionally significant to the receiver (such as those of his friends or relatives), the subject's body reacted dramatically. Blood raced from his finger, thus causing a dip on the plethysmograph chart. So while the subject was consciously unaware that he had received an ESP message, his unconscious mind and physiology had duly responded to the telepathic signal.

This little experiment indicates that all of us probably receive ESP messages continually, even though we are unaware of them.

Despite the fact that ESP is an unconscious process, many people continually report conscious ESP experiences. These usually manifest in the form of telepathic or precognitive dreams, curious 'hunches' about what is happening to somebody we know, or even full-blown visual hallucinations. Note that these are all primarily unconscious processes. Dreams, hunches, intuitive impressions and hallucinations are all vehicles by which our unconscious minds push information into our conscious awareness. So it is also likely that dreams, intuitions and similar mediating vehicles can also serve as 'tricks' which the unconscious uses to deliver ESP messages to us.

When Sigmund Freud began his probings of the unconscious mind back around the turn of the century, he was grasping to find any technique which would help his patients become better aware of information hidden deep within their subconscious minds. Hypnosis, dream analysis, and free association were all tools he used to help his patients confront these dark recesses of the mind. Parapsychologists today are using similar techniques to help people gain access to their ESP potential.

Sleep and dreaming was one of the first roads to ESP which

parapsychologists were able to isolate. Everyone dreams, and dreams seem to be natural carriers of ESP messages.

The Discovery of Experimental Dream ESP

The first researcher to realize that dreaming might be *experimentally* used as a road to ESP was Dr Montague Ullman, a psychoanalyst and parapsychologist, who in 1962 established a dream laboratory at the Brooklyn, New York-centred Maimonides Medical Center. This multi-facility lab was founded and funded for the specific purpose of experimenting with ESP and dreaming. His first co-worker was Sol Feldstein, a doctoral student at the City College of the City University of New York. He was later joined by Dr Stanley Krippner and, later still, by Charles Honorton, who directed the lab for several years and implemented its move from Brooklyn to New Jersey where today it is one of the most active parapsychology research centres in the United States. Although the original Maimonides dream-ESP research was carried out over fifteen years ago, it set the stage for even more successful research being conducted today along roughly similar lines. The following type of experiment, which was carried out at Maimonides back in the 1960s, is typical of the kind of research in which the lab was engaged for several years.

An unselected, or paid volunteer, subject (i.e., a person who made no claims to psychic ability, or a proverbial 'man off the street') would be invited to spend a night or two at the lab. He would be tucked comfortably into bed in a special room where electrodes would be attached to his scalp. These led to another room where they were linked to an electro-encephalograph which monitored the subject's brain waves and eye movements during the course of the night. Whenever the EEG chart indicated that the subject's eyes were moving back and forth, this alerted the experimenters that the subject was dreaming. While this was going on, a sender would be stationed in another room at the lab. His job was to randomly select an art print from a group of similar pictures. He would then concentrate on sending the theme of the print to the sleeping subject every time he began to dream. Each time the subject was well into a dream, he would be awakened by an experimenter and asked to report his imagery over an intercom. The next day the subject would be shown several art prints and would be asked to pick out the one he thought had been sent to him telepathically as he slept the night before.

The Maimonides team had exceptionally good luck with this procedure. For instance, one night during their first experiments, the art target was

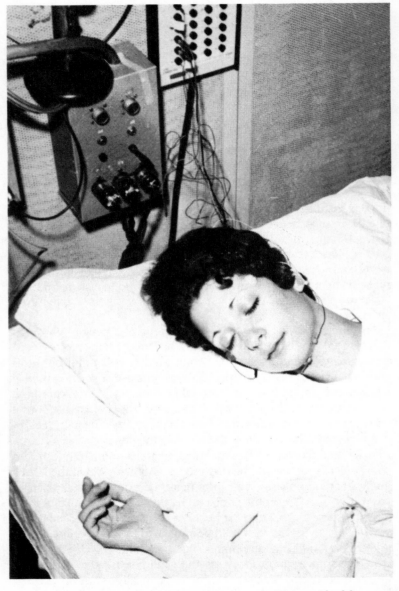

A subject taking part in a dream ESP experiment at the Maimonides laboratory in Brooklyn, New York. She has been linked up to a polygraph to monitor her brain waves. (Mary Evans)

Tamayo's savage painting *Animals*. This grotesque painting depicts two vicious dogs fighting over a piece of meat, tugging and ripping it apart. The sleep subject that night was a school teacher who did not claim to possess any great psychic talent. Yet she obviously incorporated the theme of the painting into her dreams in a most unusual way. As she reported about one of her dreams:

> I was at this banquet . . . and I was eating something like rib steak and this friend of mine was there . . . and people were talking about how she wasn't very good to invite for dinner because she was very conscious of other people getting more to eat than she got . . . That was the most important part of the dream, that dinner . . . It was probably Freudian like all my other dreams — you know, eating, and all that stuff, and a banquet. Well, there was another friend of mine, also in this dream. Somebody that I teach with, and she was eyeing everybody to make sure that everybody wasn't getting more than she was too. And I was chewing a piece of . . . rib steak. And I was sitting at the table, and other people were talking about this girl . . . and they were saying that she's not very nice to invite to eat because she's greedy, or something like that.

Notice how the theme of the print was reorganized and symbolized by the subject's mind in this dream. But the ESP message was there nonetheless.

During the succeeding years, the Maimonides team was able to demonstrate that their dream subjects could pick up more than just telepathic messages. Sometimes they asked their subjects to dream about art pictures that wouldn't be selected until the day *after* the dream session. Some of these precognition tests were just as successful as the dream-telepathy experiments. For other tests, the targets were sent from other cities, even projected on large screens during rock concerts!

The Maimonides dream work came to an end a few years ago, and it succeeded in telling us a great deal about our ESP potentials. Remember that most of the successful Maimonides subjects were not psychic superstars. They were fellow scientists, students, lay people interested in ESP, and many of them just participated because they could make a few bucks by acting as subjects. So this work tended to substantiate Rhine's view that ESP is an ability widespread among the general public. Furthermore these dream experiments indicated that, by paying attention to our dreams, we might all have a very natural and semi-consistent way of gaining access to our ESP abilities. Many people, for instance, keep dream diaries in which they diligently record all the dreams they have each night. Some of them have found that their dreams often reflect experiences they will undergo during the following day or two.

Not everybody remembers their dreams, though. So dreaming may not be the best way to gain access to our ESP talents. Dreams are often rather unclear. Transcribing them, trying to remember them in detail, and trying to decipher the symbolic language in which they communicate with us, can be a royal pain in the neck. So a few parapsychologist tried to find even simpler techniques which just about *anyone* could use to tap their ESP abilities.

The Discovery of the Ganzfeld

One of these techniques was the brainchild of Mr Charles Honorton, who (as previously mentioned) was one of the original Maimonides dream-ESP team and eventually took full charge of the laboratory. This innovative young researcher set the parapsychology scene ablaze in 1973 when he demonstrated an almost absurdly simple way of helping people gain access to their ESP abilities . . . abilities they probably didn't even know they had. Like most discoveries in parapsychology, this story, too, had a bit of a background.

For some years now, psychologists interested in visual perception have toyed with what is called ganzfeld stimulation. Ganzfeld simply means 'homogenous field.' These psychologists were interested in discovering what psychological and visual effects would occur if a person were made to stare into a totally blank visual field. (For instance, staring pointedly at a white sheet would constitute a ganzfeld.) A few of these psychologists even began wondering what would happen if these same subjects were made to listen to white noise (such as static of the sort you might pick up between radio stations) at the same time. What they discovered was interesting, to say the least. Most of their subjects began 'hallucinating' or envisioning daydream-like images against the ganzfeld.

Now as pointed out previously, ESP often manifests in the form of dreams, visions, and other types of mental imagery. So, around 1972, Honorton realized that the ganzfeld might be used to help people have ESP experiences. In other words, he figured that these artificially induced daydream-like images might be experimentally used to 'carry' ESP information from a sender to a receiver. And he was soon able to prove his point when, in 1973, he began a series of ingenious explorations into the ganzfeld setting.

For his first experiment, Honorton individually tested thirty non-selected subjects. Most of them were either lab or hospital staff members, while the others were mainly happenstance visitors to the Maimonides centre. Each subject was placed in a soundproof booth, where he was comfortably seated in a soft reclining chair. In order to establish a ganzfeld setting for the subject, halved ping-pong balls were fastened over his or her eyes. Cotton was wedged into any light leaks if the balls didn't affix tightly enough. A red light was then directed at the subject. The ping-pong balls diffused the illumination, so all that the subject could see was a perfectly uniform, reddish visual field. Earphones were placed on his head next, and the sound of monotonous ocean waves pitching to and fro was played through them.* Each subject was instructed to relax and report over an intercom all the thoughts, images and feelings he would experience during the next thirty-five minutes. While informed that an agent would send him a 'message' by ESP at some point during the test, the subject was told not to try to guess or anticipate it.

While the subject was being set up in the ganzfeld, an agent was placed in another room. At a random time during the experiment, his job was to pick out a reel of Viewmaster slides from a collection of several dozen. At another randomly chosen time, he then tried to 'send' the pictures depicted on the reel to the subject for a five minute period. When the session was over, the subject was given four reels to look at and was asked to choose which one best matched what he had 'seen' while in the ganzfeld.

Honorton's experiment was an outstanding success. Out of his first thirty subjects, close to half of them showed some indication of ESP while undergoing the test. Quite often their mental imagery closely matched or reflected the Viewmaster scenes previously sent to them telepathically. One subject's target, for example, was a reel of US Air Force Academy scenes. As the subject reported during part of her session:

'. . . An airplane floating over the clouds . . . Planes passing overhead . . . Thunder now, angry clouds . . . Airplanes . . . Ultrasound . . . A blaze of fire, red flames. A five-pointed star . . . An airplane pointing down . . '

She later continued:

'A giant bird flying. Six stripes on an army uniform, V-shaped. A face from the stripes. Now a V. . .A mountain range snow-capped. Flying through the mountain . . . The sensation of going forward very fast . . . Machine gun. A ladder.'

Another subject was telepathically sent a reel entitled 'Birds of the World.' At one point during the test he reported over the intercom, 'I sense a large hawk's head in front of me, a profile. The sense of sleek feathers. Now it turns and flies away.'

However, Honorton and his co-workers were in for a bit of a surprise when they sat down to seriously analyse their data. They found that sometimes their subjects correctly described the Viewmaster scenes *before* the agent had started sending them or even looking at them. These subjects didn't seem to be picking up their ESP impressions from the minds of the senders. It looked more as if their minds were picking up this information directly from the reels or had actually looked right into the future!

After Honorton reported on the success of the ganzfeld technique in the April 1974 issue of the *Journal of the American Society for Psychical Research*, several other parapsychologists working in other labs across the United States began experimenting with the procedure. In fact, research into the ganzfeld was being carried out both in the United States and Europe *while* Honorton was still collecting his original data.

ESP and the Importance of Imagery

Probably the most critical of these experiments was conducted by Dr William Braud and his (now former) wife, Dr Lendell Braud, in Texas at the University of Houston. These two researchers realized that the procedure their colleague in Brooklyn was using was flawed on one important count. Honorton had experimented with each and every one of his subjects in the ganzfeld and had not bothered to use a control group of subjects who remained normally awake and alert. So while the ganzfeld certainly worked as a psi-conducive induction procedure for the Brooklyn researcher, there was little evidence that it worked any better than just asking a group of people to close their eyes and *think* about the target picture. The Brauds rectified this procedural flaw by conducting their experiment with both an experimental and a control group. The formal ganzfeld was employed with half of their subjects, while the remaining subjects were asked merely to close their eyes and try to receive impressions of the target. The result of this experiment showed that the ganzfeld *was* especially linked to the emergence of ESP impressions. Their ganzfeld subjects uniformly succeeded in picking up elements of the targets being sent to them, while the control subjects just as consistently failed.

The fact that the ganzfeld is not perfect at inducing a psi-conducive state of consciousness was, however, also discovered at this same time but elsewhere. The early 1970s saw the initiation of a doctoral programme in parapsychology at the University of Edinburgh in Scotland. One of the first students to take part in the programme was Adrian Parker, a young psychologist who had trained originally in London but who was eager to embark on a career in parapsychology. Parker also began experimenting with the ganzfeld in the early 1970s, but his results were rather poor.

The fact that Parker's research did not pan out too well did not deter other researchers from exploring the parameters of the ganzfeld. By 1977 — only a few years after Honorton first reported his results — eight experiments using the procedure had been run at the Brooklyn centre alone. Seven of these turned out successfully (that is, the results were statistically significant). This is an enormously impressive confirmation rate, but the replications did not end there by any means. By 1977 replications of the ganzfeld effect had also been run at fifteen other parapsychology laboratories, and eight of these elicited significant results. This represents a 50 per cent cross-laboratory replication rate, which is an extraordinarily robust one in parapsychology.

Ganzfeld research is still going strong in parapsychology, although perhaps not with the same zeal with which the procedure was pursued during the 1970s. The cross-laboratory replication rate has continued to be impressively high, and seems to be levelling off at about 40 per cent.

This does not mean that several critics haven't tried to explain away these spectacular results. The sceptics were, in fact, able to discover an important and embarrassing flaw in some of the early ganzfeld work. Sometimes the targets viewed by the senders were the same pictures and slides subsequently given to the experimental subjects to evaluate. This led sceptics to posit that the senders could be marking the correct pictures, perhaps even inadvertently, by leaving tell-tale finger marks on them. (This became known as the greasy finger theory.) This was certainly a valid theory, and it could explain the statistical significance of the tests. It could not, however, explain the strong correspondences that often occurred between the subject's psychic impressions and the target pictures. So the greasy finger theory was only a partial explanation for the efficacy of the ganzfeld, as even some of the more reasonable sceptics were willing to admit. This flaw in the ganzfeld procedure was, however, soon rectified by the use of duplicate target pools. The success rate of these more properly designed experiments have been just as successful as the earlier and conceivably 'flawed' experiments.

But why should the ganzfeld be so efficacious in helping ordinary and very un-psychic people receive ESP impressions so consistently? There are a number of answers to this question.

We live in a fast-moving world which keeps our minds and bodies going at a frantic pace. We really don't have much time to pay attention to our innermost thoughts and feelings. We're just too preoccupied with our work, worries, finances, love-lives and business dealings to bother about what's going on in our heads. But in the ganzfeld we get the time.

Sitting comfortably and cut off from the disturbing sights and sounds which bombard us constantly during the course of an average day, we can be alone with our thoughts. While in this state, it may well be that we can *allow* ESP impressions to surface into our conscious minds, and we can tap our own inner potentials in a way impossible to us during our day-to-day bustling lives.

It should also be pointed out that the mind becomes starved for stimulation while in the ganzfeld. It can't hear or see anything, so it becomes vigilant in its readiness to latch on to any form of stimulation. In other words, our minds start wandering about *looking* for something to stimulate it and keep it from shutting down into sleep. Any incoming ESP messages might just fit the bill.

The results of ganzfeld research also hold out a very special promise to those of us interested in the possibility that some day we might be able to teach people to be psychic. I learned this lesson by way of a dramatic personal experience in the ganzfeld. I first told this story in my previous book *Our Psychic Potentials*,† but it so germane to this chapter that I would like to retell it here.

While I've had my share of little inconsequential psychic experiences, I certainly don't consider myself to be the least bit psychic, but this has never deterred me from conducting experimental work in parapsychology. I was travelling frequently to New York from Los Angeles in 1975, since at that time I had a grant to do ESP research and wanted to explore the ganzfeld. I was conducting experiments both at the University of California at Los Angeles, and at the Maimonides lab as part of this grant. Every good experimenter should know what his subjects are undergoing during his tests, so I also began using myself as a subject every so often just to get a better 'feel' for the subjective experience of the ganzfeld. I eventually began to like the ganzfeld and the sense of relaxation which accompanies the state, and every now and then, my mentation started to match the content of the ESP targets sent to me for these impromptu experiments. But then something happened which really startled me and got me thinking about how the ganzfeld might be used for ESP training.

I had just arrived in New York from Los Angeles and went directly to the lab late that morning. Since I always take night flights to the east coast, I was pretty tired by the time I arrived at the Maimonides centre, since I had missed a night's sleep. But just after arriving there I learned that a ganzfeld session was being arranged to teach a new lab-worker how to run the test and manage all the recording equipment. I was asked to be the subject.

That ganzfeld session was different from any other in which I have ever participated. I was tired . . . almost sleepy and dozing . . . and, as I looked at the red field in front of me, brilliant images kept flashing in front of my eyes. I saw an African scene, with a pool of water surrounded by tall grass. I even thought I saw an animal near the pool but wasn't sure. Towards the end of the session I saw — in a brilliant vision — a bird-like figure with outstretched wings eerily silhouetted before a pale moon.

I was amazed when I eventually saw the picture which had been the ESP target for the session. Just about all of my spontaneous imagery matched portions of the very unusual picture my agent had been trying to send me. It depicted a forest scene which centred on a pool surrounded by tall grass toward which a leopard is seen creeping. A moon illuminates the scene from high in the sky, and a bat hovers before it suspended in air with outstretched wings.

My session had been an outstanding success.

But why, I thought, had this session been so successful while my other attempts in the ganzfeld had usually failed? The answer soon dawned on me. During the session I had been super-relaxed and almost asleep. I had therefore paid particular attention to those images appearing before my eyes just before I would have normally dozed off. Had I not had to verbally report these images over an intercom, I probably would have fallen asleep right in the isolation booth! During this session I had learned to report only truly spontaneous imagery, and was able to differentiate it from the normal mental noise generated by my conscious mind.

I am certainly not the only person who has been able to find a personal road to ESP, though. Many others have found that they have sometimes been able to develop very personal methods which help them learn and use ESP. Hypnagogic imagery seems to be my key to ESP, but others have found very different ways of tapping their ESP gifts. One British colleague of mine likes to sit in the ganzfeld and generate a specific image which he holds in mind until another image spontaneously replaces it. *That* is the image he reports to the experimenters.

I do not mean to suggest, though, that the ganzfeld is the only procedure parapsychologists use to help their subjects generate psi-mediated imagery. It is only one of many techniques.

Visualization, Relaxation and ESP

Dr Elmer Green is a world renowned expert on biofeedback and is director of the Voluntary Control Program at the Topeka, Kansas-based Menninger Foundation. Although a hard scientist by training, Green doesn't 'put down' ESP and he actually uses it in his life and work. As

he explains in his book *Beyond Biofeedback*, he relies on ESP whenever
he comes across a personal problem which he needs help in resolving.

Several years ago, Dr Green decided to organize a laboratory devoted
exclusively to biofeedback research. But where, he thought? To help
answer his own question he meditated on the problem in hopes of getting
a glimpse of where he might find a possible location.

He writes:

> The grassy fields and the building where I could have a laboratory were
> clearly seen, but they were obviously not in the desert. My immediate
> question about where to work had had the limited objective of determining
> what job to take at China Lake, but I had not specified this. If my question
> had been more specific (for instance, what would be useful to do
> immediately), perhaps the hypnagogic image would have been different;
> ask a general question and you are likely to get a general answer. As it was,
> the green grass, the tree-covered hill, and the buildings and tall clock tower
> of the image I saw did not exist where we were living. If this image was
> significant, I felt at the time, it applied to a future possibility, and I merely
> stored it in my memory . . .

It was only later that Green visited the Menninger Foundation on a lark
and recognized that his 'vision' corresponded to the west campus of
the Foundation. And his ESP images were correct on another count,
too. He was soon invited to join the Menninger staff, organize his laboratory,
and has been there ever since. So meditation is another viable method
for tapping the sixth sense.

Many parapsychologists have discovered that mental imagery — which
so often occurs near sleep or during meditation — is a natural carrier
of ESP information. So to tap our ESP abilities, it looks as though we
simply need to learn how to visualize (or at least observe) our mental
imagery. Interestingly enough, both parapsychologists and conventional
psychologists have been grappling with this same problem for years.

One visualization technique that is becoming increasingly popular
among clinical psychologists is called 'guided imagery.' It is a procedure
by which a psychologist can help his client learn how to daydream in
a meaningful way. The basic techniques of this procedure were first
developed by Dr Hanscarl Leuner of the University of Gottingen. As a
psychologist, he found that 'guiding' his patients through specially
structured daydreams had considerable therapeutic value. These
daydreams usually involved conflicts the patients were trying to resolve
and the imagery often helped them confront and understand their
problems. Leuner would even go so far as to take his patients on imaginary

trips; such as following a river to its source, walking through a meadow, or a similar procedure. The patient would often be asked to elaborate on what he was seeing or experiencing during these trips. Other psychologists have learned that guided imagery fantasies can help patients gain access to deep realms of the unconscious and even control deep-seated feelings and emotions.

But could guided imagery also help people gain access to ESP powers? Some tentative findings along these very lines were presented at the seventeenth annual convention of the Parapsychological Association (held at St John's University in Jamaica, New York, in August 1974) by Edward Charlesworth of the University of Houston.

For his unique experiment (which has yet to be replicated), Charlesworth had each of his subjects undergo what he calls an 'imaginary dream.' At the onset of the experiment, each subject was given relaxation exercises to carry out. These included muscle relaxation procedures and deep breathing exercises. Once the subject was relaxed, he was told to imagine a dream he might have had as a child. He was instructed to think about getting out of bed, walking through his bedroom closet, and into a grassy meadow. From there he was guided through the meadow, up and through a forest, on to a mountain, and down to a beach. At each stage of the imaginary dream, the subject was asked to envision something unusual. For example, if the subject were being led up a mountain, he would be told to imagine something that one would not normally expect to see there.

During this imaginary trip, an ESP sender was situated in another room at the university. Each time the subject was asked to imagine an unusual object or scene, the agent's job was to open a specially prepared envelope and stare at the picture inside. Of course, Charlesworth hoped that the subject would incorporate the picture viewed by the agent into the scene he was envisioning. The experiment was successful, but for some reason never excited the interest of fellow parapsychologists. One reason may be because the procedure is so much more involved and cumbersome to use than, say, the ganzfeld which is so simple and straightforward.

Although Charlesworth's experiment has not yet been replicated by other parapsychologists, his research at least indicates that many of us might be able to use common daydreaming to help us receive ESP messages.

By this time, you might have noticed a common thread which links together the ganzfeld work, Charlesworth's guided imagery experiment and meditation states. *All these procedures seem to work best if the subject is as relaxed as possible.* If one is looking for a solution to the ESP mystery, this certainly might be a critical clue. Physical relaxation may just be the simplest way yet known by which to help people develop ESP. And thanks to the outstanding research of two brilliant parapsychologists working in Texas during the 1970s, there exists considerable experimental evidence that indicates a crucial relationship between relaxation and ESP.

Dr William Braud, who was formerly a psychology professor at the University of Houston where he first conducted replications of the ganzfeld effect, is now a researcher in Texas at the San Antonio-based Mind Science Foundation. He and his former wife remain, even today, two of parapsychology's most eager young researchers. During the heyday of ganzfeld research, which preoccupied parapsychology in the 1970s, they experimented with everything from the ganzfeld to brain hemispheric dominance studies in their search to discover ESP-conducive states of mind. Beginning in 1973, the Brauds began regularly publishing a series of reports which indicated that simple muscular relaxation is an 'open sesame' to the psychic sense.

The following is just a sample of the type of experiments the Brauds conducted.

For one critical test they carried out at their Texas lab, the Brauds taught sixteen volunteer subjects to enter into a state of deep physical relaxation by having them progressively tense and relax each and every muscle of their bodies. The subjects were then asked to mentally image about a picture being sent to them telepathically from another room. Before learning how well they had done on the test, however, each subject was asked to rate himself on a ten point scale of relaxation. A low number represented extreme relaxation, while a high number indicated a normal to tense physical state.

The Brauds discovered that those subjects who had been successsful at the ESP task had given themselves a mean rating of 1.81.[§] They had, indeed, felt relaxed. The unsuccessful subjects only reported an average score of 3.12.

To further demonstrate a relationship between relaxation and ESP, the Brauds soon designed an even more stringent test. For this fascinating experiment, the couple did away with self-rating scales completely and instead hooked each subject to electrodes which monitored the tension levels of their forehead muscles. By continually monitoring these muscles, the experimenters were able to determine objectively just how relaxed their subjects were becoming during their ESP tests. The catch to the experiment was that two groups of volunteers were actually used for this test. One group was given relaxation exercises to carry out before the actual ESP test, while the others were led through *tension* exercises.

After this procedure was completed, each subject was asked to image about an art print being sent to them by ESP from another room.

As you might have guessed, the results of this experiment were just as the Brauds had anticipated. The electromyographic recordings objectively proved that the muscle-relaxation group had become more physically relaxed than the muscle-tension group. And also as they had expected, the relaxation subjects had done much better on the ESP tests than their competitors.

The important point to remember about these experiments is that the Brauds used totally unselected subjects. They were mostly just volunteer students from the University. This indicated to the Brauds that *anybody* might be able to use relaxation as a method to develop and control ESP, just as anyone might be able to use the ganzfeld as a royal road to ESP.

Some Personal Conclusions

So in conclusion, what is this research *really* telling us? Are there virtual roads to ESP? Can anyone develop ESP powers? What meaning does all this research have for you and me?

Personally, I would have to answer that all this research into dreams, mental imagery, relaxation, and ESP is telling us a great deal . . . not only about our ESP potential itself, but also about how we might tap it, be able to make it more reliable, and perhaps even control it. The research of such parapsychologists as Honorton, the Brauds, and others have begun to show that ESP is not a God-given gift. It is a potential that we all obviously possess and can use in our daily lives. ESP appears to be a normal aspect of our minds, much the same as vision and hearing are normal aspects of our physiology. But it is a form of cognition which can only function on a conscious level when we enter into certain *states of mind*. This might sound a lot easier than it really is, though. Mastering even relaxation (which is just as much a state of mind as of body), not to mention meditation, is not easy. But by learning how to control our minds — instead of allowing our minds to control us — we might yet learn how to make use of our psychic powers at will. And once we gain access to our ESP potentials, who knows what other hidden powers of the mind we might eventually be able to tap and control.

End-Notes for Chapter Two

* The ocean wave sounds tended to make the subjects conjure up sea imagery, so in later tests the sound of undifferentiated static was employed.

† Englewood Cliffs, New Jersey: Prentice Hall, 1984.

§ The Brauds evaluated the results by asking their subjects to pick out the target picture previously sent to them from a pool of six thematically different ones. They ranked all six in order of their resemblance to their (the subject's) previous imagery. Those subjects who ranked the picture 1-3 were considered 'successful', while those placing the targets in the lower half of the rankings were considered failures. This procedure gives the subject a 50 per cent chance of success, although the procedure works well statistically when a large number of subjects is used.

3.

ESP Goes to the Races

'If ESP really works, why hasn't somebody used it to win at the races'
It sounds like a refrain from an old '50s song. But it is actually one
of the chief clichés used by the sceptics. It isn't even a good cliché either,
for like so many stereotypes, the retort is a curious mixture of truth and
fiction. It is true that no one ever got rich by using ESP at the races. But
this doesn't mean that it has *never* been used to successfully pick the
winners of horse-races — either intentionally or unintentionally.

Some Historical Perspectives
Some of the best cases of race-related premonitions were collected in
the 1930s by Dame Edith Lyttelton, who had been long fascinated by
the phenomenon of precognition. Mrs Lyttelton was herself an
extraordinary woman, who was born a member of the politically and
socially prominent Balfour family in England. She served as a delegate
to the League of Nations, but her first love was psychical research. She
began receiving automatic writing shortly after the death of her husband
in 1913, and some of her scripts seemed to predict events to come during
the First World War. She also contributed several evidential scripts to
the famous cross-correspondences. (The cross-correspondences
consisted of several hundreds of scripts received by an international group
of psychics. They purportedly came from the deceased founders of the
Society for Psychical Research.) Mrs Lyttelton also served on the council
of the SPR and was elected its president for 1933.

In 1934, the BBC broadcast a series of talks on psychic research, and
Mrs Lyttelton devoted her presentation to the subject of precognition.
She ended by inviting her listeners to send their own experiences to
her. She received a flood of mail in response and then systematically
followed up on those cases for which corroborative evidence could be
collected. The results of this task were published in 1937 in her book
Some Cases of Prediction. The volume's chief importance rests with the
independent documentation which Mrs Lyttelton was able to provide

Dame Edith Lyttelton, a member of the politically and socially well-known English Balfour family, served on the council of the Society for Psychical Research and was elected president in 1933. (Mary Evans/Society for Psychical Research)

for each case. These documents were usually provided by a witness, such as a friend or relative, who knew of the prediction before it was fulfilled. The wide selection of cases included in the book range from predictions of personal tragedies to premonitions of public events. But probably the most commonly recorded type of premonition dealt with the results of horse-races or other sporting events.

For example, the following case is rather typical of these reports. Mr W.L. Freeman of North Leicester wrote to Mrs Lyttelton about a personal psychic experience which had occurred twenty years prior:

> Somewhere about the year 1911 to 1913 I dreamed that I visited Lincoln. The dream occurred in November, the event dreamed of transpired in the March following. I had not up to that time been interested in Horse Racing and did not know the names of the race horses. In the dream I visited Lincoln Cathedral and remained so long inspecting the interior that on arriving at the race course I feared I had missed the first race. I inquired of a gentleman just leaving the course 'Has racing started?' He replied, 'Yes, over an hour ago and the big race (The Lincoln Handicap) is over and Outram has won it.' Upon waking in the morning I outlined the dream to several of my friends and not until then did I know there was such a horse as Outram. This was in November and the list of entrants was not published until I think January of the New Year. In this list I saw the name of Outram and in March the race was won by a horse of that name and rather long odds were laid against it.

Mrs Lyttelton checked and found that the race was run in March 1914. Luckily, her correspondent had told his wife about his dream long before the time of the race. She remembered the incident and was willing to corroborate it for Mrs Lyttelton. The woman added in her letter that, 'I do not think Mr Freeman took any interest in racing at that time, which made the dream the more remarkable.'

Probably the most elaborate racehorse premonition collected by Mrs Lyttelton also came by way of a dream. The focus was the Grand National race of 1933 which was somehow precognized by Mrs Phyllis Richards of London. She wrote to Mrs Lyttelton in 1934:

> I crossed from Belfast to Liverpool on the night of Thursday, March 23rd in order to see the Grand National which was being run the next day. On the boat I discovered that I had forgotten my mackintosh and felt a little worried. I went to sleep and dreamt that I was at the race, that it was pouring with rain and that a horse beginning with K and ending with Jack had won the race although he was not the first horse past the winning post. Before going to see the race I had lunch with some friends and told them my dream.

They looked up the list of the horses that were running and suggested Pellorus Jack, but I said 'No, his name began with a K'. They read on and found Kellesboro Jack and I told them that was the horse. I had told them that in my dream it was pouring with rain and this made them so sceptical (as the actual day was heavenly) that I did not say anything about my impression that Kellesboro Jack although winning the race was not the first horse past the winning post. Kellesboro Jack won and he was not the first horse past the post as a loose (riderless) horse was.

Mrs Richards was so sure of her dream that she bet a pound on the horse.

Mrs Lyttelton investigated this case in collaboration with Theodore Bestermann of the Society for Psychical Research. They were able to track down one of the people with whom Mrs Richards had spoken. He verified the account, and added that his wife had bet on the horse after hearing the story.

Unfortunately, the detail concerning the riderless horse rests solely on Mrs Richard's word, since she had been too reluctant to mention this part of her dream. But this odd event did, in fact, take place during the 1933 competition. The BBC had covered the race and by checking their files, it was discovered that a riderless horse had been among the race's top finishers. They could not, however, document whether this horse finished in front of the others.

Two related cases were collected in which the winning horses were not revealed through dreams, but by way of waking impressions. The most thoroughly documented of these was reported by a Mrs G. Ling, who also wrote to Mrs Lyttelton in February 1934:

The year April the Fifth won the Derby I was trying to win the prize offered for the first three horses in the *Daily Express*, etc., newspapers. I had no tips and knew no one in the racing world to give me any, incidentally I did not win. I have occasionally put 1/- on horses I fancied but have never won anything except on the occasion which I am about to explain.

About a week before the race took place I was awoken early in the morning by a voice saying 'April the Fifth will win the Derby'. I saw no one in my dreams only heard the voice. I roused my husband to tell him. I also told people at the breakfast table and the morning before the race was won I spoke of it in a fishmonger's shop when several customers were present. I modestly put 1/- on the race myself and my husband and son did the same. We listened over the wireless in the afternoon. Another horse was in front for some seconds and then the man broadcasting explained 'April the Fifth is in it' and continued calling the name until it won. A most peculiar feeling almost making me faint was on me but almost immediately I burst into tears, it all seemed so uncanny. I have had two distinct other dreams with the same voice waking me four years ago and about two months ago, but the one four years ago proved true, the other one has not had time to prove itself and they were over private matters.

Her account was signed by two members of her family who knew of the prediction before the race, while Mrs Ling named three other potential witnesses in a footnote to her letter. By checking the appropriate records, Mrs Lyttelton learned that April the Fifth won the Derby in 1932.

Probably the most unique case collected by the SPR researcher represents a 'tip' delivered by way of automatic writing. This personal experience was reported by Miss Edith L. Willis of Norwich. The incident occurred on 4 July 1929 while Miss Willis was working at home waiting for a photograph to develop. Remembering that the Derby was scheduled to be run the next day, she decided to try for the winner's name through psychic writing. She did not know the names of the horses entered in the race, so the name 'Trigo' made little sense to her when it was received. But by checking a list of entrants, the name was duly found there . . . registered with odds of twenty-one to one against winning. Miss Willis told the members of her household about the name, and she and a friend both bet five pounds on him — the only time she had ever bet on such a race. She received a hefty return.

Miss Willis ended her story by writing:

> I think it is of interest to note that caring nothing about horse racing I had not consciously either read or heard the names of any of the horses, not even the name of the favourite, nor should I have been likely to have heard the race discussed among my circle of acquaintances. After the event I looked up back newspapers to see if by any chance I might not have seen the name Trigo and forgotten it. This of course is not impossible but improbable, as being such an outsider his name was difficult to find anywhere.

This case, too, was corroborated by a relative familiar with the prediction before the race was run.

Mrs Lyttelton included a few other cases of horse-race predictions in her book but these reports lack enough details to be properly evaluated. They consist merely of brief claims backed up with corroborating affidavits collected from secondary witnesses.

The most striking finding that we can draw from Mrs Lyttelton's study today concerns the range of people who experience horse-race predictions. Some seem to be people who are definitely interested in racing, while others seem to be indifferent to the sport. Or at least they are when they have their experiences. So why some extraordinary people suddenly focus their psychic talents on forthcoming races remains a mystery. But one thing is certain. No one can claim that ESP has never helped make money at the track.

The Experiences of John Godley

The cases collected some fifty years ago by Mrs Lyttelton were primarily once-in-a-lifetime experiences. While some of her correspondents reported several precognitive experiences during the course of their lives, there was no evidence that they had ever successfully predicted a *series* of races. ESP seems to be too capricious and unreliable for that! However, a case in which the winners of several horse-races were predicted *has* been reported and documented. The races were run over a period of three years and the story is told by John Godley, Lord Kilbracken, in his book *Tell Me the Next One* published in 1950.

The incidents began while Godley was an undergraduate at Oxford. Suddenly he found himself receiving the names of the winners in his dreams. He was so impressed by these dreams that he began betting on the basis of them. He even supplied some of his friends with his psychic tips, and soon they were all cashing in on the premonitions. Godley won a series of three races during the first week the dreams manifested, but then the dreams stopped. They only recurred a year later, by which time the surprised young man decided to properly document them. He began by calling up the *Daily Mirror* in London to report his premonitions and the paper duly documented his next two wins. The newspaper was so impressed by the predictions, in fact, that they offered Godley a job! He eventually took it and began his career as a journalist.

Mr Godley's performances were not perfect, though. His next 'test' dream failed to come up with the winning name. For this race, though, he had already placed a bet on one of the horses. He therefore rationalized that he might have influenced or interfered with his dream by taking this action. Godley experienced three more dreams concerning the races during the course of the coming year. Two of his psychic choices won their respective races, while the third should have won but stumbled while still in the lead near the last fence. So in the space of three years Godley's record was seven for nine — odds that most horse-race enthusiasts would envy.

Nor do we have to rely solely on Godley's personal testimony concerning the predictions. Aside from the two premonitions documented by the *Daily Mirror*, Godley often wrote down the names of the forthcoming winners. He would then ask some of his friends to witness the predictions.

A Modern 'Test' Case

People who feel that they have a curious penchant for picking winning horses at the races show up every so often. It is usually difficult to evaluate their claims, but a good start was made when one of these people approached two parapsychologists in 1969. What resulted was an elaborate research project that was eventually reported to the annual convention of the Parapsychological Association in 1970. The researchers responsible for conducting the research were Dr Thelma Moss and Harry Sands, a student volunteer at her (former) parapsychology laboratory at the University of California at Los Angeles.

The idea for the project came in 1969 when the researchers were visited by a self-confessed psychic they call 'Mrs Rare the Medium' in their report. She was rather eccentric and in her late sixties, but described a creditable number of psychic experiences. She added that she had a special talent for picking the winners of horse-races. She never bet on them, she claimed, but merely played a personal game with her talent. Her basic procedure was to sit at home and dowse the names of the horses scheduled to run in a particular race by holding a pen or pencil over the newspaper page where they were printed. When her hand came to the winner's name, she would feel a pulling sensation. She told the researchers that she had been successful playing this game for several years, and they were impressed enough by Mrs Rare's claim to recruit her for a controlled experiment. Mrs Rare was at first apprehensive, but decided to collaborate with them.

The test was eventually run for a two-week period, which comprised ten days of racing and eighty individual races. During this experimental period the psychic used her sixth sense by working at home with published racing charts, which she would send to UCLA after marking her predicted winners. Mrs Rare actually provided two sets of possible winners to Dr Moss and her assistant. The first list was based on dowsing the index numbers of the entrants, while the second was compiled by way of Mrs Rare's psychic impressions when she read the names of the horses. (With one exception, the two lists were completely different.)

In order to best judge the results of the experiment, the UCLA researchers employed the services of two research assistants. One of these was a psychology student who considered himself a dunce when it came to racing and gambling. The other psychology student considered himself to be a racing buff. This second student was cynical about the experiment, since he felt that anyone could win at the races by shrewdly judging the handicapping and the favoured horses. Both of the students were asked to put their expertise (or lack of it) in competition with Mrs

Rare's, although the psychic was not told about their involvement in the experiment.

When Mrs Rare returned to Dr Moss's lab, she clearly felt that she had done poorly on the test. She had been keeping track of the races herself and was not pleased by her showing, claiming that her best day's choices included only four winners from a set of eight races. While this would probably please the casual racing enthusiast, Mrs Rare could do nothing but keep repeating the phrase, 'Why did I flunk the horse test?' But was the psychic's performance really that bad?

Because of the enormous statistical problems complicating the study, the UCLA researchers decided to judge the results in a simpler way. They put it into terms of dollars and cents by trying to figure out the earnings their subjects could have collected if they had placed two-dollar bets on each of the races.

The self-proclaimed dunce was clearly the loser on the basis of this criterion. By the end of the two weeks, he would have lost $111.40. He only won fourteen of the eighty races, which constituted a success rate of 17.5 per cent.

The racing buff did considerably better. He had told Dr Moss that a racing enthusiast could normally count on a 28 per cent success rate, and that's almost exactly what he achieved. He had successfully selected twenty-three winners, which represented a success rate of 28.8 per cent. Clearly this young man knew what he was talking about; but since his selections were based on favourites and safe betting practices, he wouldn't have collected very high profits. His hypothetical earnings would only come to $67.80.

Even though Mrs Rare was unhappy with her performance, she did tolerably well during the experiment. The results of both her psychic divining techniques (dowsing versus psychic impressions) were positive and they resulted in the choice of fifteen and seventeen winners respectively. These choices would have earned her $49.60 and $30.80. This wasn't as good as the success reported by the racing buff, but Mrs Rare successfully picked a higher percentage of long shots. The combined success rate of her ESP and dowsing procedure was a whopping 40 per cent — which was also higher than either of the selected strategies employed by the students.

Because of the complexities of their study and its results, Dr Moss and her colleague did not conclude that Mrs Rare was able to demonstrate psychic powers on their test. They merely concluded that her results were encouraging. Their initial hope was that they could convince Mrs Rare to co-operate in a follow-up study. The psychic was favourably inclined to the idea, but the plan was dropped and this second test was never conducted.

Can ESP really help you win at the races? It seems that it can. But because of the vagaries to which the sixth sense is prone, I wouldn't suggest that you bet on it.

Or maybe I would. When I phoned Dr Moss in March 1986 to get some further details on her study, the former UCLA psychologist told me a fascinating story . . . a story that had prompted her interest in the subject of ESP at the races. She explained that, some years back, a school psychologist she knew began dreaming about the winners of forthcoming horse-races. Since the woman had some background in parapsychology, she thought enough of the dreams to report them to her husband. He was impressed by her claim and even placed large bets on the basis of them. The result? Within a relatively short period of time the couple were able to buy a Cadillac with their winnings. Then, unfortunately, the dreams stopped and never recurred. Dr Moss personally knew the people involved in the case and today, fifteen years or so later, was still willing to vouch for their honesty.

When Dr Moss told me the name of the psychologist, I had to chuckle. She turned out to be a researcher whose experimental work in the field of ESP in children is standardly referenced. She is also currently an associate member of the Parapsychological Association. So it would seem that even parapsychologists have used their ESP to win at the races!

4.

The Psychic and the Stock Market

Some of the stories included in the last chapter are rather old, dating back some fifty years or so. They hardly represent psychic breakthroughs being made today. I have included them in this book, however, since they bear crucially on a subject currently coming to the forefront of parapsychology — is there a practical side to the sixth sense? Parapsychology's sceptics often ask why gifted psychics can't use their precognitive gifts to cash in on the stock market, win at the horses, or break the bank at Monte Carlo. I showed previously that the psychic sense *has* been successfully used to predict horse-races. Research conducted in the 1960s even showed that it could be used successfully to predict roulette outcomes.* Now it appears that there might be yet another practical application for the sixth sense. This story first came to public attention in January 1984 when *Nova*, the highly acclaimed British-produced PBS program, announced that some investors in California had used psychic help to cash in on the futures market. *Nova* revealed that the businessmen relied on the talents of Keith Harary, a San Francisco psychologist and psychic, to predict the silver market. Over $100,000 in profits was the reported outcome of the undertaking.

I was just as amazed as the rest of the viewing audience by this disclosure. Keith and I have been friends for well over ten years. I first met him in 1973 when his ability to induce out-of-body experiences voluntarily was being explored at the Psychical Research Foundation (then) in Durham, North Carolina. (This research, too, will be discussed in a forthcoming chapter.) Keith left Durham after taking his degree with honours in psychology at Duke University, and he recently acted as a consultant to the Stanford Research Institute (now SRI International) on their psi research programme.

Keith had mentioned to me long ago that he and some of his colleagues were playing around with predicting the stock market, but this was the first I knew of the profits involved. I could hardly wait to learn more about the project and since I was flying to San Francisco weekly to teach,

I was able to discuss the project with him in depth.

The idea to apply Keith's psychic gifts to a practical endeavour was a result of the SRI's intensive research on remote viewing. This project was spearheaded by Russell Targ and Dr Harold Puthoff, both trained physicists. Back in 1972 they conducted some highly successful experiments demonstrating that a psychic can 'tune in' on a distant location and describe the local geography. (This procedure will be discussed in greater depth in the following chapter.) Targ and Harary subsequently extended their research and now the term 'remote viewing' is sometimes applied to a number of clairvoyant tasks. The idea for the silver futures project was a result of this expanded exploration of the remote viewing work. It should be noted, though, that the experiments were not undertaken simply to make money, but also a prove a scientific point.

'Our work' Harary told me, 'is about integrating psychic abilities into people's lives in a normal, productive way. Now we're doing applications work. Past research work [in parapsychology] is just sitting around in journals and not really impacting people's lives on the street. So we need to do things that have impact and that gets the point across.'

It was this idea that led Harary and Russell Targ, who recently left the SRI staff, to form Delphi Associates with San Francisco businessman Anthony White, an MBA from Stanford University. This organization is devoted to the practical applications of the sixth sense. It also advises businessmen on their high-risk decisions by exploring possible courses of action through remote viewing, but neither Targ nor Harary really believe that they are proposing anything radically new. 'Successful businessmen are using their intuitive capabilities all the time, anyway', says Harary. 'They call it going on a hunch, a gut feeling, or something like women's intuition.'

The Procedure and the Experiment
For the actual (and highly successful) silver futures project, a procedure called 'associative remote viewing' was used. This protocol is rather simple. The experimenter merely chooses a number of simple objects and assigns each to a possible future event of interest. The subject is then asked to remote view into the future and describe the object he or she will be shown or handed at a future date. If the psychic's impressions match one of the objects in the target pool, this gives the experimenter information about the future event. This all may sound a little more confusing than it really is.

Let's say that you want to predict who the Democrats will be nominating for president at their forthcoming convention. You would simply create a target pool of four objects and assign one to each of the candidates — e.g., a spool of thread for Walter Mondale, a pencil for Gary Hart, a red ribbon for John Glenn, and a comb for Jessie Jackson. You would then ask your subject, who you would keep ignorant about the selected objects, to describe the one you will be showing him or her the day *after* the convention concludes. The subject may then describe for you something 'red, long and sleek', which would obviously refer to the ribbon designating John Glenn. So you would place your bets on the Senator and later show the ribbon to your subject at the appropriate time. (The associative remote viewing procedure is based on the principle that the future event actually affects the remote viewing session through backward causality.)

Before running the formal silver project, Delphi Associates conducted some preliminary sessions to see if Harary could predict fluxes in the stock market in just this way. The physicist chose objects that would indicate downward or upward trends. These pilot studies indicated that Harary could reliably predict changes in gold prices and the Dow Jones Industrial Average. His successes were clear-cut enough that Delphi Associates was able to round up a group of investors willing to place their money on Harary and the remote viewing technique. Tens of thousands of dollars were at stake.

The formal experiments began on 16 September 1982. Delphi Associates conducted nine associative remote viewing sessions on the silver futures market over the succeeding two months. For each experiment, Russell Targ called Harary at his apartment in San Francisco on a *Thursday* and asked him to describe an object that would be placed in his hand the following *Monday.* Harary would give his psychic responses right over the telephone.

Then the complicated part of the protocol began. Targ would then make a list of possible market fluctuations — i.e., up or down, more than 0.25, or less than 0.25. Only three discriminations were made for other sessions — up more than 0.25, down further than 0.25, or an insignificant change. The numbers one to four or one to three were then randomly assigned to the possibilities. The physicist would next call their associate Anthony White and instruct him to choose four or three very different items in his home and assign numbers to them. They would then break the 'code' so that each object was associated with one of the three or four market changes. Only then would Targ read Keith's target responses to White, and together they would determine which object, if any, had been described. If there was a clear-cut description of one of the objects in the target pool, White would then advise the investors of the predicted flux in the silver market over the weekend. This, by the way, is the hardest part of the week to make a commodities prediction.

The Results of the Experiment

While I was investigating this story, Russell Targ kindly supplied me with the transcripts of the first and second sessions. The successes really were clear-cut. During the second session, for instance, Harary kept getting impressions of a smooth texture. He added that the object was a 'tubular ring of some kind . . . like a fluorescent tube light fixture.' He also said that it was like 'a tube inside of a paper towel' that had '. . . a funny smell.' The objects later chosen for the target pool consisted of a three-inch long, cylindrical vial of perfume, a plastic bag of washers, and a pair of eyeglass frames. It wasn't hard to see that Keith's remote viewing focused on the cylindrical perfume vial. The code designated that this object was associated with a rise of over 0.25 for silver futures. The market did rise over the subsequent weekend as predicted, and Delphi's investors scored a profit.

Nine sessions were run using this technique, and seven transactions were made. Every one of them was successful. Statistically speaking, such results would occur by chance only fourteen times out of every *one million* times the experiment was run.

'The pressure was intense,' Harary admitted. 'I was able to keep very calm and clear while doing it, but I wouldn't want to keep that particular pace up indefinitely. That's to say, I think it requires a rest after a while.'

When I spoke with Mr White in February, he was still very enthusiastic about the silver project. Since he has been managing investments for over fifteen years, he is well aware how hard it is to predict the stock market. He wouldn't tell me who the investors had been, nor how much money was involved, since such information had to be kept confidential. *Nova* claimed that over $100,000 in profit was made on the project, and no one with whom I spoke disputed that figure. Thousands of dollars were obviously invested since the fluctuation in the silver market between September and December 1982 were not exceptionally great. Mr White did, however, give me the purchase history for one of the investors. It aptly revealed his cogent reliance on Harary's associative remote viewing.

During the first session, Harary predicted a drop in the market between Thursday, 16 September and the following Monday. The investor sold when he heard the news at $9.20 and the futures dropped to $8.87 by Monday. When the same investor was informed on 8 October that the market would probably rise over the weekend he bought at $9.07 and sold on the eleventh for $9.62. Harary designated a rise in the market later that month and once again the investor profited. Silver futures suffered some dips in November. So when Keith's remote viewing indicated a drop in the silver market over the weekend of the twentieth, the businessman sold short at $9.89 and repurchased the futures on Monday at $9.17. Similar transactions were made twice in December.

Needless to say, the investors were more than gratified by their earnings.

When *Nova* first heard about the project and considered airing a report on it, they decided to do some of their own follow-up. After learning about the success of the project from Anthony White, they tried to determine whether Harary's performance was within the bounds of what any broker could reasonably forecast. It was obvious that *Nova* had only a very vague idea that the silver forecasts were based on psychically-described household items and were not really 'direct' predictions of the market. The show's producers didn't realize that the existing market conditions and its fluctuations could not have influenced Harary as he did his associative remote viewing. In any event, even *Nova's* own expert couldn't believe that Delphi's accurate forecasts could have resulted from marketing analysis. This is interesting in itself.

'The most unusual aspect of these people,' he explained in the documentary 'is their ability or their willingness to predict not only the direction of a move and the magnitude, but to give you, on silver, a 25 per cent prediction for Thursday to Monday, which is really sticking one's neck out. I'm sure they're the only people that I've heard of in the business that would get that far . . .'

The expert was also stunned when *Nova* explained that Harary had been correct in making nine separate predictions. 'Being right nine times out of nine is unheard of,' he said. 'And in this business it's . . . incredible is a weak word . . . I would say impossible.'

Having determined that coincidence couldn't explain Harary's success, *Nova* still wanted to see if perhaps the predictions could merely have followed existing trends within the silver market. This theory was denied by the broker who handled the transactions for the investors and who wished to remain anonymous. He pointed out that the market between September and December was generally in an uptrend.

'But some of the most spectacular and successful trends were on the short side,' he pointed out. 'That is, they sold before they bought back. So in other words, they were making money in anticipation . . . or making a prediction in anticipation . . . of the market coming down.'

So Harary's predictions were sometimes opposed to the advice a stock expert would have given the same investors and opposed to the general trend of the market itself.

But in light of these continual and reliable successes, why didn't Delphi continue to predict changes in the silver market psychically?

Keith Harary explained to me that apart from the pressure he found himself working under, it was the attitude of the investors that finally got to him. Delphi was conducting one experimental session per week on the average. This was about all the young psychologist wished to undertake. Since psychic ability is a delicate potential, it simply can't be abused or overworked. The investors, on the other hand, were not trained in the delicacies of the sixth sense and couldn't understand his reticence about increasing the frequency of the sessions. Things finally came to a head when one of the investors started pressuring Delphi to do more and more sessions on a greater variety of stocks. The pressure was just too much and Keith decided it was time to withdraw.

I was curious about other possible reasons for Harary's reluctance to continue the pace. There is an old tradition that psychics cannot use their abilities for personal financial gain without it backfiring on them. Since Delphi was getting a commission on the transactions, I wondered if this stigma influenced Harary's decision. He denied this flatly, saying 'I didn't have any qualms about using psychic abilities in that way. The purpose of the experiment was to show that psychic abilities can be useful in the real world and in the market-place.' The *Nova* documentary also stated that a replication of the silver futures project (conducted the following year) failed, which may have caused Harary to become disenchanted. But he explained that this report was incorrect.

'There were some continued trials in January by which time I was getting very tired,' he told me. 'Everybody was; even the judges. We began working with more people [as viewers]. The problem we got into later was that we would see accurate psychic functioning in which the viewer would correctly describe one of the objects in the target pool, but that object would not correlate with the change in the market.'

Harary feels that the problem was partially one of fatigue and boredom — that by this time everyone was tired of the procedure and that their viewers' ESP talents were simply penetrating the *entire* target pool. What was obviously needed was a new and innovative approach that would help the viewers re-focus. 'We tried a new approach,' Harary continued, 'and even had some success with it. So the important thing with psychic functioning, I think, is to keep making it new. If we use the same method indefinitely then the method gets tired. You have to give it a rest and change. So when we started getting tired, we changed things around a little and now we're getting good results again.' He didn't elaborate further.

Both Russell Targ and Keith Harary feel that there were a number of reasons for the success of the silver project, apart from the fact that the young psychologist obviously possesses formidable psychic gifts. Chief among them is that the researchers saw their work as meaningful and not merely as an exercise in experimental design. It was certainly no academic parapsychological foray. The research was meaningful not only because of its obvious practical application, but because it had direction and potential. These potentials are now being explored further.

But in the long run, Harary considers his silver predictions a scientific project more than as a commercial one. The research was just a new expression of his deep commitment to parapsychology, or psi research as he prefers to call it. This is a field to which he has dedicated the last fifteen years of this life.

'You have to show that psychic abilities are useful,' he said and he told me that society must learn to accept the reality and importance of ESP. 'We must establish the reality of psychic functioning not only in the scientific journals . . . but also in the *Wall Street Journal*.

Since conducting this experiment, Targ and Harary have extended their research even further. It is their view that the sixth sense can be used for all sorts of practical purposes and that just about anyone can make use of it. I decided to explore this possibility with them when they started teaching seminars in psychic functioning in California in 1986. It was an eye-opener.

End-Notes for Chapter Four

* See the chapter 'Psi application' by Robert Brier and Walter V. Tyminski in *Progress in Parapsychology* edited by J. B. Rhine. Durham, N. Carolina: Parapsychology Press, 1973.

5.

A Workshop for Psychic Development

Up until a few years ago, the subject of personal 'psychic development' was frowned upon by conventional parapsychologists. Certainly no scientifically-trained researchers taught the skill, or even claimed that they could. People who tried to teach their clients to be psychic, offered courses, or wrote books on the subject were either considered charlatans or simply self-deluded.

But this was before parapsychology came of age, and before researchers started taking an interest in the practical side of the sixth sense. Several bold researchers have recently been coming to the forefront of the field who believe you *can* learn to be psychic.

The latest parapsychologists to take an open and controversial stand on psychic development are Russell Targ and Keith Harary, as I explained in the last chapter. Both of these researchers originally worked at SRI International in Menlo Park, California, where they conducted research into the mysteries of remote viewing. Remote viewing is the ability of an experimental subject to psychically 'see' and describe a geographical site located miles away. Researchers at SRI have been exploring this phenomenon for over a decade, and their opinion is that you don't have to be a gifted psychic to successfully remote view. Given a little training and practice they have come to believe that most people can learn the skill.

To prove this point, Targ and Harary began teaching workshops on understanding and using the sixth sense. The first of these was held in San Francisco, California at Fort Mason Conference Center, just off the Marina with its blue water and multicoloured sails. Russell Targ and Keith Harary first presented their opinions in their book *The Mind Race* which I had favourably reviewed in the *Journal of the American Society for Psychical Research*, so naturally I wanted to see for myself if their remarkable claims would bear up when put to the test. When I flew to San Francisco to act as an observer and to participate in their inaugural seminar, I didn't realize I would be in for a lot of surprises.

*   *   *   *

The story of the SRI's research programme is a long one, but it is extremely germane to the work in which Targ and Harary are now engaged. It sets the stage for the psychic development work they are now undertaking.

Remote viewing research began at SRI in 1972 when Russell Targ and Dr Harold Puthoff, his original co-worker, discovered that some of their best subjects could 'send their minds' to any number of distant locations. The experimental protocol used by the researchers required a co-worker to randomly pick one of several locations in the Bay area, drive there, and simply observe the site for half an hour. In the meantime, the experimental subject was kept sequestered at SRI and would be asked to describe the chosen area. While they originally used only gifted psychics, they eventually learned that all sorts of people can successfully remote view. The first volunteers they tested were government officials. Since much of the original SRI work was being secretly funded by the US military, government agents often came to Menlo Park to see what the physicists were up to. When the researchers talked about the nature of their experiments, the officials tended to be sceptical. So Targ and Puthoff invited their guests to try their own hands (and minds) at remote viewing. The government representatives were usually so successful that they left California shocked and bewildered.

When the general public eventually learned about the research activities at SRI, Targ and (later) Keith Harary were often asked to appear on television talk-shows. To best demonstrate remote viewing, the two researchers refused to bring along any of their 'star' subjects. Instead, they usually recruited the hosts of the shows to do the viewing. The television production staff were asked to choose the target sites and drive there. The programme hosts tended to perform extraordinarily well too . . . certainly as well as SRI's best psychic superstars. So soon the two researchers decided that it was time to go even more public with their discoveries. They therefore decided in 1986 to begin teaching seminars on psychic functioning.

The First Day of the Workshop

There were about seventy people that weekend in San Francisco. We had come on Saturday, 8 March, 1986 to learn remote viewing and to see whether we could employ it in our own lives. For the first hour, the two researchers showed us clips of successful remote viewing sessions filmed either at SRI or at various television studios they have visited around the country. They constantly reinforced that psychic ability is neither rare nor bizarre, but a normal faculty into which we can each tap. Their second claim was that, through their experience at SRI, they had learned specific skills that people can learn in order to become psychic.

The key, they explained, was the use of uncensored imagery. We were told to focus on the pictures that are constantly forming in our minds as we tried to learn psychic functioning. The problem, they went on to say, was that few of us ever pay close enough attention to our inner experiences. We also tend to interpret or critically analyse our mental images. This, we were warned, was the worst mistake we could make. Speaking boldly and repetitively from the podium, Targ and Harary emphasized that our job was to learn to report what we saw within the mind's eye without trying to evaluate any of it — in other words, to report and sketch whatever we saw or experienced without stopping to label it. It is for this reason that successful remote viewing required a 'team approach.' The two researchers explained that it helps if the remote viewer is guided through his session by an interviewer, who like the experimental subject, is kept totally ignorant of the target location. His task is to simply encourage the viewer, keep him from analysing his imagery, and ask him meaningful questions to help him focus on the chosen site. The former SRI researchers believe, in fact, that the role of the interviewer is critical to the remote viewing process.

It took Targ and Harary the entire morning and part of the afternoon to explain the fundamental skills of remote viewing. By 3.00 p.m. we were ready for the acid test — would we be able to learn remote viewing skills ourselves? We were told to break down into small groups and test each other. The first exercise required one of us to select a small object and conceal it, while a second person tried to use remote viewing to describe it. The third person in each group was to serve as the interviewer. My little group was comprised of four people: a blonde middle-aged woman, a college graduate student, a rather overbearing self-proclaimed gentleman psychic, and myself. Even though I've worked in several parapsychology laboratories throughout the United States, this was the first time I had ever been part of such a 'team' experiment. The critical use of the interviewer was certainly innovative, and I was eager to see if it worked.

By the mutual choice of the group, Carol (the middle-aged housewife) went first. She became nervous when I explained that my target object was concealed in my clothing.

'I'm trying to get out of my mind anything that I *think* could be on you,' she said as she closed her eyes. This was a good beginning since it showed that Carol was trying to subvert her critical thinking processes. But her promising start didn't pay off.

'I'm not getting anything,' she said. 'Absolutely nothing.'

It was clear that her try at getting impressions from my concealed object was going nowhere. The college student was acting as her interviewer, and he seemed befuddled by Carol's lack of response. I didn't want to intrude, but by this time Targ, Harary and their assistants were mingling with the teams in order to help those who were having trouble with the exercise. Elizabeth Targ, who is Russell's daughter and herself an expert remote viewer, was only a single table away, so I motioned for her to join us. I explained that Carol has having considerable difficulty, so Elizabeth gently prodded and encouraged her. The Stanford medical student assured Carol that she *was* getting pictures of the target and encouraged her to draw whatever shapes or forms came into her head . . . and warned her not to censor anything.

This form of benign cajoling seemed to break the impasse. While still claiming that she was receiving no information about the target, Carol finally grabbed a pencil and sheet of paper and drew four parallel lines. 'This is nothing, just nothing,' she complained. But then she boxed in the lines. What resulted was a sketch of a rectangular object with a set of parallel lines running across it. She closed her eyes for a moment and then said that the only real impression she got was *printing*. There was printing covering whatever object she was trying to view. She repeated this claim three times.

I was grinning when I finally took my target object out of my jacket pocket. For this experiment I had especially chosen a cassette tape package. It was a simple rectangular plastic case, with two parallel red lines running across it — a box virtually identical to the one Carol had drawn only moments before. Printing on the label covered half of the package. What really impressed me, however, was that Carol had picked up a considerable amount of psychic information from the case while continuously denying that she was getting anything from the target.

For the next segment of our group experiment, we decided that Don (the graduate student) should try his skill at remote viewing. I served as interviewer while the self-proclaimed psychic kept his object in his shirt pocket. I had to coax Don for a good ten minutes before he was ready to begin. He, too, constantly complained that he couldn't grab hold of any mental imagery, so I suggested that he take a pencil and draw whatever forms — no matter how vague — entered his consciousness. Don finally executed a rough drawing that really didn't make much sense. While reporting that the target object was white, he drew a simple square. He followed this up by running a line from the square and connected it to a rectangle about twice as large. This was all he could get.

It was another hit! Bob withdrew his laminated ID card from his pocket.

It was a white card encased in clear plastic. The only two markings on it were a square (that contained his picture) with a rectangle by its side (where his name and address were printed). The dimensions and relative positions of the card's markings uncannily matched Don's simple drawing.

Now it was the psychic's turn to try remote viewing. Bob was sure he could do better than any of us, but the competition was certainly getting tough. It was Carol's turn to serve as the object-holder. 'My object is in a little bag in my purse,' she said.

Bob closed his eyes and then quickly drew his impressions. First he outlined a cigar shape, but told us that the target object consisted of several items somehow linked together. He couldn't focus on it any further, but started drawing circles around his sketch. 'That's connected to it,' he said as he finished.

Carol was all smiles. 'You really are good,' she said as she plopped down a roll of pennies on the table.

The group went through two more complete rounds of testing, but I didn't get to witness any of these trials. Everyone agreed that working with four instead of three people was cumbersome, so I walked outside for a while to take stock of what I had just witnessed. I was impressed by the fact that three *entirely different target objects* had been used by us for the first round of experiments. Carol, Don, and Bob could have sketched *anything*, but they didn't. Each of them had executed sketches that closely matched the targets chosen for them to view. Could this have been coincidental? I tended to doubt it. It seemed unlikely that three such remarkable 'coincidences' would crop up in such suspicious succession. It really did look as if my little group was learning to use extrasensory perception fairly reliably.

The Second Day

When we regrouped the next day, it was clear that very few people had dropped out of the workshop. Everyone was more relaxed and I took some time to talk to several of the participants. It was surprising to learn that not everyone taking part in the workshop was from the Bay area. Visitors from several other states had flown in in order to work with the former SRI parapsychologists. The people with whom I spoke represented a good cross-section of the general public: they included housewives, successful businessmen, a few college students, one professional nurse, and some retired folk. The more relaxed atmosphere of the workshop's second day also provided some time for me to speak with Targ and Harary concerning their views and seminars. I was especially interested in their controversial beliefs that anyone can learn remote viewing.

'We haven't worked with everyone in the world,' Harary cautioned me as we spoke, 'so it's hard to make a blanket statement and say that absolutely everyone can do this. However, we've worked with a large cross-section of people and we've found that a tremendous variety of people are able to use their psychic abilities, even if they've never had a psychic experience that they were aware of. There are definite skills involved in learning to do remote viewing, and these skills are learnable.'

Russell Targ agreed totally with his younger colleague. He explained that they weren't too interested in working with self-proclaimed psychics — people, he felt, who were too ego-involved with their own abilities. He preferred working with people such as professional businessmen, people who were self-confident and who were required to make decisions every day. These people expect success in their lives and bring this state of mind with them when they train for remote viewing. But the physicist did feel that psychic training programmes had their limitations.

'We would not make the statement that everyone can do remote viewing,' he said, echoing his colleague's sentiments. 'But a great number of the people we've worked with have been able to do excellently. We assume that psychic functioning is a talent or an ability like any other ability. Like vision or musical ability, some people have more of a talent than others.'

But why, I wondered, did they feel that it was time to train the general public in the skills of remote viewing? Why not stay in the scientific laboratory and do more process-oriented research?

'It's important to get good information to the public,' explained Harary in answer to my questions. 'People are having psychic experiences, and they are interested in understanding more about their abilities. We have to get information out there in a way that isn't distorted, that separates the wheat from the chaff.'

The young psychologist also felt that parapsychologists should take on the ethical responsibility of helping people to explore their psychic potentials.

'It gives people a way to explore their capabilities without joining a cult or being exploited,' continued Harary, who, before working at SRI specialized in counselling cult defectors. 'It is the responsibility of the researcher to educate the public. There is so much bad information out there that if we don't do anything, then by default we let all the bad information just take over.'

But why, I felt, should people *want* to develop psychic powers? What good does it really do for anyone?

'Remote viewing is part of a range of experiences that people have in their lives, and it de-mystifies things that are otherwise very mysterious,' countered Targ.

'Like psychic phenomena in general?' I asked.

'Yes,' continued the physicist. 'People are interested in psychic experiences not because they are reading about them, but because they are having them. In these seminars and in our book *The Mind Race* we're teaching people about the laboratory evidence for psi, and we're showing them how to incorporate these abilities into their lives in a straightforward fashion. It shows them that psychic functioning is not the bizarre ability that they see in movies such as *E.T.* and *Carrie*, but an ordinary human capability.'

Keith Harary took a different perspective on the issue.

'There's a continuous barrage of things we don't know about,' he said. He was speaking of our growing alienation from the world in which we live. 'Computers and the like — the world is getting more and more complex. People don't need more reasons to feel inadequate; that there are psychic people out there in the world who are different from us. This is just another way of feeling that they themselves lack something other people have. It is empowering for people to realize that they have an ability that they didn't know they had. It doesn't matter who they are, it makes them feel better.'

With that, our interview came to an end.

Learning Remote Viewing

The second day of the Bay Research Institute's workshop promised to teach us the skills of geographical remote viewing and the use of psychic skills in real life situations. It was a natural progression from the work with hidden objects we had practised the day before. The morning session began with a special address by Dr Charles Tart who spoke on parapsychology's implications for building a meaningful philosophy of life. When he finished an hour later, the real work of the day began.

To help prime us for the day's activities, Targ and Harary began by showing us more film clips of successful remote viewing. The most impressive of these was taken from an old *In Search of . . .* television episode, which showed Ingo Swann — a psychic from New York and SRI's first star subject — remote viewing from a mini-submarine. He was able to correctly guide the sub to a (hitherto) unknown submerged wreck site.

The problem with training and testing us for geographical remote viewing was obvious, though. It was impractical for the researchers to send one of us to a distant site, and then drag along seventy or so people to see it for themselves half an hour later. So instead, Targ and Harary asked us to pair up with the person next to us and form teams. Our task would be to remote view *slides* of geographical sites, which we would soon see projected on to a screen behind the podium. That sounded easy enough! This time my partner turned out to be a painfully shy young man named Ted. He was a Bay area resident, and remained sceptical whether he could ever learn remote viewing skills.

For the first exercise I chose to go first. I was still excited by the successes I had witnessed the day before. By this time, I was figuring that I could do just as well as anybody else. So I closed my eyes and immediately sensed that, whatever the nature of the target, it had water in front of it. I sketched a pond, and then drew a brick or stone wall behind it. My only other impression was that trees could be seen in the background of the location.

The target slide was projected for us five minutes later. It was a picture of Palo Alto, California's city hall, which is an enormously tall white building. I had missed the building completely, but my other impressions weren't that far off. There was a fountain in front of the building and four trees could be counted in the background.

It was Ted's turn for the next session, but he was so shy he could hardly talk about his imagery. He kept telling me that he couldn't see anything, so I finally motioned for Russell Targ to do some interviewing with him. Targ put some friendly pressure on Ted by convincing him that, of course, he was experiencing the target. He just had to zoom in on it a little better. The physicist told him to just wait a few moments, assuring him at the same time that an impression of the slide would soon enter his mind as he kept his eyes closed. Ted seemed rather annoyed by the researcher's presence, but after a few more silent moments he quickly sketched something that looked like an obelisk.

'There,' he said curtly to Targ and me, 'I got something. Now are you happy?'

Ted explained that he had momentarily glimpsed a white tower. He closed his eyes again and then filled in the picture. He told me that he saw green grass and flowers next to the tower, and then drew something running along the side of the scene. He thought it might be a brick wall, but eventually reconsidered and felt that it could be a walkway of some kind.

When we both eventually saw the slide, I was impressed with the percentage of correct information my partner had picked up. The slide depicted a column of bleached white pillars, bordered to one side by a green quad of grass. (There were no flowers.) A cement walkway bordered the column on the opposite side. Ted's sketch wasn't too accurate, but each of his impressions — the white tower, the grass, the walkway — were correct. The only true error he made was when he added flowers to his sketch.

I congratulated my partner on his success, but he wasn't impressed by his own performance. I had to point out that if the components of his drawing were separated, he really had incorporated a great deal of psychic information into his sketch.

The third slide showed a mangled oak tree, but both Ted and I missed it completely. When Targ asked later whether anyone had received the impression of a tree during the viewing period, only two people raised their hands. That didn't strike me as being beyond the realm of coincidence.

The second session of the day commenced at 2.00 p.m. after a rather long lunch break. Everyone was still hanging in there, and several people seemed to be pretty self-satisfied by their performance and burgeoning skills. Because we were sitting at large tables, it was hard for me to see anybody else's drawings. But I did manage to catch some impressive conversations as some of the participants shared their sketches with each other. It struck me that the enthusiasm pervading the room was probably contributing to the successes we were seeing.

This was certainly the opinion of both Targ and Harary. 'An expectation of success is important,' Targ had explained to me earlier that day.

From what I had seen during the past two days, this sort of Dale Carnegie technique for psychic development was certainly paying off. So to close the workshop, the two researchers explained the practical uses to which remote viewing could be put. They referred once again to the contribution remote viewing was making to the field of archaeology, where it has been used to locate new dig sites. They continued by explaining that remote viewing has recently been used to help find drill locations for oil companies and even to make successful stock market predictions. The workshop went into its closing phase when we were told that we would now be asked to use our newly developing powers to resolve a real-life problem. We were going to help the researchers find oil!

During the preceding break (directly after the slide experiments), the researchers had placed two wooden boxes on the podium. Behind each of them was a covered cup. Russell Targ pointed to the boxes and explained that each of them contained a distinct object, but he warned us that only one of the corresponding cups represented a possible oil deposit. We were to use our remote viewing skills to gain impressions of the hidden object that signified the oil. We were then given ten minutes to gather up our psychic impressions.

This little experiment was still being described to us when an image flashed into my mind. When I closed my eyes I could see an old-fashioned silver dollar.

This was too good to be true, I thought. I figured that the image was probably wrong but that it contained information *incorporated* into the target. So I took a piece of paper and wrote down three impressions: that the target was a round object, silver in colour, and metallic.

Five minutes later Targ opened the first wooden box. It contained a wooden carving of a hand, which didn't fit any of my impressions by a long shot. Then the physicist opened the second box and my heart skipped a beat. The target was a round, silver, metal apple slicer. My three impressions had been correct.

Russell Targ then asked for a show of hands concerning each of the targets. Only ten people or so raised their hands when the physicist asked if anybody had received impressions of the carving. But when he asked how many of us previosuly received the impression of a circular or metallic object, fifty hands shot up! Our psychic impressions were obviously telling us that the second cup probably represented the oil deposit. We all got a good laugh when Targ took off the top of the cup — and showed us a little bottle of commercially-processed oil! Of course, the fact that we made the correct choice could easily have been coincidental. But as I looked around, I saw that many people had indeed sketched circular objects of one form or another.

Retrospections

While I was getting ready to leave San Francisco the next day, I spent some time re-evaluating the weekend while waiting for my plane. What had I learned about the sixth sense? It seemed to me that Russell Targ and Keith Harary had proved their point — that most of us have the potential to develop psychic capabilities. Not only had I seen it unfolding in the few people with whom I had worked, I had even seen it functioning in myself. This was really a shock, for as a parapsychologist I had been trained to believe that psychic functioning is a rare experience. My experiences that weekend forced me to conclude that my training had been misguided.

While he was tracking the sixth sense at Duke University during the 1930s, the late Dr J.B. Rhine discovered, demonstrated, and claimed that one in every five people probably possesses psychic abilities. Even this modest claim struck the parapsychologists of that time as too radical.

But perhaps today parapsychology is ready to take the next step, by demonstrating that fully 60 per cent of the general public is really psychic. Russell Targ and Keith Harary seem well on the road to proving this new, and even more radical, claim. Only time will tell whether they are on the right track.

6.

Psychic Phenomena
and the Brain

The late J.B. Rhine believed that ESP was a totally non-physical as well as non-sensory information channel directly linked to the human mind — that mysterious essence that is both one with, yet separate from, the brain. He believed further that ESP could never be truly captured by the cold art of science nor authoritatively measured by its technology. All we could do was measure it, using statistics and the laws of probability as our tools.

This concept of ESP (and even psychokinesis) as limitless and non-physical forces literally dictated the way most research in the United States was carried out for over thirty years. No one ever thought that we might be able to find a receptor organ for ESP in the brain, or be able to objectively determine when someone was actually receiving a telepathic message. But times are changing. The last decade has seen rapid advances in the neurosciences, biology, biochemistry, and in our understanding of the vastly complex central nervous system. By gently and provisionally dismissing Rhine's dogma, a few bold parapsychologists are now entertaining the heresy that psychic phenomena may actually be integrally linked to the varied functions of the brain. The search is now on to discover what areas of the brain might conceivably be linked to different forms of psychic phenomena. Although the results have been meagre, they have also been fascinating. So when over one hundred parapsychologists met at Fairleigh Dickenson University in Madison, New Jersey to attend the 1983 convention of the Parapsychological Association, it often seemed as though the brain was on their minds just as much as psi itself. Looking at the workings of the brain seemed to be a natural follow-up to the research on psi-conducive states that had preoccupied the field in the 1970s, and which was reviewed in an earlier chapter.

I had gone to the convention just as another participant, and it was lucky for me that I had spent the last few months boning up on neurology. Never before at one of these conventions had there been so much discussion of the brain, the nervous system, and how they may play important roles in the strange world of psychic phenomena.

ESP and Brain Hemispheric Dominance

It should be well known to the readers of this book that the brain is divided into two large hemispheres. They seem identical, but psychologists and neurologists learned many years ago that their functions differ in several respects. For the normal right-handed person, for example, the left hemisphere contains the body's language centre, while the right plays a lesser role in verbal skills. This basic finding was extended shortly before the Second World War, when research with brain-damaged patients (such as stroke victims) indicated that the two brain hemispheres controlled several different functions. The general finding was that the left hemisphere is more skilled in analytical tasks such as language use and problem solving, while the right hemisphere is dominant when it comes to space relations, emotional responses, and other more holistic tasks.

It should be emphasized, though, that the differing functions of the brain's hemispheres are not exactly dichotomized. The two hemispheres actively co-operate in most tasks, while one merely tends to be *dominant* for any specific function.* The role of the brain's hemispheres is even more complicated by the fact that their dichotomized functions are more pronounced for right-handed people than for left-handers. They are also more pronounced in men than in women. Nonetheless, even these limited recent findings have exerted their influence on experimental parapsychology.

One of the central issues facing parapsychology today is whether ESP information is *processed* by the brain or somehow overrides the central nervous system altogether. The CNS is regularly saddled with the job of processing and relaying information coming to us from the outside world. And if the CNS *is* crucially involved with processing ESP information, does ESP work through a specific hemisphere of the brain? The (non-analytical) right hemisphere has long been suspected. It was portentous that one of the first presentations made of the 1983 PA convention was specifically directed to this problem.

Michaleen Maher recently completed her doctoral studies in psychology at City College in New York, and has been making these key issues her primary concern. Her bold presentation, one of the most original at the meeting, sought to show just *how* the brain processes psychic information.

Her experiment was complex and nothing short of brilliant. The New York researcher began by recruiting twenty adults as subjects for her experiment, which was conducted at an EEG laboratory at the City University of New York. The subjects were each tested individually for ESP while sitting in an acoustically shielded chamber and monitored by an EEG, which recorded their brain waves. After taking part in some relaxation exercises, they were instructed to sit back and merely describe all their mental imagery over the next several minutes. The catch was that a sender was busy in another room watching segments drawn from two films. One picture was called the *Love Tape* since it consisted of several people discussing the nature of love. This film was meant to stimulate the right hemisphere of the brain, which monitors emotionally-toned information and facial expressions. The other tape was called the *City Tape*, and was a highly structured documentary on New York city designed to engage the left hemisphere's affinity for processing analytical material. Ms Maher was interested in determining if her subjects would describe any mental pictures that related to the films, but also wanted to see what was happening to their brain waves at the moments when the signals were being sent.

After the experimental period was over, each subject was taken out of the room and chatted with the experimenters. They were then told that their brain waves were going to be monitored under more neutral conditions, such as might occur if they were watching television. The subjects had no idea that they were about to watch the same cassettes that had just been sent to them by ESP. This allowed Ms Maher to determine how her subjects' brain waves normally processed information, which she could then compare to what was going on inside their brains during the preceeding ESP test.

Ms Maher was able to identify a number of subjects who showed strong indications of ESP during the test. These were the subjects who seemed to actually describe those scenes watched by the senders. She had little difficulty finding that the brain waves of her subjects *showed the same general patterns and changes when they were receiving the ESP messages as when they were merely watching the cassettes.* It didn't matter one bit just which brain hemisphere was activated by the information, either. In other words, information that was normally processed by the left hemisphere was also assimilated there during the ESP sending and vice versa. These findings demonstrated to the young experimenter that the brain processes ESP information the same way it handles normal sensory messages. So it would appear that ESP is not necessarily limited to the right hemisphere of the brain, as so many parapsychologists have been speculating.

Whether or not ESP is somehow related to hemispheric lateralization is also an issue that Dr Richard Broughton, a researcher at the Institute for Parapsychology in Durham, has been exploring. Dr Broughton conducted his original research while he was still a doctoral student at the University of Edinburgh. His research was especially designed to see if the left hemisphere of the brain might perhaps be *interfering* with the reception of ESP information. He therefore instructed his subjects to count backwards by three's or four's while sitting in front of a table on which were placed five objects of differing shapes. The subject tried to guess which one of the objects was being touched or thought about by a friend in another room. It was the researcher's theory that the counting task would distract the subject's left hemisphere, thereby allowing the right to respond to the ESP signal. The results of his research, and the many extensions he made of it, seemed promising at first but then faltered and Broughton could find no consistent right hemispheric effect cropping up in his research.

The upshot of these experiments is that Dr Broughton, too, has now shifted his thinking away from the idea that ESP is localized within one specific hemisphere of the brain. He was quite in evidence at the Fairleigh Dickinson meeting and shared his thoughts on ESP and the functions of the brain with his colleagues.

He began by pointing out that it was, after all, quite logical to look to the right hemisphere as the processor and seat of ESP, since ESP messages are often encoded in dreams, through mental imagery, or in visions. These are phenomena that are all rooted in right hemispheric activity. But his own research, in which he tested his subjects for ESP while their left hemispheres were kept distracted and 'out of the way', had disappointed him. Speaking about the recent work of Ms Maher, the Durham parapsychologist admitted that, 'the hypothesis which [she has] advanced, that each hemisphere handles ESP as it does other cognitive functions, is a perfectly reasonable one and it serves as a useful antidote to the frequently encountered propensity to ascribe anything we do not understand to the right hemisphere, ESP included.'

Later in his presentation he even went so far as to admit that, 'I do not think we have made any progress in understanding the relationship between ESP and brain specialization.'

The reason, if Ms Maher's recent findings hold up, may be that there simply isn't any.

But if ESP isn't specialized in either hemisphere of the brain, might it possibly be linked to a specific system within this complex organ?

Psi and the Temporal Lobes
One researcher who thinks this may be the case is Dr Vernon Neppe,

a psychiatrist from the University of Winwatersrand in Johannesburg, South Africa, who was attending his first PA convention in 1983. He has long been one of South Africa's leading researchers and has been proposing that psychic phenomena might be focalized in the temporal lobe or lobes of the brain. (They are sometimes referred to in the singular.) These are the lobes that 'fold under' the frontal lobes located behind the forehead. The temporal lobes play a vital role in memory, hearing, and they are the seat of some hallucinatory experiences.

Dr Neppe's interest in the temporal lobes goes back several years, when he first began studying the lives and personal testimonies of gifted psychics. He explained to his colleagues that he became fascinated by the fact that, apart from their psychic adventures, his informants described a number of anomalous psychological experiences that suspiciously resembled temporal lobe disturbances. These included smelling odd odours and frequent *déjà vu* experiences, both of which are prone to occur when tiny seizures occur there. His suspicions about the temporal lobes were confirmed when he discovered that many of his temporal lobe patients also tended to report frequent *psychic* experiences. But just *how* and *why* should the temporal lobes be saddled with such a bizarre function as producing or relaying psychic information?

'Theoretically,' explained Dr Neppe, 'the temporal lobe is the great integrator of the brain. It receives information from all perceptual modalities admixed with the emotions and memories. Thus, in theory, psi processes could also be integrated in this area of the brain.'

Dr Neppe is not alone in his thinking. Some provisional support for his theory comes from the work of Dr Gordon Nelson, a South African electroencephalographer of international repute. Dr Nelson published a study in 1970 in which he reported on the EEG examinations he had made of several trance mediums. A majority of them showed specific disturbances in the temporal lobes, though none had any history of actual epilepsy.

Perhaps the strongest support for the Neppe/Nelson temporal lobe theory has emerged from yet another country. Canada has never been noted for its parapsychological research, but for several years Dr Michael Persinger has been engaged in some highly original research there at Laurentian University in Sudbury, Ontario. Dr Persinger is a psychologist by training who also commands an impressive expertise in neurology. He has been focusing his interests on the specific interrelationship between psychic experiences and the functions of the temporal lobes, and he has been making some interesting discoveries.

Dr Persinger's work first came to public attention in 1984 when he published a survey showing a correlation between his respondents' propensity to report both psychic experiences and temporal lobe symptoms. This first survey study was flawed, however. It was based on his subjects' responses to several questions concerning their possible temporal lobe disturbances and previous psychic experiences. The problem was that few of the 'psychic experiences' Dr Persinger asked about were typically psychic at all! His survey items focused on out-of-body episodes, experiencing imaginary playmates in childhood, feelings of oneness to God, inner voices, etc. Now none of these experiences are indisputably psychic, and out-of-body experiences as well as feelings of religiosity can even result from temporal lobe disturbances! Only two of the seven questions included by Dr Persinger on his psychic experience index concerned events resembling commonplace extrasensory experiences. These concerned the respondent's feelings that he or she could read somebody else's thoughts, or whether the respondent ever thought about a person right before running into him or her.

Luckily, Dr Persinger was able to replicate his research using a more concise and (to my mind) valid set of questionnaires. The first consisted of 140 items which contained several questions directly or indirectly involved with the measurement of temporal lobe signs. The same subjects who filled out this survey completed a second one a week later. This form included five statements pertaining to their possible psychic experiences:

1. When a close friend or relative died, I just knew something had happened.
2. When a close friend or relative had an emotional conflict, I just knew something was wrong at about the same time.
3. I have had dreams that later turned out to be true.
4. I have seen or experienced the apparition of a close friend or member of the family.
5. I have had vivid dreams in which I was looking through the eyes of a person who lived long ago.

The people surveyed by Dr Persinger also reported the number of personal psychic experiences they had undergone during the previous year.

This short questionnaire is still not perfect, since it seems to me that only the first three items genuinely relate to true psychic experiences. (Seeing an apparition can result from temporal lobe problems, as we will shortly see, while the fifth item seems to be referring to some sort of 'reincarnation' dream. These are reported only rarely by the general public and may not represent a valid form of psychic experience.) But the survey was certainly better than the first one he employed.

Despite these problems, Dr Persinger found a strong correlation (with odds against chance of a thousand to one) when he compared the results of the two surveys. To put it more simply, those subjects who tended to report psychic experiences also reported temporal lobe problems. It is therefore Dr Persinger's working hypothesis that psychic experiences may be generated by transient electrical activity deep within the temporal lobes, perhaps within the structures of the upper brain-stem that regulate emotion.

Of course, the problem with evidence collected from surveys of this type is that it cannot tell us whether the temporal lobes are the core of the psychic sense, or merely help to process ESP information arising from other sites in the brain. But one could freely speculate about the possible role the temporal lobes might play as the brain goes about its normal activities of regulating the body. Some researchers believe that ESP only comes to our conscious attention when a flaw occurs in the nervous system's ability to reject subliminal information (including ESP) from reaching consciousness. It seems that the brain-stem, that primitive part of the brain directly linked to the spinal cord, probably regulates the flow of sensory information to which we are regularly exposed. Yet the research of Drs Neppe and Nelson indicates that perhaps ESP information actually makes it through the brain-stem and is trapped by the temporal lobes before being sent on to the higher cognitive areas of the brain. Chronic disruptions within the temporal lobes might inhibit their ability to censor ESP information from relaying to other areas.

A report which actually suggests such a possibility was delivered to the Parapsychological Association in 1976 by Dr James McHarg of the University of Dundee in Scotland.

The case concerned a most curious apparitional experience. Dr McHarg reported that one of his patients, who suffered from temporal lobe disturbances, was visiting the new home of a friend one afternoon in 1969. Suddenly she suffered the very symptoms that presage a seizure. A funny milkish odour caught her attention and she felt her surroundings becoming 'unreal.' These symptoms are often accompanied by visual hallucinations, and this seizure was no different. The patient saw a woman with soft brown hair standing by a cooker at the far side of the room in which she and her friend were standing. The figure seemed to be staring at her in astonishment. Then it faded from view.

The amazing upshot came when the friend, realizing that a cooker had indeed been located exactly where her guest had seen it, decided to trace the history of the house. Research uncovered the fact that two sisters had previously lived there. A photograph of the sisters was found, and the patient recognized one of the women as the apparition she had seen. This may all sound like a conventional apparitional sighting, but the catch to the story is that this woman was still alive at the time her 'apparition' appeared.

It is Dr McHarg's view that the apparition was the result of his patient's temporal lobe seizure, but that the woman had used her ESP to modify the specific content of the hallucination.

While most research in parapsychology is conducted with otherwise non-exceptional volunteer subjects, investigators interested in focalizing ESP within specific brain functions have been exploring the lives of gifted psychics in the hope of finding some clues. This certainly has been the approach of Dr Neppe and Dr Nelson. Another researcher who is currently studying the experiences — and the nervous systems — of gifted psychics is Dr Elson de A. Montagno, who, over the last few years, has been issuing a series of reports to the Parapsychological Association: 1983 was no different. Dr de A. Montagno is at present co-operating in several projects at the Psychical Research Foundation in Chapel Hill, North Carolina, where he and W.G. Roll, the PRF's long-time project director, have been deeply exploring the mysteries of the brain.

Psi, Epilepsy and the Upper Brain-stem

It is well known that the human brain is the result of a series of evolutionary steps, and actually represents three brains in one. These include the hindbrain, which is the most primitive part of the organ, and which is an outgrowth of the spinal cord. Evolving from the hindbrain is the midbrain, which serves somewhat as a relay station for sensory impulses. It is also the seat of much of our instinctual behaviour. The newest part of the brain is the forebrain, which is the core of our higher thought processes. W.G. Roll and Dr de A. Montagno have long believed that since psychic phenomena probably represent very primitive communication channels, their neurophysiological bases may reside deep inside the older parts of the brain.

W.G. Roll explained to the 1983 Parapsychological Association convention just how he and his colleague came to adopt this viewpoint. It was all an outgrowth of his own investigation of several poltergeist cases.

Roll first suggested a link between psychic phenomena and brain functions to the PA in 1975 when he reported on a bizarre poltergeist case he had recently investigated. The geist was pestering Mr and Mrs Mueller and their two sons, Peter and Thomas, at their home in an undisclosed town in Michigan. The phenomena were varied and violent. Poundings were heard on the walls, exploding noises rocked the house and even put a crack in the kitchen ceiling, pillows and household lamps flew about, and mysterious fires flared up. But the weirdest part of the case was how all the disturbances related to twenty-one-year-old Peter's epilepsy. The development of the poltergeist seemed to progress right along with Peter's escalating medical problems, which culminated in several *grand mal* seizures. This led Roll to posit that perhaps poltergeist eruptions are somehow linked to disruptions within the central nervous system. He thereupon rechecked the EEG recordings he and other investigators had made of other poltergeist agents over the years. Several of the tracings indicated that the subjects of these investigations were also suffering from some sort of disturbance similar to epilepsy.

These data eventually led Roll to take a detailed look at the limbic system of the brain. This system includes a number of mini-organs and lies between the forebrain and the upper brain-stem. It is the neurological base of our instinctual behaviour, houses our pain and pleasure centres, and is the seat of our aggressive tendencies. What better place for the poltergeist to have its roots? This research also led the Chapel Hill researcher to begin wondering if *all* psychic phenomena might not have integral relationships with subsystems within the brain. And it was in search of these possible relationships that Roll began teaming up with Dr de A. Montagno, a physician and parapsychologist who harbours similar sentiments about the relationship of psi to the brain.

Dr de A. Montagno, who is currently teaching at the University of Berlin, has been studying and investigating several psychics both on his own and on behalf of the Psychical Research Foundation. He believes that if ESP has a neurological basis, it will be found in the upper brain-stem, which is one of the most primitive parts of the brain.

Dr de A. Montagno was first alerted to the possible role of the brain-stem in 1971 when he met and became friends with a psychic who suffered edema of the ankles and feet. No medication seemed to work, and the problem was causing the poor woman no end of misery. Even though she was a psychic healer, she couldn't cure herself. Dr de A. Montagno eventually came to the conclusion that the problem was water retention caused by a syndrome of inadequate anti-diuretic hormone. This hormone is regulated by the upper brain-stem, particularly the hypothalamus. It didn't really strike him that the edema had anything to do with the woman's psychic abilities, though, until he met another gifted psychic with the same condition. This psychic was a thirty-one-year-old housewife who developed two peculiar conditions right after her pregnancy a year earlier. She began retaining water abnormally and she began having psychic experiences. As her mediumship developed, so did her condition.

The story doesn't end there, however. Eventually the astounded physician investigated a third psychic who suffered once again with the same problem.

By this time, Dr de A. Montagno realized he was on to something. His suspicions were more than confirmed when he discovered that a French psychic investigator had published a report in the *International Journal of Parapsychology* back in 1963 in which he noted that gifted mediums often suffer water retention. The fact that two researchers had stumbled on to the same syndrome was more than suggestive. It indicated that a causal link between psychic phenomena and the upper brainstem may well exist.

The limbic system is rather complex, since particular organs within the system often contribute to a number of different activities. So neither W.G. Roll nor Dr de A. Montagno have any specific suggestions about the role it plays in the production of psychic phenomena. They pointed out, though, that the limbic system is the seat of our emotions, and it is well known that telepathy often occurs between people — such as relatives or close friends — who share a tight emotional bond. So perhaps a clue lies not so much in how the brain reacts to ESP, but how it normally handles emotionally laden information.

Is There a Neurological Basis for Psychic Phenomena?

So have today's core of bright, young, energetic, and capable parapsychologists solved the mystery of ESP and the brain?

It is pretty obvious that they haven't. But there is equally impressive evidence that they have begun to make a good start. Probably the biggest handicap researchers devoting themselves to this area of enquiry confront is that the brain is still a great mystery. Experts on neurology are still trying to figure out such basics as how the brain encodes memory, and they are still puzzled by how it processes and retrieves information. How ESP functions within the central nervous system is just one more item on the long list of enigmas brain researchers are just beginning to grapple with. Nonetheless, the study of psychic phenomena and their links to the brain promises to help resolve a number of debates which have an important bearing on the nature of man and his mind. For this reason it is a pre-eminently important area of study, despite the limited gains it has made.

In his comprehensive book *The Conscious Brain*, the British biologist

Steven Rose argues that eventually all human behaviour will be explained in terms of brain function. He is impatient with anyone who even dares to think that what we call the 'mind' is anything more than a peculiar essence that has evolved out of the electrical and chemical activities within this organ. Yet another one of the world's leading authorities on the brain, the British neurologist Sir John Eccles, has recently proclaimed that every bit of knowledge we have gained about the brain suggests that the 'mind' is something inherently distinct from it. Perhaps it is for this reason that Dr Rose takes a very dismal view of parapsychology, while Dr Eccles has been a long-time supporter of the field. *If* parapsychologists eventually learn that ESP is a normal outcome of the brain's electrochemical capabilities, perhaps this finding will confirm a rather reductionistic and unspiritual view of man. But if they ultimately fail to discover a causal link between psychic phenomena and the brain, such a finding would bear significantly on such issues as man's immortality, the existence of 'mind', and the nature of the soul.

Parapsychology today is finding itself in a curious dilemma. It is hoping to find a neurological basis for psychic phenomena. But the most challenging issues will only be raised if it *fails* in this quest.

End-Notes for Chapter Six

* Some of the different functions of the two hemispheres are based on cases where their connecting links have been cut, or during experiments for which half of the brain is anaesthetized. These are very abnormal conditions, and it is a moot point whether the findings from such studies are representative of the brain's functionings under normal conditions. For more on this position, refer to *Two Sides of the Brain* by Dr Sid J. Segalowitz (Englewood Cliffs, NJ: Prentice Hall, 1983).

7.

Can the Weather Make You Psychic?

Over ten years ago, a private conference on 'Parapsychology and the Sciences' was convened in the Netherlands by the New York-based Parapsychology Foundation. Twenty researchers from around the world (including myself) met in Amsterdam to discuss the relationship between psi and everything from abnormal psychology to chemistry. One topic that came up was considerably more off-beat. Could meteorological factors influence our ability to function psychically?

This possibility was initially raised by the late Dr Solco Tromp, former director of the Biometeorological Research in Leiden. Dr Tromp, who was also a widely acknowledged expert on dowsing, reminded us that meteorological conditions can subtly affect several of the body's physiological functions — such as white blood cell count, blood clotting time, and the reactivity of the nervous system. Such environmental factors as the weather can also influence the restlessness of schizophrenics, suicide rates in the general population, and several parameters of animal behaviour. It seems that there somehow exists a mechanism in the brain that registers weak signals from the physical environment. This, suggested Dr Tromp, could eventually help us to understand the mechanism that lies behind extrasensory perception.

'The study,' he concluded, 'of the various physiological mechanisms of mental processes in man in relation to those meteorological stimuli that are unconsciously perceived will prove to be a valuable tool in the future for the study of the mechanism and mode of perception of parapsychological phenomena.'

Dr Tromp's opinions prompted no little debate at the conference. George Zorab — one of the deans of parapsychology in the Netherlands — took strong issue with his colleague. While he didn't believe that weather or cosmic factors could materially influence the psi process, he did tell us about a curious incident dating from 1946 when several experimenters in Holland, following the work of J.B. Rhine at Duke University, tried to determine if psychokinesis could influence the fall of ordinary playing dice. 'There was one of the members of the Dutch Society who threw about 120 times,' Zorab reported. 'But no significant effect. No significant results. Only when there was, in the afternoon, a tremendous thunderstorm, suddenly the results jumped up to a high level.'

Mr Zorab didn't know whether the connection was coincidental or not. But, he added, the subject himself claimed that the shock and fright of the storm suddenly increased his psychic powers.

This certainly was an unusual result, since some prominent psychics dislike working or exhibiting their powers when the atmosphere is electrified. This is especially true of Nina Kulagina, the Soviet psychic so well know for her displays of PK. It is also true of Keith Harary, whose powers of leaving the body were documented in the early 1970s at the Psychical Research Foundation in Durham.

Despite this small controversy, no one ever followed up the leads suggested at the Parapsychology Foundation's 1972 conference.* Determining if the weather can influence psychic functioning was a topic that was virtually ignored for over a decade, but recently there has been a surprising resurgence of interest in this possibility. I made this discovery in August 1985 when I flew to the Boston area to attend the annual convention of the Parapsychological Association, a body consisting solely of professional or serious researchers in the field. The meeting convened at Tufts University, and the subject of meteorology turned out to be a prominent feature of the convention.

The most important contribution to the discussion was a paper by Dr Michael Persinger of the Neuroscience Laboratory at Laurentian University in Canada, whose research on psi and the brain was discussed earlier in this volume.

ESP and Geomagnetic Activity

For some years now, Dr Persinger has been attempting to map out what geophysical, electromagnetic, and/or atmospheric factors might be feasibly influencing extrasensory perception. The Tufts University convention marked Dr Persinger's first assay at bringing his data specifically to the attention of his parapsychological colleagues. It was therefore unfortunate that he was prevented from personally delivering his paper due to a last minute emergency. This situation placed his paper in some jeopardy at first, since the rules that govern PA conventions dictate that papers cannot be delivered by proxy. Luckily though, Dr Persinger's assistant *was* present and since he had been instrumental in collecting some of the data that served as the basis for the paper, the programme committee was willing to make an exception. George Stauch is currently finishing up his psychology degree at Laurentian University, and was eager to get a hearing for the findings he had helped uncover.

It has long been Dr Persinger's belief that telepathy and clairvoyance result from information carried over extremely low frequency (ELF) electro-magnetic waves, presumably generated by the brain. This view has led him to look at the level of geomagnetic activity present during days when psychic experiences tend to be reported. Since ELF waves are affected by geomagnetic factors, he expected to find some sort of positive correlation. So to test his theory, the Canadian psychologist used what is called the antipodal (aa) index, which records half-day measures of the world's geomagnetic activity from which monthly and weekly averages can also be determined. Day by day records are extant back to 1868, and Dr Persinger set about trying to correlate reports of dramatic psychic experiences to the index listings.

He began by looking into a collection of telepathic impression cases (cases in which the experiencer had a waking but non-hallucinatory impression or intuition of a distant event). These had been collected, studied, and subsequently published by Dr Ian Stevenson of the University of Virginia in 1970. Twenty-five of the cases in the collection were specifically dated, so Dr Persinger graphed out the levels of geomagnetic activity for the target dates and for the several days before and after them. He found strong evidence (with odds to 1000 to 1) that Stevenson's cases were reported from days of relatively low geomagnetic activity . . . often even lower than the *monthly* average.

Twenty-five cases really aren't too much to go on, so Dr Persinger expanded his study by going back into the past. One of the richest collections of spontaneous telepathy cases was published in 1886 by the founders of the Society for Psychical Research in London. *Phantasms of the Living* is a massive two-volume set of well-documented reports that still ranks today as one of parapsychology's true classics. Many of the cases included date back before 1868, for which meteorological data are not available. But Dr Persinger was able to extract seventy-eight usable accounts from the study, and the pattern he had previously found in the Stevenson cases cropped up once again. This was more of a trend in the data than a firm finding, but again the target days tended to be less geomagnetically active than the monthly or yearly averages.

To serve as an added control, Dr Persinger carried out a further statistical test. He compared his key collection of seventy-eight cases to thirty-one cases included in *Phantasms* that contained discrepencies — i.e., errors suggesting that the subject's psychic experience was questionable or incorrectly dated. These cases, as predicted by the researcher, did *not* conform to the geomagnetic activity pattern linked to the more evidential cases.

For a final check on his data, Dr Persinger asked his assistant (George Stauch) to comb through back issues of *Fate* magazine from 1960-70 for even more usable cases. *Fate* has the largest circulation of any psychic-oriented magazine in the United States, and it regularly publishes two columns in which its readers can report their personal psychic experiences. Persinger and Stauch were able to collect and classify fifty-seven of them as telepathy/clairvoyance experiences. This became their new database, while they catalogued an additional fifty-six reports as probable instances of precognition to serve as a control base. (These cases did not enter into their primary analysis since Persinger and Stauch were postulating that geomagnetic factors only influence 'real-time' ESP, such as telepathy and clairvoyance.)

By consulting the antipodal index, the researchers were again able to show that strong psychic occurrences tend to be reported from days of low geomagnetic activity relative to the weekly average. That such incidents tend to fall on days of geomagnetic activity lower than the monthly or yearly average also held up. Since Dr Persinger does not believe that precognition is necessarily contingent on ELF waves, he and Stauch did not expect to find any correlation between the antipodal index and *Fate's* precognition cases. Their hunch was correct, for an analysis of the control data revealed no significant link between the cases and cosmic factors.

Since these results are hard to refute, it really does seem as though meteorological, environmental and geomagnetic activities influence the ESP channel. But what could be the nature of this exotic influence?

Since Dr Persinger wasn't attending the conference, I couldn't ask him about this question directly. My primary concern was that he and his assistant were actually isolating a reporting artifact — in other words, they might be telling us something about the days on which psychic experiences get *reported* rather than when they are actually experienced. It was my hunch that people who experience striking instances of ESP on days of low geomagnetic activity simply remember and/or report them more often for some reason. Why? Days of less intense geomagnetic activity are 'easier' on us and our system, which tends to be less biologically agitated during such times. If an episode of ESP were to be experienced on such a day, it might simply jolt us and burn into our memories especially vividly. We might therefore be more prone to report it and place it into print.

I broached this idea to George Stauch after he reported on Dr Persinger's findings, but he was sceptical. He pointed out that my theory could not explain why only telepathic and clairvoyant experiences seem linked to geomagnetic activity and not spontaneous premonitions. My response was that there is good evidence that cases of real-time ESP are more vivid and carry with them more of a sense of conviction than precognition experiences.[†] Geophysical factors might enhance the *sense of conviction* cases of real-time ESP bring with them, a factor to which precognitive experiences may be immune.

Whether or not the Persinger data is a genuine finding or a reporting artifact is moot, however. For some further data presented at the conference could *not* be due to reporting effects, but seem to represent a genuine connection between psi and meteorological factors.

Replications of the Geomagnetic Effect

The Time Research Institute is a relatively small organization currently based in Woodside, California just south of San José and the San Francisco Bay area. The primary goal of the group has been the study of how our behaviour is influenced by the environment, but recently they have begun looking into some parapsychological matters. One of their researchers is Marsha H. Adams, who has obviously been nurturing a long-lived interest in extrasensory perception. She must have been heartened by the fact that her paper caused as much interest as had Dr Persinger's. Her results were even more startling! The main focus of her interest was the remote viewing procedure first developed at the Stanford Research Institute (now SRI International) in the early 1970s.

As I explained in an earlier chapter, this procedure is becoming of increasing importance to parapsychology. As was noted, the subject stays at SRI with the primary experimenter, while a second (or outbound) experimenter drives to a randomly selected point in the Bay area. The subject is then asked to psychically visit the target location and describe what he or she sees there. Several sessions are typically run with each subject and the transcripts are then turned over to a blind judge. His job is to determine if it is possible to match up the descriptions with the actual target sites, which he either visits or evaluates from photographs. The protocol has now been replicated at other parapsychology laboratories as well.

By consulting an unpublished data pool at SRI, Dr Adams was able to collect data from over 500 remote viewing sessions contributed by twenty-three subjects, which she broke down into successful versus unsuccessful trials. These two sets of information were then compared to records drawn from several geomagnetic indices, even those affecting specific three-hour slots of time before and after the specific experiments were run. While the findings of the California researcher were a little more complicated than those presented by her Canadian colleague, they seem to be pointing in the same direction. It turned out that geomagnetic activity tended to be more active one or two days *before* an unsuccessful remote viewing session, but quieter before a successful one. These results would indicate that the days directly preceding a parapsychological experiment are just as critical as the target days themselves. Such a finding could possibly help parapsychologists watch for especially good days on which to run their tests.

Despite the fact that she is clearly on to something, Dr Adams remains perplexed by the fact that the critical factors seem to precede the days on which remote viewing experiments are run. 'Relationships with lead or lag times of up two or three days are puzzling,' she admitted. 'They may indicate that the relationship between the geomagnetic field and remote viewing performance might not be directly *tied* to GMF values, but rather to another geophysical factor which co-varies with the GMF, or to some more subtle aspect of the GMF than can be found in the indices available today.'

Solar flares might be one factor to look at, since they influence both human behaviour *and* the geomagnetic field.

When I talked with George Stauch again after Dr Adams concluded her presentation, I found that he, too, was puzzled over what specific mechanism could be responsible for his own results.

'Trying to isolate the precise mechanism by which [geomagnetic] energies could interact with us during psi experiments would be difficult to determine,' he told me. 'It's difficult to speculate how organisms would be able to code or decipher the information.' He also explained that, even granting the existence of a causative link between the geomagnetic field and ESP-carrying ELF waves, we would still be somewhat in the dark. We would then have to ferret out which components, bands, or waves from the ELF-EM (electromagnetic) field influence the psychic channel.

Dr Adams is not the only researcher who has replicated Dr Persinger's findings. The research presented by Dr Persinger, his assistant, and Dr Adams was so persuasive that other researchers are beginning to look back at their old data. When the 1985 conference was over, Dr Stanley Krippner — who was once part of the famous dream telepathy laboratory team at Maimonides Medical Center in Brooklyn — decided to check the lab's records. He reported back to me in December (1985) that his *post-hoc* analysis was confirming his Canadian colleague's data. Dr

Krippner recently prepared a report on his findings.

Explanatory Models for the 'Persinger' Effect

There is an old saying in science that a good experiment will answer one question, while unlocking a box full of even more provocative ones. Such can certainly be said of the research on whether meteorological factors possibly influence our psychic potentials. *Whether* there exists a relationship has obviously been answered, but it is the precise nature of the interacting factors that remain a puzzle. Certainly there is no lack of speculation on the issue. Some people will, no doubt, favour Dr Persinger's view that a strong connection exists between the earth's geomagnetic field and ESP because of the way the field interferes with electromagnetic waves generated by the brain and body. But the idea that geomagnetic flux is itself a response to more primary cosmic factors simply can't be dismissed.

There is also a more behaviouristic position that the sceptic can take, which happens to be my own bias. Many atmospheric and environmental conditions may simply make us more 'open' to psychic impressions. Days of low geomagnetic activity, for example, may have a calming affect on the mind. It has been known for years that mental and physiological quiescence is a primary requisite for receiving ESP information.

But perhaps the final word will come from neither psychology nor physics, but from the rapidly evolving neurosciences. There has been a great deal of speculation that brain functions may be instrumental for the reception of ESP information. Could there be a link between brain functions, psi, and the geomagnetic field?

Such a line of speculation was inadvertently contributed by Serena Roney-Dougal, a young British parapsychologist who was also attending the conference. Her presentation was devoted to whether the psychedelic drug harmaline might help to chemically induce ESP experiences, since several native tribes in South America have been using it for that purpose for many years. Ms Roney-Dougal's primary point was that harmaline is chemically similar to a molecule found naturally in the brain's pineal gland, which — according to yogic tradition — is the legendary seat of mystical powers.

I perked up as Ms Roney-Dougal was reading her paper, for it took me back to the conference I had attended in Amsterdam. Solco Tromp had specifically stated there that the pineal gland was probably instrumental in our ability to register and respond to cosmic influences. Connections?

Whether or not there is a connection between the sixth sense, cosmic factors, and brain biochemistry is a far-reaching line of speculation. But perhaps it is one we should be exploring vigorously.

End-Notes for Chapter Seven

* The only possible exception occurred in 1973 when Dr Livingston Gearhart of the State University of Buffalo (New York) researched whether poltergeist outbreaks tend to occur on days of extreme geomagnetic perturbation. He analysed twenty cases reported between 1915 and 1969 but found no firm relationship.

† *Conviction* is Dr Louisa Rhine's term for the flash of insight that tells the percipient that he has had a genuine psychic experience.

8.

The Search for ESP in Animals

I was still attending college in my home town of Los Angeles in 1971, and had just moved into my own apartment. It was across town from my parents' home, but much closer to the campus. I did have a few regrets about moving out. Not getting home-cooked meals was one of them, but I especially missed my two dogs. One was an old beagle named Freddy, and the other was a much younger mutt named Peanut that I had found abandoned in a parking lot six or so years earlier. I had left them at my parents' house, where they had a large yard in which to romp and roam.

Freddy was almost fifteen years old at this time, and twice that year my parents had to rush him to the vet when he took ill. Peanut took these emergencies in his stride. He seemed perfectly indifferent about the entire situation. Then, one morning in September, my parents found Freddy very sick again and immediately took him to the vet. Later that day the vet told them that there wasn't much he could do . . . there was just too much wrong this time. My parents regretfully gave permission for Freddy to be put to sleep.

When my parents came home later that day they went to tell our neighbours about the events of the day. But when my mother reported what had happened, she was in for a surprise.

'I know all about it,' my neighbour's wife explained.

'How?,' my mother replied nonplussed.

'Why, Peanut told me all about it. He howled all day long.'

This was really weird, since Peanut had never reacted during the other times when Freddy had been taken to the vet, and never in his life had he ever howled. Barked, yes. But *howled*? Never.

Was this a coincidence? Did Peanut somehow sense Freddy's imminent death? Or did he somehow reach out telepathically and tune in on what was happening?

This little story is representative of a great deal of anecdotal material that has come to the attention of those of us who have made a career out of the study of parapsychology, the scientific study of ESP and other forms of psychic phenomena. These include reports telling of dogs that inexplicably cried when their masters were involved in accidents far away, cats that become restless when some horror befell their littermates, horses that began neighing and bolting just before some natural disaster struck, and a host of other stories right out of a Ripley's 'Believe it or Not' column.

Of course, stories such as these will not impress the sceptic, who will naturally just brush them aside as coincidences. But anecdotes such as these have led many of us in the field to look deeply into the whole area of animal ESP — and the possibility of capturing this elusive faculty (if it exists) in the laboratory — with a great deal of optimism. If animals possess ESP, perhaps this finding will help us to understand why *we* possess it as well.

The fact that some excellently documented cases of ostensible animal ESP have been placed on file has also encouraged some of us to believe that the key to solving the riddle of ESP may rest in the animal world. One such incident was reported as a human interest item in 1956 by the late Danton Walker, a well-known, syndicated, Broadway columnist. He told a story that had come to him from Mr and Mrs Donald S. Rockwell of Westchester County, New York. Mrs Rockwell explained how she had been home one afternoon when, at about three o'clock, her Great Dane began acting rather strangely. He would bolt upstairs and bring down articles of clothing belonging to Mrs Rockwell's sister, who was staying with them for a while. Mrs Rockwell really knew something was wrong when the dog laid down on the clothing and began whimpering. Later that day, the police called to inform her that her sister had been killed at about 3.00 p.m. during an airborne sightseeing tour.

This case, *if* it occurred the way it was reported, is hard to explain away as a coincidence. The dog had apparently never acted in this manner before and the correlation between his behaviour and the accident is too bizarre to easily dismiss.

The Phenomenon of Psi-trailing

A case I personally looked into during my day-to-day work as a parapsychologist specializing in field investigations, is similarly provocative. This incident, which I studied in 1981, constitutes an intriguing case of what has been called 'psi-trailing'. These are cases where a lost or abandoned animal will somehow be able to find its master, even by travelling through unfamiliar territory. My case wasn't spectacular, but strange enough to indicate that ESP was a likely explanation.

I learned of the incident directly from the chief witness, a twenty-two-year-old photographer living in a Los Angeles suburb, whose mongrel had apparently traversed seven miles through an unfamiliar area of town to find him. The event occurred after Tim had moved out of his parents' house and into a converted garage behind one of their rental properties. His dog, who he had left behind, had never been to the garage. In fact, the dog had never in all his life travelled more than a mile or so from his home since he got violently carsick if driven anywhere. Several weeks after Tim had moved, though, the dog escaped from the backyard and disappeared. A few days later Tim and his room-mate were ready to leave their makeshift apartment when there . . . standing outside and sniffing the house . . . was the dog. The fact that he showed up within a day or so of his disappearance is inferential evidence that it was actually seeking out his master and did not simply stumble upon the right house.

There is, of course, certain limits to the value contributed by this type of material. Incidents such as these, when evaluated independently, tell us nothing about the inner workings of ESP, nor anything about its nature. My only approach to the case was to track down all the witnesses and make sure the story panned out properly and that everyone's evidence was consistent. Such a case doesn't even tell us very much about the nature of ESP in animals. We are left wondering if *all* animals possess this capability, if ESP in general is a widespread animal supersense, or what.

Nonetheless, some researchers have made a valiant attempt to study similar cases of psi-trailing in hopes that large collections of such data might reveal something important about the nature of animal ESP. In the 1950s, researchers at the famous Duke University Parapsychology Laboratory (which had been founded in 1937 by the late Dr J.B. Rhine) began taking a serious look at these cases to see if they might reveal anything of unusual interest. Their major finding was that psi-trailing seemed to be a widespread phenomenon distributed through several species of the animal kingdom, perhaps akin to the 'homing instinct' possessed by some of them.

One case which Rhine himself investigated and documented was reported in 1951 by Mr and Mrs Stacy Woods of Gage, Oklahoma. Mr Woods had been a school principle in Anderson, California, but he and his wife decided to leave in order to take up farming in Gage. The move was what initiated the incident they reported. The Woods had long owned a cream-coloured Persian cat named Sugar. Their original plan was to take Sugar with them, but the cat was terrified of automobiles and refused to stay in the car when the Woods prepared to leave. The only thing the couple could do was leave her behind with neighbours. They left broken-hearted, but knew at least that their pet would be well taken care of. What they didn't know was that Sugar ran away shortly after they had left and was never seen by the neighbours again.

The upshot to all this came fourteen months later in Gage. Mrs Woods was working in the barn of the new farm when a cat suddenly jumped through the window and landed on her shoulder! It was a cream-coloured Persian cat. Mr and Mrs Woods adopted the stray and toyed with the idea that it really was Sugar, since it looked identical to their former pet. But they couldn't believe that she had actually got all the way to Oklahoma from California. They just shrugged off the uncanny resemblance between the two animals as a coincidence. Then Mr Woods made a curious discovery. While petting the cat on his lap one night, he noticed that it had a curiously deformed hip-bone. Sugar had been born with this identical deformation and the Woods now knew that this cat *must* really be Sugar. It was only then that they contacted their former neighbours and learned of Sugar's mysterious disappearance.

Rhine journeyed to Gage when this case came to his attention and personally verified the deformed hip-bone and took down the testimony of the Woods.

Another similar case was reported from Summerville, West Virginia where a twelve-year-old boy had found a homing pigeon in his backyard. It was tagged with a metal band numbered 167. Hugh, a young honour student, adopted the bird and cared for it until he had to be taken to a hospital some 115 miles away for medical treatment. A week later Hugh was sitting in bed when he heard a fluttering at the window of his hospital room. It was snowing outside and he asked the nurse to open the window and let whatever was out there come in. She did . . . and in stepped a pigeon. Hugh immediately recognized it as his pet, and confirmed the fact by the metal band and number on its leg. The pigeon had apparently flown seventy straight miles to find his master.

The press had a field day with the story when it was originally reported. A radio station in Columbus, Ohio even tracked down the nurse who had opened the window and interviewed her over the air.

Of course, these reports *are* only stories. But there seems no logical reason to dismiss them just because of their anecdotal nature. But the real case for ESP in animals does not rest with such anecdotes and field studies. For years parapsychologists both in the United States and in Europe have been actively experimenting in the laboratory with canine, feline, and even rodent subjects. Science is primarily experimental. Discoveries can only be made when a theory generates testable hypotheses that can be empirically verified or falsified. It was therefore inevitable that experimental parapsychologists would take the area of animal ESP out of the wilds, so to speak, and subjected it to controlled experimentation.

Let's take a detailed look at these studies and see if they actually do demonstrate ESP in animals; and if so, just what they seem to be indicating about the ability.

ESP in the Aquatic World

Probably the most basic question about animal ESP is whether it is widely distributed throughout the animal kingdom. Just how many *kinds* of animals possess ESP? Parapsychologists have long been interested in this question. If ESP is a natural ability normal to life, one might expect that all animals — not just highly evolved ones like dogs and cats — would possess the sixth sense. This has led some researchers to experiment with very primitive animal forms to see if they have some control over extrasensory powers. Parapsychologists in Great Britain, for example, demonstrated back in the 1950s and '60s that even such tiny animals as paramecia (one-celled animals that have to be viewed through a microscope) and wood-lice can at least receive ESP messages. The experimenters placed the little critters on glass plates and then 'willed' them to swim or crawl either up, down, to the left, or to the right. A different direction was chosen for each trial, of course. This simple experiment was repeated over and over again, and the animals often actually moved in the direction toward which they were telepathically commanded. Similar experiments have been conducted with sea worms, caterpillars, and ants.

Even fish seem to possess ESP powers. Dr Robert Morris, a former colleague of mine at the Psychical Research Foundation in Durham, demonstrated this when he was still working at the Institute for Parapsychology, which is also located there. (This is the old Duke University Parapsychology Laboratory. It moved off campus in 1967 where it became the Foundation for Research on the Nature of Man and the Institute became its research organ.) Dr Morris made use of a simple T-maze for his experiment. This is a maze shaped like a 'T'. An animal is released at the base of the maze and will be forced to turn either to the left or right when it reaches the junction at the cross-area of the stem. Morris filled the T-maze with water, released fish into it, and then tried to mentally will them to turn either to the left or right. His attempts were marginally significant. In order to substantiate his findings further, he went on to design a more complicated experiment in which the fish were tested for precognition. Once again this test was conducted under the auspices of the Institute for Parapsychology. Morris, being an animal behaviourist, knew that fish tend to become agitated when faced with a threatening situation. So he placed three goldfish in a tank and had a research assitant monitor their behaviour. His job was to determine which of the fish acted most agitated. This was established by seeing which fish swam about more than the others. After the assistant had made his observations, Morris caught one of the fish in a net and held it aloft over the tank — which is certainly a very traumatic experience if you happen to be a fish! He chose the fish randomly and found that the one he caught in his little net was often the fish which his assistant had found to be particularly active as it swam about. His conclusion was that the fish had actually *foreseen* that its life was about to be momentarily threatened.

Unfortunately, the results of this experiment were still only marginal. It didn't strike Dr Morris that the results were very stable, reliable or replicatable.

There was actually very little work done with animals during the 1950s and '60s. Most parapsychologists felt that it was more fruitful to work with people than fish, dogs, cats, or rodents. The few research projects that had been executed were intriguing, but they just didn't show very strong or reliable results. All this was soon to change, though. The world of animal ESP research (or *anpsi* research, for short) received a charge in 1968 when two scientists in France, writing under the pseudonyms of Pierre Duval and Evelyn Montredon, reported on a new technique they had developed to test the ESP powers of mice. This experiment was easy to run, harmless to the animals, and — according to the scientists — highly reliable. They conducted their research at the Sorbonne in Paris.

ESP Goes to the Rats

The design of the Duval-Montredon experiment was quite simple. They used a specially constructed box which was divided in half by a low barrier. A grid was constructed at the bottom of the cage which was capable of conducting an electrical current. The box was then hooked up to a generator which delivered a series of shocks to either side of the cage in random order. A shock was sent every minute or so. Since most animals have a strong aversion to electrical shock, the experimenters were interested in determining if mice placed in the apparatus could precognize which side of the box was about to receive the shock by jumping over the barrier and escaping it. So they started placing the rodents in the box, turning on the generator, and watching what would happen. Now the mice would, of course, jump over the barrier when they received a shock in the side of the box in which they were situated. This was a normal response to the discomfort. But the French researchers started paying special attention to those moments when the mice jumped across the barrier for no apparent reason. These they called 'random behaviour trials.' By testing the mice over and over again, they discovered that the rodents tended to jump over the barrier when the side of the cage in which they had been placed was *about* to be shocked. This tendency was too consistent to have been due to coincidence. The mice seemed to *know* when and where the shock was coming and had jumped the barrier to avoid it.

Duval and Montredon conducted a series of such tests before submitting their research for publication in the *Journal of Parapsychology*, which is the official publication of the Institute for Parapsychology. The Durham people were extremely excited when they learned about these experiments, for it seemed that the French researchers had discovered a consistent way of studying ESP in animals. The test was very easy to run. It could also be totally automated. The box and the generator could be hooked up to special equipment which would keep a record of where the mice were when the shocks were delivered, which side of the cage was given each charge, and so on. All the experimenter had to do was to set up the experiment and let the equipment do all the work. Then he could either busy himself with other matters or enjoy a casual lunch!

The actual task of replicating the French rodent research fell to Dr W.J. Levy, a young doctor who had only recently joined the Institute staff. Dr Levy was able to report a series of consistent replications of the French research, but this research was called into question in 1974 when he was caught faking some of his later research. So it is an open question whether the French work was really confirmed at Rhine's laboratory.

The Levy work did, however, leave parapsychology with a considerable legacy. The success of his early work stirred other parapsychologists, both in the United States and in Europe, to begin their own experimentation with small rodents.

Researchers in Europe were especially fascinated by the original Duval-Montredon work and Dr Levy's initial and alleged replication of it. They, however, tended to be put off by the fact that the animals had to be punished by shocks if they didn't show off their psychic capabilities. The result was that several European researchers began designing rodent ESP tests which rewarded the animals if they succeeded. This allowed them to conduct their tests with a clearer conscience. It was also a lot easier on the rodents!

Some of the first work along these lines was conducted by Sybo Schouten at the University of Utrecht, which has long maintained an excellent parapsychology laboratory. Schouten's plan was to see if his mice could use ESP to get nourishment. He began by training the mice in a special cage equipped with a waterfeeding tube. A lever inside the cage controlled the feeding system. A light bulb was located inside as well. The mice were taught that they could get a drop of water by pulling the lever down, but only when the light bulb flashed on. After the mice had learned how to work the lever and water system, they were tested for ESP. They were placed in a new box which had two levers. A generator randomly determined that only one of the levers would release water from the tube at any given time. Schouten hoped that each mouse being tested would be able to choose the correct lever once the light bulb went on. The test was successful since, after a great many trials, Schouten was able to determine that the mice were able to choose the correct lever more than the expected 50 per cent of the time.

Schouten went on to design what may be called the first experiment in 'mouse telepathy'. He conducted the same experiment as outlined above but with one catch. A second mouse was placed in a separate but identical box and was *shown* which was the correct lever to push. It was Schouten's theory that the second mouse might be able to telepathically inform his little cousin which lever to choose. This experiment was also successful.

Unfortunately, there has only been one independent attempt to replicate the Schouten work. This was conducted in the United States by Jim Terry who teamed up with Susan Harris, a student at Mount Holyoke College in Massachussets. However, they used rats instead of mice and were successful in their endeavour.

Researchers in England also began testing rodents for ESP by using rewards instead of punishment. They, too, were successful. So all in all, the small-rodent ESP effect did hold up reasonably well despite the disqualification of the Levy research.

There was also another intriguing development which came to parapsychology's attention during this time as well. The fuss and *furor* caused by the Duval-Montredon work gradually led a few researchers to ask an even more provocative question. If animals can make psychic contact with the outside world through some sort of sixth sense, might they also be capable of actually controlling it? In other words, do animals possess PK as well as ESP?

The Case for Animal PK

The pioneering work in this controversial area of parapsychology was the brainchild of Dr Helmut Schmidt, a physicist from Germany who originally settled in Seattle, Washington where he worked with the Boeing Laboratories. Because he had long nurtured a strong interest in parapsychology he eventually moved to Durham where he joined the staff of the Institute for Parapsychology. He has long been concerned with whether animals possess PK, and experimented first with very simple forms of life such as algae and even yeast cultures. But it wasn't until he began working with cockroaches at the Institute that he hit the jackpot!

Dr Schmidt conducted his first successful experiment there in 1970. It was an ingenious test. He placed the cockroaches on an electric grid which was hooked to a generator. Every so often the generator would activate and would either deliver a shock to the grid or would withhold it. The order was entirely random. This meant that when the cockroaches were placed on the grid for a series of trials, the generator would deliver shocks when activated 50 per cent of the time. The other 50 per cent of the time no shock would be administered. It was Dr Schmidt's belief that the cockroaches, should they genuinely possess PK ability, would use their powers to 'zap' the inner workings of the generator, run by a high speed oscillator, and cause it to malfunction so that it would deliver the shocks somewhat *less* than 50 per cent of the time. To use a terrible pun, they had to put a 'bug' in the machine. Schmidt tested several cockroaches before making a most amazing discovery. It seemed that the cockroaches were causing the generator to deliver *more* shocks than expected. It looked as if the insects were actually seeking out the shocks as a form of stimulation! This certainly didn't make much biological sense, since animals try to avoid unpleasant experiences just as we do.

This finding alerted Dr Schmidt to a major problem in his research. Since he had run the tests with the cockroaches himself, could it be that he might have used his *own* PK on the generator? This idea does make some sense, since many people have a natural and emotional aversion to insects. Schmidt once readily admitted to me, as well as to his colleagues in Durham, that he really didn't like working with the cockroaches one bit. So his aversion to his own test might have led him to unconsciously punish the insects by unknowingly zapping the generator into producing even more shocks than it normally should have. Dr Schmidt soon realized that he would have to revise his test in order to get around this thorny problem.

For his next test Schmidt decided to use his pet cat and to automate the experiment so that he wouldn't have to monitor it. That way he wouldn't interfere with it, he hoped. He began by placing the cat in a shed behind his home in Durham. It gets pretty cold at night down there and the only source of heat in the shed was an electric lamp that was hooked to a generator which would randomly turn it on and off. The lamp was programmed to stay on precisely 50 per cent of the time after the generator had been activated. Schmidt's theory was that the cat would use its PK powers to cause the light to remain on more than the expected 50 per cent of the time in order to stay warm. Since the test was automated, Dr Schmidt left the shed for the duration of the experiment. By remaining inside his house when the test was being run, the physicist hoped that no PK would escape from his mind to help out his trusty little pet.

The results of the test confirmed Dr Schmidt's theory. The cat was indeed able to make the light stay on above the 50 per cent rate. He was not able to replicate this experiment, however. The temperature in Durham started to warm up and the cat soon got wise and learned to hate the shed. She would run away from it as soon as anyone tried to get her to go inside. Even animals can sometimes be uncooperative subjects, so Dr Schmidt was never able to finish his hoped-for follow-up.

Dr Schmidt's PK test with the heat lamp did prompt many other researchers at the Institute for Parapsychology to design similar experiments, however. They ran a host of replications using lizards, chicks, and even unhatched chicken embryos with some reported success.

Although there has been relatively little research conducted to explore the PK powers of animals, most of the work which has been done followed closely along the lines of Schmidt's original experiment. The only major exception to this rule has been a very clever experiment which was run only a few years ago by Dr William Braud of the Mind Science Foundation in San Antonio, Texas. Dr Braud spent most of his early career studying the learning capacities of freshwater fish at the University of Houston before turning to parapsychology. Since his early work utilized freshwater fish, it wasn't long before he began wondering if fish might also be gifted PK subjects.

Braud soon designed a novel test to explore this possibility. First he procured two Siamese fighting fish. These fish are very aggressive and will even attack their own reflections. They were placed in a special tank that was equipped with a mirror which could be turned either towards the fish or away from them. The mirror was then hooked to a generator which produced a high-speed oscillation. As long as the generator was running smoothly, the mirror would only activate and turn towards the tank a specific number of times. Of course, as soon as the fish saw their reflections they would become very agitated. They would change colour, extend their gills, beat their tails and put on quite a show. It was Braud's theory that, once placed in the tank, the naturally aggressive fish would use PK to interfere with the oscillations being produced by the generator and cause the mirror to turn towards them more frequently than it should under normal conditions.

He was right. After several days of testing, Dr Braud discovered that the fighting fish did seem capable of affecting the oscillations. To check his findings, he also tested two other species of aggressive fish as well as common goldfish which are rather placid. As he expected, the aggressive fish were all capable of affecting the generator while the goldfish were not.

Dr Braud's test is certainly an ingenious one. Hopefully it will soon be replicated by other parapsychologists interested in anpsi research.

The world of animal PK has not, unfortunately, been as thoroughly researched as has the world of animal ESP. It is for this reason that it is hard to draw any firm conclusions from the relatively few studies that have been carried out in this area. So do these tests really indicate that animals possess psychokinetic abilities? This is a pretty tricky question and one that is very hard to answer. The problem with most of the PK tests that we have been looking at is identical to the possibility Dr Schmidt faced during his cockroach experiments. It is practically impossible to tell if the animals were employing their PK powers during the tests or if the experimenter was contributing the talent himself. Just look at Dr Braud's tests. Who is to say that he wasn't using his *own* PK to affect the generator? The same is true even of Dr Schmidt's tests with his cat. We don't know any limits which restrict PK power, so there is no reason that the good doctor couldn't have projected his mind-power all the way from his house to the shed. ESP can function over great distances. Perhaps PK can too.

So far we have talked about the psychic world of paramecia, cockroaches, goldfish, rats, mice and many other animals with which we interact very little during our day-to-day living. But you must remember that, having discovered that animals possess ESP, it was absolutely essential for parapsychologists to learn just how widespread psychic abilities are within the animal kingdom. This includes the search for PK as well as ESP. But the story of experimental ESP research with animals doesn't end here by any means. Dogs and cats have also made some surprising débuts in the parapsychological laboratory.

ESP and the Feline World

Back in the 1960s, two enterprising experimenters at the Duke University Parapsychology Laboratory became interested in testing the psychic capabilities of cats. Dr Karlis Osis, a psychologist who originally came to Durham from Latvia, and his assistant at the lab, E.B. Foster, ran two series of tests with kittens who were made to run a 'T-maze. They secretly placed food cups at one end of the 'T' during each trial. Osis and Foster ran each kitten separately and expected the animals to turn into the arm of the 'T' where they would find the food. The kittens did tend to go for the food more often than expected by chance, but the tests really do not serve as strong evidence for ESP. Although the experimenters placed a fan above the maze which blew the odour of the food away from the kittens, it is still possible that the cats caught a whiff of it and were thus directed to the food cups.

Unfortunately, no one ever followed up on the Osis-Foster work and the realm of feline ESP has been relatively ignored by experimental parapsychologists. The only other attempt to experimentally demonstrate ESP in cats was conducted by John Stump and Dr Robert Morris at the Institute for Parapsychology some years later. They, too, worked with kittens and a 'T-maze. They released the kittens in the maze and then attempted to telepathically influence them to turn either right or left at the cross-piece of the 'T.' They only worked with two kittens; one of which seemed to respond well to their unspoken commands, while the other tended to semi-consistently turn the wrong way.

ESP and the Canine World

Despite the fact that many cases of telepathic dogs have come to parapsychology's attention over the years, there has been relatively little experimental exploration into whether all dogs are generally psychic. The most notable exception to this fact was some early work by Dr J.B. Rhine, which he carried out while he was still at Duke University. The story is a fascinating one, since the tests were backed by the US Army.

Several years ago representatives from the Army approached Dr Rhine and asked him if he thought dogs could be trained to clairvoyantly locate buried mines in battlefields. This was a serious concern of the military's. If dogs did possess such a capability, many lives could be saved in battle. Rhine admitted that he didn't know but said that he would be willing to experiment and find out. The Army co-operated by supplying the funds for the project. Their only condition was that the tests must be kept secret.

The tests weren't conducted in the Durham area, but in San Francisco,

J. B. Rhine was certain that ESP was not a physical or sensory information channel but was mysteriously separate from although at the same time one with the brain. (Mary Evans/Society for Psychical Research)

California where several experiments were carried out along a beach north of the city. Rhine had his colleagues bury small wooden boxes along the shoreline. These served as 'dummy' mines and five boxes were buried for each test. Then a dog trainer who did not know where the boxes were located, would lead his dogs along the beach and mark the spots where a buried mine was indicated. The dogs were trained to sit down when they detected one of the boxes. These experiments were run over a three month period during which 203 tests were made. The dogs were successful in locating the mines a little over 50 per cent of the time. This is well above what coincidence could account for. However, the dogs tended to do best at the beginning of the tests and then their accuracy diminished.

The US Army eventually abandoned the test, despite the fact that the results had been encouraging. The results weren't consistent enough and training dogs for ESP wouldn't be truly practical. Their main concern was that the dogs didn't seem capable of independently searching out and locating the mines. They had to be led through the mock minefield by a trainer.

Probably the most sophisticated experimental work with canine subjects was conducted years after the demise of Dr Rhine's project when Dr Aristede Esser, a psychiatrist at Rockland State Hospital in New York, undertook a whole series of ingenious tests in 1975. Dr Esser's tests were apparently prompted by some rumours that were rife during the 1960s which reported that Soviet scientists were testing animals for ESP. One of these rumours was that Soviet officials had sent out a submarine carrying some baby rabbits while the mother rabbit was kept at a laboratory on the mainland. The story was that when the baby rabbits were either killed or frightened, the mother became very agitated at that very same moment. The truth or fiction of this story has never been truly determined, though Sheila Ostrander and Lynn Schroeder, two news-reporters who went to the Soviet Union to investigate parapsychological research there, repeat the tale in their book, *Psychic Discoveries Behind the Iron Curtain*. Whatever the case may be, this report gave Dr Esser the idea for his tests . . . or so it would seem.

Dr Esser eventually conducted a number of tests to determine if dogs could telepathically respond when their masters or canine cousins were threatened in any way. In one initial experiment, he made use of two rooms located at different ends of the hospital in which he worked. Two beagles that had been trained as hunting dogs were placed in one of the rooms. This room had an observation window which led to an adjoining area, so the dogs could be watched carefully during the test.

The owner of the dogs was then escorted to the other chamber, given an airgun, and was instructed to 'shoot' at colour slides of animals that would be flashed on a wall of the room at random intervals. The experimenters then waited to see how the dogs would react during the 'shootings.' They were able to watch them bark and whine as soon as the hunter began shooting, even though they could neither see nor hear what was going on in the chamber where he was positioned.

Dr Esser was so pleased with his results that he later wrote that there was 'no doubt in my mind that some dogs, especially those with a close relationship with their owner, have highly developed ESP.' He made this comment when he reported his experiments in 1967.

Dr Esser also conducted a series of follow-up tests. One of these was designed to see if a boxer would react when its owner was threatened. The dog was placed in a soundproofed room and attached to a device which kept a record of its heartbeat. The dog's owner, a young woman who had volunteered to take part in the experiment, was asked to wait in a different room in another part of the hospital. She had no idea that she was about to take part in the test; so she was justifiably surprised, when a mysterious man suddenly barged into her waiting room and started yelling violently at her! The woman was scared half to death. Of course, this was all part of the plan. Dr Esser was able to determine that at the exact time the woman was being so badly frightened, her dog's heartbeat suddenly accelerated for no apparent reason. The boxer seemed to have sensed that its owner was in trouble and became very agitated.

The doctor also conducted a similar test with two boxers. One of the dogs was a female, and the other was one of her male offspring. Each dog was placed in a separate room. When one of the experimenters threatened the younger dog with a newspaper, the mother dog was seen to suddenly cower in the other room.

Unfortunately, little research with dogs has been done since this time, although Dr Esser believes that his tests have 'proved conclusively that some dogs have the power of telepathy.' So it will be up to future researchers to follow up the many leads presented by this promising line of research.

The Results of the Search

The search to demonstrate that animals possess ESP has been a long and varied treasure hunt. Has this search paid off in the long run? This is probably the most important question we should be asking ourselves. I personally think that the experiments we have discussed have, by and large, been very fruitful. Other parapsychologists hold a variety of differing attitudes about the importance and success of animal ESP research. Dr Morris, who is probably the world's leading authority on animal ESP, has admitted that 'there is some evidence that psi communication is not restricted to humans', but he refuses to offer any speculation about the long-range meaning of this work. 'Before more specific speculation on the evolution of psi and its ecological significance can be seriously considered', he wrote in 1977, 'we need much more data on more species'. He goes on to point out that while it certainly looks as though animals possess ESP, we still know virtually nothing about the hows, whys and wherefores of the capacity. We are especially in the dark about the conditions under which animals can best make use of their psychic powers. Yet not all conventional parapsychologists agree with Dr Morris. Dr John Randall, an English biologist who pioneered research there on ESP in animals, is much more enthusiastic about the evidence. Nor does he hedge when it comes to speculating about the long-range meaning of this work. He believes that ESP may have been a power which significantly guided and shaped the process of evolution itself.

Parapsychologists are not the only scientists who have become intrigued by the new vistas opened by the discovery of ESP in animals. Even many conventional biologists and zoologists are finding this body of evidence rather exciting. There has been some speculation from these scientific circles that ESP may be an 'X' factor that contributes to the hive behaviour of communal insects such as ants and bees, helps pigeons to home, controls the behaviour of migrating birds, or which helps animals learn better ways of adapting to their environment.

These ideas are very speculative at this point, but they at least remain as scientific possibilities. So only time will tell what role ESP plays in the daily lives of animals, although the evidence that they possess psychic abilities seems unimpeachable.

9.

The World's Greatest Psychics

Probably the most poignant look at the life and times of the American Indian was originally published in 1932. Black Elk was one of the last of the great medicine men of the Oglala Sioux — the tribes of the central region of the United States who once controlled the land. These tribesmen keep their spiritual secrets well guarded. But before his death, Black Elk told his life story to the late John G. Neihardt, who recorded it in his classic book *Black Elk Speaks*. The book is about a contemporary shaman, written with respect and sensitivity by a man who was both an educator and poet.

After telling his story and sharing his memories, Black Elk took his scribe to a peak in South Dakota where he first experienced his shamanic visions. He wanted to say something to the kind spirits who had revealed the secrets of the world to him.

'Something should happen today', the old and half-blind medicine man told Dr Neihardt. 'If I have any power left, the thunder beings of the west should hear me when I send a voice, and there should be at least a little thunder and a little rain.'

That day was bright and cloudless, and the Dakota badlands were suffering from a severe drought . . . in fact, one of the worst in recent memory. Black Elk and his small group of friends continued their climb to the peak's summit, where the old man pointed to the place where he had undergone his initiation. He then dressed and painted himself in the great tradition of his religion. Only then did he recite his exaltations to the spirits who had been his guides and protectors. The sky remained clear until Black Elk was almost finished. Then it changed.

'We who listened now noted that thin clouds had gathered about us,' recorded the astonished professor. 'A scant chill rain began to fall and there was a low, muttering thunder without lightning.'

Tears rolled down Black Elk's cheeks as he finished his chant. He grew silent and stood nobly with his face towards the sky. The rain stopped and the sky cleared.

Dr Neihardt explained in his book that he was reporting this incident to his white readers as 'merely a more or less striking coincidence.' But it is clear that he didn't believe his disclaimer for even a moment.

*   *   *   *

Shamanism is the art of primitive mediumship. Many technologically undeveloped cultures have evolved similar traditions, whereby one of their members takes over the role of intermediary between the world of the living and the supernatural realms. The shaman may inherit the title, learn the trade through apprenticeship, or develop the talent spontaneously after receiving a 'call'. He also functions as both healer and psychic. His or her duties include not only diagnosing and healing, but bringing through communications from the dead or the Gods, counteracting spells and black magic, and sending his soul to the netherworlds on behalf of his tribe or clients.

There exists a rich anthropological literature on shamanism, which is still practised today among the Eskimos, Siberians, Mongols, and all through South America and Africa. The late Mircea Eliade, until the time of his death an historian of religion at the University of Chicago, was the world's leading authority on the subject. His classic book *Shamanism — Archaic Techniques of Ecstasy* cites over 500 major works on the subject written between the mid-nineteenth century and the present. Yet despite this large body of literature, few anthropologists have ever bothered to study the psychic side of shamanism. Most ethnologists have addressed their research purely to the sociological significance of the practice. Eliade, for instance, suggests that the art of shamanism arose as a ritualized method of attaining deeply meaningful altered states of consciousness. Professor I.M. Lewis, one of England's most renowned anthropologists, has countered this view with his own theory that shamanism evolved as a method of social control whereby one member of a tribe acts as a voice-box (through his 'communications') for the established norms and mores. Neither of these eminent researchers has ever grappled directly with the issue of whether shamanism developed as a practice because, in all cultures and religions, certain people have sought and developed powerful psychic abilities and have institutionalized their practices over the ages.

When parapsychology began to broaden its horizons in the 1970s, it began looking at several neglected areas of study that now seemed pertinent to it. Chief among these was anthropology, and several anthropologists began to wonder whether primitive or technologically unsophisticated cultures might be a roosting place for psychic abilities. Limited research projects had been conducted among the Australian aborigines in the 1950s, but now researchers began re-examining the legendary feats of the shaman — wondering if there was truth as well as fiction to their claims. A whole new area of conventional anthropology called 'transpersonal anthropology' opened up as both parapsychologists and anthropologists became determined to study this possibility.

Psi and the Shamanic Tradition

By tradition, the shaman is supposedly endowed with several specific supernatural powers. The same phenomena are mentioned over and over again even within widely separated cultures. These include the power to heal, diagnose and 'read' people clairvoyantly, control the weather, levitate, become immune to fire, and project the soul from the body. There is good evidence to believe that some shamans actually control such powers, and even a few Western anthropologists have been fortunate enough to witness sometimes stunning displays of their psychic capabilities.

Most shamans are certainly not reluctant to talk about their supernatural powers. Dr Joan Halifax, a medical anthropologist on faculty at the New School for Social Research in New York, discovered this fact in the 1970s when she was travelling the world interviewing these fascinating wonder-workers. She was lucky to meet Maria Sabina, a celebrated Mazatec shaman in Mexico, in 1977. The old woman, then eighty-three years old, enthralled her visitor with accounts of the many psychic experiences which had arisen from the development of her powers. These included a vision of her own son's death and its tragic inevitability. 'I saw the entire life of my son Aurelio and his death and the face and the name of the man that was to kill him, and the dagger with which he was going to kill him,' she explained. 'It was useless for me to say to my son that he should look out because they would kill him, because there was nothing to say. They would kill him and that was that.'

Nor is Dr Halifax the only anthropologist who has heard such claims. Dr Marlene Dobkin de Rios, an anthropologist from California, learned during her studies of shamanism in Peru that most of the local healers openly bragged about their psychic experiences.

But the most remarkable eyewitnessed accounts of primitive shamans and their powers no doubt appear in a fairly obscure report by Vladimir Bogoras, a Russian ethnologist who made an intensive study of the Chukchee Eskimos of Siberia and the St. Lawrence Islands at the turn of the century. Shamanism has practically died out among the Chukchee today, especially in Alaska, but a few powerful shamans were still practising their mediumship when Bogoras was conducting his field work. He was lucky enough to witness several displays that read today like something right out of a Victorian spiritualist seance.

Bogoras' most incredible encounter with the strange world of shamanism took place during a seance he attended on the St Lawrence Islands. The scene was the shaman's tent, and the wonder-worker sat directly in front of him as the seance commenced. As the shaman proceeded to invoke the spirits and enter a trance, his followers placed a walrus skin over his shoulders but did not attach it. The demonstration then began and Bogoras found his attention directed increasingly to the skin. It had taken on a life of its own! The part draped over the shaman's back began elevating and contorting about, though it never actually left the shaman's shoulders. Bogoras finally grabbed the skin to see how the trick was being done, but found it impossible to pull the skin off the shaman — despite the fact that it was obviously not permanently affixed. Bogoras was even thrown about the tent by the skin's contortions. The shaman sat quietly throughout the whole display.

Later during his investigations he watched another shaman perform an amazing feat of psychic surgery. A young boy of fourteen was brought to his tent and the healer magically produced an incision in the lad's body. Later he closed it up without leaving a trace. Bogoras actually examined the body and was able to confirm that an opening had somehow been made in the skin.

During his extensive investigations, Bogoras heard many stories about the 'spirit voices' that whistle and speak during Chukchee seances, and was eventually able to document this rare phenomenon. The scene was a Chukchee tent in Siberia, and the subject of the investigation was a shaman famous for his spirit voices. Bogoras wanted to make a recording of the vocalizations, though it never crossed his mind that the voices might actually be real. The Russian anthropologist had long believed that the spirit voices of the Chukchee shamans were produced by clever ventriloquism and nothing more. He wanted to record them for posterity nonetheless, and was hardly prepared for what he was about to discover.

Before the seance began, Bogoras placed a recording funnel some distance away from the shaman, who sat stationary throughout the demonstration. There was little light in the tent, so the seance was conducted in almost total darkness. The shaman invoked the spirits and it wasn't very long before the spirit voices commenced to break out in the tent. Several of them manifested. Bogoras was startled to realize that the voices sometimes emanated from various points in the tent and not merely from the shaman's immediate vicinity. This curious effect was also caught by the recording apparatus, which had recorded the entire demonstration. In writing about this experience sometime later, Bogoras openly admitted that there existed 'a very marked difference' between the voice of the shaman himself, which sounded from afar, and the voices of the 'spirits', which seemed to be talking directly into the funnel.

The Russian researcher was never, however, able to break through his scientific training and bias to admit that he had witnessed the miraculous. In his final report, published in 1904 by the American Museum of Natural History, he explained that everything he witnessed was no doubt due to trickery . . . though he never offered any hint as to how the feats could have been fraudulently performed.

Bogoras' research and observations were later corroborated by an anthropologist from the U.S.A. Riley Moore was a celebrated physical anthropologist who visited the Chukchee several years after Bogoras published his findings. He, too, attended several shamanic seances and later admitted to several of his colleagues that he had heard the same independent voices. He also heard odd poundings on the door to a structure in which one of the seances was held. Moore was intrigued enough by his observations that he interviewed several of the local Eskimos and collected accounts of the sometimes spectacular telekinetic displays they had witnessed during similar seances. Unfortunately, Moore never published any of this material.

Probably more observations have been made of the Eskimo shamans and their purported psychic ability than any other group. The well-known Canadian anthropologist Diamond Jennes researched the Copper Eskimos, who live on the coast of the Arctic Ocean in the Northwest Territories of Canada. He, too, ran right into the world of the unexplained. Their shamans divine the future and seek out clairvoyant information by way of dreams, and Jennes had at least one opportunity to personally authenticate the art. In a book on his research published in 1922, Jennes talks about his friendship with an Eskimo shaman named Ilatsiak, who often claimed that his spirit helper came to him in his dreams to deliver important messages and prophecies.

The anthropologist reports how one day the shaman, 'entered our house and reported that during the night his spirit had told him that something had gone wrong on our schooner; it was the thing, he said, that made the vessel move. We thought that he must mean the propeller, for we had put a new one on during the winter and had to keep the ice open around it. By a strange coincidence, however, we discovered during the day — what Ilatsiak could hardly have been aware of — that a boom we were using to roof our provision cache had snapped during the night owing to the weight of snow above it.'

Surveying the evidence

This little anecdote illustrates the fact that ESP is also part and parcel of the shaman's repertoire. There is no dearth of literature on this subject, either. Dr David Read Barker, an anthropologist until recently affiliated with the University of Virginia, made an in-depth study of the literature on anthropology and the paranormal in the 1970s and was able to uncover not a few such accounts by searching through a large body of ethnological writings dating back many years. He presented his research in 1979 at a meeting of parapsychologists held in Vancouver, Canada under the auspices of the Parapsychology Foundation. Most of the accounts he was able to unearth are brief and hard to analyse, but a few are more impressive. He found, for instance, that a French missionary in New Caledonia reported how he had eyewitnessed a remarkable display of travelling clairvoyance by a native shaman in 1930. The seer was also the chief of the tribe the missionary was visiting, and the event took place during a public meeting.

'In the course of a great joyous feast,' the missionary wrote in his memoires, 'he suddenly plunged himself into despair, announcing that he saw one of his illustrious relatives in Arama [a town several miles away] agonizing. A canoe was speedily sent to Arama, a three hour trip from there. The chief had just died.'

An equally impressive story was collected by an American anthropologist working among the Saulteaux of the Beress River in Manitoba, Canada. The researcher had become so intrigued by the supernatural that he actually attempted to gather direct testimony about the psychic abilities of the local shamans. A. Irving Hallowell's research was later published by the University of Pennsylvania Press in 1942. There he reports how one of his informants was present at a seance, the purpose of which was to locate her son, who had been missing for a week. The woman had brought tobacco and tea for the conjuror in payment for his services. Hallowell explains how the lost man was found. 'After the performance had progressed for a while, the voice of a young man manifested right through the entranced shaman, explained that he was all right, and even where he was currently camping.' The woman left the seance reassured.

The young man arrived home two days later. During the night of the seance he had been asleep at the very location indicated through the shaman, yet he had no idea that his 'soul' had been called forth by the conjuror's power.

Shamanism Today

By far, though, some of the best witnessed and most contemporary accounts of shamanic wonders have come down to us from the late Adrian Boshier, an amateur anthropologist who witnessed several psychic displays during the many years he lived in the wilds of Africa. Boshier, who was born and raised in England, always felt a deep affinity for the dark continent even before he actually travelled there. When his family finally emigrated to Africa he was little more than a teenager. Though totally inexperienced in the fine art of wilderness survival, he immediately decided to live the life of a nomad. He lived without provisions in the bush for many years, and eventually became a respected authority on African customs, folklore and archaeology. Because he was epileptic and refused to take medication for his seizures, the local natives believed that he had a special talent for shamanism and even apprenticed him to a sorcerer for extensive training. Boshier eventually adopted much of the world view taught by the natives, including their belief in the supernatural.

Much of this belief evolved from his own encounters with the local sorcerers. When he addressed a meeting of parapsychologists in London back in 1973, he explained how he had visited one shaman who divined his past and future by throwing bones in front of her and 'reading' their configurations. He reported that she was able to reveal many 'personal details concerning my life, which were absolutely correct.' His chance to thoroughly test an African shaman didn't come until sometime later, though.

This incident took place when Boshier was working in conjunction with a museum in Swaziland, where he was conducting research on shamanism in co-operation with a celebrated local diviner named Ndaleni.

He reported to the conference: 'Ndaleni first came to the Museum some sixteen months ago in the company of another witch-doctor, and immediately agreed to my testing her spirit. Leaving her in my office with the other witch-doctor and Miss Costello, I went to a neighbouring building and took out the skin of a gemsbok. This I hid beneath a canvas sail on the back of my Land Rover. I then called her outside and told her I had hidden something which she must find. With the aid of the other witch-doctor, she knelt down and began to sing softly. Then, in trance state, she informed me that I had hidden something across on the other side of that building, over there. She told me that it had more than one colour, that it came from an animal, that it was raised up off the ground. Suddenly she got up, ran around the building, out into the front where the Land Rover stood and knelt down beside it. Again she began singing softly and within five minutes of this she tore off one of her necklaces and holding it in front of her like a divining rod, she walked around the Land Rover, climbed into the back and took out the skin.'

The levitational feats of yet another African shaman were even filmed in 1975 in a small town between Togo and Dahomey. This film, later incorporated into a documentary released by Burbank International Pictures, was taken at a camp-ground by a lake where a fiery pit had been constructed. A local shaman named Nana Bwaku was filmed standing before the pit, raising his hands in preparing for the levitation. The film actually shows the shaman levitating into the air about three feet and then floating across the pit. A second camera was stationed at another location and caught the levitation from a different angle.

Alan Vaughan, who was at the time on the staff of *Psychic* magazine in San Francisco, California, was able to interview the producer of the film in 1975, and came away from the meeting convinced that no cinematographic fraud was involved. He also learned that it was the director himself who had chosen the site where the miracle had been performed.

Unfortunately, the scene was photographed at night and the setting is quite dark. Even though two cameras caught the performance from two different angles, the quality of the film is far from ideal. Vaughan summed it all up nicely when he quipped that 'a black man against a black background lit by flickering fires does not provide ideal viewing conditions.' I have been personally trying to track down more information on this film through those in Germany and Austria who were present at the demonstration. I've been unable to come up with anything further on the conditions under which the film was made.

Shamanic Weather Control

By far, though, the shaman's chief duty in some cultures is to control the weather. Times of severe drought are common in Africa and in other strongholds of the shamanic tradition, and these wonder-workers are expected to remedy the situation . . . or stop the rain should it become too plentiful! Tales of shamanic weather control feats are commonly reported in the literature, and not all of them can be easily dismissed.

Back in the 1950s, the husband and wife team of Ronald and Lyn Rose pioneered the study of 'primitive' parapsychology with their work with the natives of Australia. The Roses had two goals in mind when they embarked on their adventures in the central regions of the country. They wanted to test the aborigines for both ESP and psychokinesis, using conventional card-guessing and dice-rolling procedures. But they also hoped to witness the feats of the great shamans at first hand. They succeeded with their first goal, and were able to show that the Australian natives make fairly successful ESP subjects. (Their scoring on conventional PK tests wasn't nearly as good, though.) But they failed to witness the miraculous feats of the local shamans, although they did encounter some crude fraud. Luckily, though, they ran into plenty of natives who recalled witnessing their tribal shamans working their miracles, and several of these stories concerned weather control demonstrations. Nor were all of these informants superstitious; for some of the stories came from de-tribalized natives living close to modern civilization.

While travelling in New South Wales, for example, one elderly native woman in Woodenbong told the Roses the following story. It concerned a shaman still living in a nearby village:

> . . . to do this clever thing he had to take his clothes off, proper-naked-fella-like. He was pretty wild with some other fellas, he was, missus, and I was pretty scared when I watched him. He stood there without any clothes on, and the sky was clear, without any clouds. He sang the song and a wind came up and blew about him. He talked to the wind — those old fellas could do that, you know — and told it to bring some storm clouds.
>
> Wasn't long before them clouds came, either. Big, black fierce clouds with thunder and lightning. I remembers seeing this old fella there making the storm to send away and hurt these other peoples; yes, I remembers it like it was yesterday.

Another native in Woodenbong explained that he had seen his own grandfather conjure up a storm on an otherwise clear day:

> . . . it was clear until this old grandad of mine started to sing the storm song. Then the clouds started to come up and my father covered up my face with his waistcoat. There was so much thunder about I shivered with frights. But I sneaked a look and, so help me, there was the old fellow waving his arms about, singing his song, and the storm was getting fiercer and stronger. There was another old doctor fellow with my grandad, and he saw me looking, and they were both pretty angry. They were so angry, so help me, they broke up the storm right then and made it go away so I wouldn't see no more.

This same native went on to explain that the clever-men can break up existing storms as well:

> It was at Kilcoy in Queensland. We could all see a terrible storm coming

straight towards the town and everyone was frightened. Well, them old fellows took off their clothes and sang a song to the storm. It got closer and closer and then, so help me, it split into two parts. One part of it went to one side of the town and the other went to the other side. Them white peoples that knew about it were pretty glad my grandad and the other old fellow saved the town.

The Roses were sceptical of the story, so the native gave the couple the names of some other witnesses capable of testifying to similar events. Even with this testimony in hand, though, the Roses were never convinced that these rain-making feats were genuinely psychic. They felt that the events probably occurred as reported, but resulted from the clever-men's shrewd ability to judge weather conditions which enabled them to discern when a storm was brewing. 'Waiting for inspiration to go ahead with rain-making ceremonies,' writes Mr Rose, 'is, in this area, probably little more than closely observing the seasons and noting such signs of nature as atmospheric conditions and the movements of ants that would indicate the imminence of rain.' Rose also noted that rain rituals were usually conducted during those times of year when rain was often expected. So rain probably did follow the rituals . . . at least eventually.

'This type of rain-making is an interesting example of the confusion between cause and effect that is superstitious thinking,' the psychologist concluded.

Rose may have been too hard on the natives, especially since he and his wife specifically asked their respondents whether the storms they witnessed were conjured up on *clear* days. The natives uniformly agreed on this important point. The speed with which the rains came strikes me as more than coincidental as well. The Roses also ignored the fact that the aborigines are at the continuous mercy of the weather. Being that they spend a considerable time out in the open, they are probably very sensitive to weather conditions and changes. I doubt if their clever-men are specifically gifted with this ability. The average tribesman is therefore probably very capable of distinguishing whether a rain-making ritual has been efficacious or not, or has resulted from coincidence.

The evidence for psychic weather control does not, however, rest solely with the stories collected by the Roses and other sceptical anthropologists. Even a few contemporary researchers have seen these displays and have remained puzzled by them. One of these fortunate researchers is Dr David Read Barker, whose psychic survey was reported earlier in this chapter. Dr Barker conducted his doctoral research among the Tibetan refugees in Nepal and India between 1970 and 1973. These settlements were established when the Tibetans fled their homeland after the Chinese invasion of 1959. Dr Barker was able to successfully integrate himself within the Tibetan culture and community, and on one occasion eyewitnessed a successful weather control ritual executed by a Tibetan lama. Dr Barker spoke of his experience during a convention of parapsychologists which convened at Washington University in St Louis, Missouri in August 1978. He stunned his audience with his report.

Tibetans believe that *lamas* or shamans can influence the weather for benevolent or malevolent purposes,' Barker explained, 'and many sacred texts tell of priests who caused hailstorms to descend on the ripe grain fields of enemies or caused a long stretch of good weather for a monastic celebration.'

Barker, of course, knew of these traditions, but had hardly expected to see anything of this sort when he travelled to Nepal and India. He was wrong.

He continued:

> In Dharamsala in Northern India, there is an annual gathering of Tibetans to mourn the flight of the Dalai Lama from Tibet on March 10 1959. My wife and I attended the fourteenth annual gathering, held on March 10 1973. Storms had been rolling down the southern slopes of the Himalayas for weeks, bringing cold torrential rains, sleet, and hail. An elderly lama, Gunsang Rinzing, who is greatly feared and revered locally for his powers of meteorological control, was employed by the Dalai Lama to stop the storms long enough for the day-long festival of mourning to occur.

Since he was living so close, Barker decided to watch the lama's ritual. The day before the scheduled celebration, at about eight o'clock in the evening, the lama arrived on the grounds and built a fire. He had to work hard to keep it alight because of the rain.

> He was in a state of intense concentration, and recited *mantras* and a *sadhana*, frequently blowing on a trumpet fashioned from a human thigh-bone and beating the two-headed drum of a shaman. After several hours of watching him from a respectful distance, we retired to bed, certain that the weather would be as miserable the next day as it had been for the preceding days. Early the following morning the rain had dimished to a drizzle, and by ten o'clock it had become only a cold fog over a circle with a radius of about 150 metres. Everywhere else in the area it continued to pour, but the crowd of several thousand refugees were never rained on during the six hours they were assembled. At one point during the speech of the Dalai Lama a huge hailstorm swept past, causing a tremendous clatter on the tin-roofed houses adjoining the festival grounds, but only a few dozen hailstones fell on the crowd.

Dr Barker told his colleagues that the event so shocked him that he was slightly disoriented for several days.

Testing the Shamanic Power

The incidents summarized above certainly indicate that at least some shamans possess genuine psychic abilities. But do all of them make use of these powers, or is the average shaman no more psychic than you or I?

This is a difficult question to answer, especially since shamans — like so many of the great mediums of the Victorian Age — are notorious for resorting to trickery in order to impress their clients. Yet it certainly seems likely that some cultures habitually produce shamans of great power, since these societies actually *test* their shamans for ESP during their apprenticeship. The apprentice can only become invested as a shaman if he passes!

The Tungus people of Siberia prescribe one such test. The initiate must appear before a more experienced shaman, who calls forth a particular spirit before the entire tribe. The initiate must relate the biography of the spirit and also name the other shamans through whom it has manifested. The Korekore tribes of Rhodesia take the test one step further. Their apprentices are required to bring through a specific spirit known to the village, who must be able to correctly recite his life story and tell where his shrine is located. The shaman must then pick out the staff, concealed within a bundle of similar ones, which the spirit's last shaman had used. And pity the poor Manchu shamans of Mongolia. They are required to walk over burning coals before being accepted as genuine seers and healers.

Legend or Fact?

These traditions, tests, and anecdotes all point in the same direction — that the shamans of so many world cultures are neither clever tricksters nor instruments of social control, but may indeed represent psychics of great power and advanced development. Perhaps parapsychologists here in the West should be taking a less casual look at these gifted practitioners, who seem to possess powers that often exceed even the best capabilities of our own home-grown psychics. The mystery of the shaman and his powers may, however, remain an unsolved riddle. Many anthropologists interested in shamanism have reported on the widespread belief held in many cultures that the glorious days of the *truly* great shamans are over. Many of Dr Halifax's informants explained that the shamans of today possess only a vestige of the powers once available to them. So perhaps we will never know whether the shamans of the primitive world are indeed the world's greatest psychics, or merely the current practitioners of a lost but psychic art.

10.

The Threat of Psychic Warfare

Rock superstar Dan Merriweather has discovered his own astonishing psychic powers. His 'out-of-body mind voyages' have revealed rival Russian and American installations for developing deadly psychic weaponry. Now Russia wants him. America has sent a psychic general to track him down. The war merchants covet him as the ultimate weapon of terror. But the weapon has found himself a strange and terrifying 'hiding place' to wait and plan the future of the world.

These dramatic words appear as part of the publicity blurb for *Star Fire*, a shocking novel by Ingo Swann published in 1978, which chronicles the world's first psychic war. A superpsychic of no mean accomplishment himself, Swann has already written an autobiography and there are probably in excess of two dozen books currently available which discuss him and his remarkable talents. So *Star Fire* is certainly a unique novel. It is about a superpsychic *by* a superpsychic and, according to Swann himself, the book is just as much a warning as it is an enthralling yarn of suspense.

We'll be returning to Swann and his views shortly.

Military Uses for Psychic Power

Parapsychology sometimes breeds more rumours than politics. Is the United States military using psychics for espionage purposes? Are the Soviets trying to harness psychic energy to use against the Western world in some forthcoming war? Will the next war be a psychotronic rather than a military one? Are the few Federal agencies currently funding parapsychology research in the United States fronts for covert military operations?

These are some of the questions and rumours that have made their way through and around parapsychology circles ever since it became known that the US military helped fund psychical research projects undertaken in the early 1970s at the Stanford Research Institute in Menlo Park, California. This led to SRI receiving a $47,000 grant from the Naval

Electronics Systems Command to encourage their research into remote viewing. Rumours about top-level military interest in psychic research have also been flying about like deranged sparrows ever since Sheila Ostrander and Lynn Schroeder, as a result of their visits to the USSR in the 1960s, reported on the interest Soviet military commanders are taking in parapsychology. And at the annual convention of the Parapsychological Association which convened at St Mary's College in Moraga, California in 1977, Barbara Honneger, (then) a graduate student at John F. Kennedy University, reported on the secret high-level interest US government officials and agencies are beginning to have in parapsychology.

The truth and fiction concerning many of these rumours have now come to light thanks to two major documents released by the Defense Intelligence Agency, a division of the Department of Defense in Washington, DC. The first of these documents, 'Soviet and Czechoslovakian Parapsychology Research,' is a hitherto classified, seventy-one page, report which the defence department commissioned in its attempt to keep tabs on what Soviet scientists were learning about psychic phenomena. Their second and earlier report is more sinister. Entitled 'Controlled Offensive Behaviour — USSR,' it surveys the potential military uses the Soviets might be planning to make from any results stemming from their parapsychological research. Both documents, once top secret, have been released as a result of the Freedom of Information Act.

The first report was authored by Louis Maine and Major J.D. La Mothe, MSC, and surveys what the military had learned about Soviet parapsychological research up until 15 April 1975. According to the report's preface, some of the material was based on 'intelligence reports' the authors had access to. This, of course, suggests that the military is still in possession of classified material concerning parapsychology. It can be easily seen that the compiler(s) of this report were very concerned with the possible military uses which could be made from control over psychic phenomena, since it is concerned with telepathy, telepathic 'behaviour modification,' research on 'storage' and using 'psychic energy,' remote viewing, and so on.

A great deal of the report is a 'state of the art' analysis of parapsychology in the Soviet Union and Czechoslovakia. These sections are based on Soviet and Iron Curtain literature, readily available to the general public, and a general history of Soviet parapsychology dating back to the 1920s is given. Since this material is available in such volumes as Leonid Vasiliev's *Experiments in Mental Suggestion* (reissued in 1976 as *Experiments in Distant Influence*), these sections of the report reveal nothing new. But they do indicate that the US military, circa 1975, was very interested in keeping abreast of what the Soviets were up to and as completely as possible. And the authors also note, in the form of a veiled warning that '. . . it is important that the increased degree of sophistication which has occurred in Soviet ESP or telepathy research since 1960 be understood.'

This 1975 report is more concerned, however, with what Czech scientists call 'psychotronics' — the study and use of psychic energy. Psychotronics had its greatest advances as a scientific study when a Czech inventor, Robert Pavlita, began developing psychotronic 'generators'. These are little devices which Pavlita builds, and he claims that they can store psychic energy for later use in the production of psychokinetic effects. On a more sinister note, Pavlita feels that these generators can be used to kill insects and small animals. One merely has to point the little devices at the target. While Pavlita has given a few informal demonstrations of his devices, he has not allowed them to be critically tested by Western parapsychologists. So whether they are genuine controllers of psychic energy, or whether Pavlita is just a clever con-man, is an open issue.

Nonetheless, the US military was apparently very concerned with the possible military uses of psychotronics. They linked it with the use of 'telepathic behaviour control' as two possible psychic threats to civil populations outside the Soviet Union. Ever since the 1930s, the Soviets have been interested in the induction of hypnosis by telepathy over fantastic distances, and the US military was justifiably concerned about the implications of this research. To them, psychotronics appeared to be just one method of manipulating the human mind and body over vast distances.

'Outside of the Soviet and Czech research on the manipulative possibilities of PK and psychotronic generators, the emphasis on manipulation by means of telepathy still involves the use of hypnosis,' the report reads. 'Many Soviet and Czech scientists are using this technique as a means to try and identify the "carrier" of telepathy but others may be conducting such research for more devious reasons.' The document goes on to state:

> Dr Stefan Manczarski of Poland predicted that the field of telepathy will open new avenues for spreading propaganda. He feels that . . . telepathy can be amplified like radio waves. Telepathy would then become a subtle new modus for the 'influencers' of the world. Some Western followers of psychic phenomena research are concerned, for example, with the detrimental effects of subliminal perception techniques being targeted against US or allied personnel in nuclear missile silos. The subliminal message could be 'carried' by television signals or by telepathic means.

The potential applications of focusing mental influences on an enemy through hypnotic telepathy have surely occurred to the Soviets. The bulk of recent telepathy research in the USSR has been concerned with the transmission of emotional or behavioral impulses and the study of physiological responses to PK exercises, etc. In their exploration of telepathy, they are seeking the eventual capability to reproduce and to amplify the phenomena so that control is feasible. Control and manipulation of the human consciousness must be considered a primary goal.

And as for Pavlita's psychotronic generators?

Ever since these little devices became known to the West, there has been some speculation that Soviet and Czech scientists have been building huge psychotronic generators and are currently beaming deleterious psychic energy at the United States. One well-known US parapsychologist with whom I spoke about this very problem told me that Soviet scientists are actively using secret psychotronic generators to alter US weather.

Such stories have always struck me as the result of borderline paranoia, but they seem to be proliferating. If such generators *do* exist (which is doubtful) the US military was apparently not aware of them in 1975. Nonetheless, the Defense Intelligence Agency's report on Iron Curtain parapsychology does point out that:

> In their present form and size, Pavlita's devices could probably exert an effect on humans at only relatively short range. It is possible that their size could be enlarged or their energy amplified, thereby extending their range. If the Czech claims for these devices are valid, biological energy might be an effective anti-personnel weapon. It would be difficult to defend against, since it apparently penetrates most common forms of insulation and its reported effects (changes in brain wave characteristics, disturbance of equilibrium, dizziness) could result in personality changes or physical discomfort which might alter combat effectiveness.
>
> Soviet or Czech perfection of psychotronic weapons would pose a severe threat to enemy military, embassy, or security functions. The emitted energy would be silent and difficult to detect electronically (although the Soviets claim to have developed effective biological energy sensors) and the only power source required would be the human operator.

But the document adds that 'no information is available on Czech efforts to develop psychotronic weapons.'

The Threat of Psychic Attack
Just as enlightening as what the US military was able to learn about Soviet and Czech parapsychology was what they were unable to ascertain.

Towards the end of their report, the Defense Intelligence Agency lists nine gaps in their knowledge of Iron Curtain research. Some of these areas include the need for more information on the construction of psychotronic generators; whether the USSR military is recruiting psychics for research purposes; and whether the Soviets are actively attempting to disrupt US personnel or communication systems with the knowledge they are gaining.

The Defense Intelligence Agency's report on 'Controlled Offensive Behavior' is even more disturbing and was drawn up by the Medical Intelligence Office, the Office of the Surgeon General and the Department of the Army. It was primarily authored by John La Mothe, who was one of the main authors of the Agency's report on Soviet and Czech parapsychology. This report was written in 1972, and was scheduled for declassification in 1990.

This paper surveys Soviet research on, and methods for, psychological control of the human mind. It is a huge report, over 175 pages in length, and covers Soviet research on such topics as psychological manipulation; hypnosis; psychopharmacology; and the effects of light, colour, and sound on the human mind and body. One large section is devoted to parapsychological phenomena as a technique leading to 'controlled behaviour.' It is rather clear that much of this information prompted the Defense Intelligence Agency to make their in-depth survey of Soviet and Czech parapsychology in general three years later. But this report differs from the 1975 report in that it is more directly concerned with the far-reaching military implications of parapsychology. In fact, according to the report, Iron Curtain support of parapsychology research was instigated by the Soviet military and KGB, and that 'the energy and resources being allotted for the work' were specifically encouraged 'because of its military implications especially in mind manipulation and controlled offensive behaviour.'

Apparently the US military also seems to think that Soviet parapsychology researchers are interested in the phenomenon of 'apports.' Their report states that the Soviet military would have an important tool if they could learn how to control the production of them. It is also apparent from this report that our own military has developed a similar interest, since a reference is made to a document prepared for them in 1970 by G.A. Welk entitled 'Proposed Use of the Apport Technique as a Means to Strengthen the US Intelligence System.' To quote from the Defense Intelligence Agency's report:

> According to Welk, a costly weakness in our intelligence system, to a large extent, is an inability to use effectively the resources of the science of

parapsychology . . . Whenever parapsychology is mentioned, most people are likely to think of ESP. However, there are other types of parapsychological phenomena which are just as important militarily as ESP. Welk claims, based on many Soviet sources, that the so-called 'apport' technique is likely to meet valuable intelligence needs. When fully developed, this technique would make possible the abduction of actual objects (including documents) in enemy territory and their transfer to friendly territory. Objects so abducted [teleported] are known as 'apports'. They could be returned to the point of origin without the enemy becoming aware of this temporary abduction.

It is now also clear that the US military was (and probably still is) concerned about the military advantage the Soviets would have if they learned how to produce 'materialization' at a distance. The authors of the Agency's report feared, or at least suggested, that Soviet diplomats might eventually be able to sit in their offices and steal vital documents from foreign countries through the controlled use of teleportation! They especially noted the potential espionage uses that controlled induction of out-of-body experiences might have.

So just what can we conclude from these now declassified Defense Intelligence Agency reports? Are their concerns over the military use of psychic powers well founded or not?

On one hand, there is growing concern within some US parapsychology circles that psychic forces could be effectively relied upon should another major war break out. It was these concerns that led a top US psychic, Ingo Swann, to write his novel *Star Fire* about the first *psychic* war. The idea for the novel, claims Swann, came from information which he has received clandestinely from apparently top-level government sources. Duane Elgin, a futurologist on staff at SRI, has even written a hypothetical scenario on what a psychic war would be like, and predicts one by the 1990s.

A Psychic Speaks on Psychic Warfare

Swann is himself every bit as fascinating a subject as the story of his novel. He was born high in the mountains near Tulleridge, Colorado in 1933 but his family eventually moved to Utah where Swann took degrees in art and biology at Westminster College. After a three-year stint in the army, he packed off to New York in 1958 to pursue his dual careers as a psychic and professional artist while earning a living wage by working for the United Nations Secretariat. A Scientologist by philosophy, Swann credits the late L. Ron Hubbard and his teachings with helping him to unlock and develop his psychic potentials. It was, in fact, shortly after converting to Scientology that he first came to the attention of the

Ingo Swann, a well-known psychic, wrote a novel entitled *Star Fire* that described the world's first psychic war. (Mary Evans Picture Library)

parapsychological community and rapidly became one of the best known and widely tested psychics within contemporary decades: To date, he has been tested at the American Society for Psychical Research, the Stanford Research Institute, and at the City College of the City University of New York. An 'all purpose' psychic, under controlled conditions Swann has been able to demonstrate his ability to alter the temperature of termisters placed several feet away; employ his mind-over-matter abilities to disrupt magnetic fields and delicate mechanical equipment; and 'send' his mind away from his body and correctly describe distant locations in great detail.

Ingo Swann is a rare breed of psychic in more ways than one. Not only is he gifted with both ESP and PK, but — owing to his scientific background — he can write and comment about his abilities objectively and with astute insight. It is, in fact, Swann's masterful introspection which makes his novel so enthralling. It is not 'merely' fiction, since it is based on his own experiences as both a psychic and psychic investigator.

'Psychic espionage' is the basic theme in his book. Can a psychic, once properly trained, project his mind hundreds of miles away from his body to view and describe secret military installations, probe into the minds of enemy strategists, or even foul up their computers by PK? These are all distinct possibilities, according to Swann. For years, he points out, parapsychologists have been wondering just what practical applications ESP and PK might have to offer us, and the idea that psychics might eventually be employed for covert spy operations is not really all that absurd. In fact, the basic themes so vividly enacted in *Star Fire* are actually based on research in which Swann has himself been involved at the SRI in the past.

SRI is not, as is so often mistakenly believed, associated with Stanford University, but is a private research and think-tank operation. Although certainly not primarily a parapsychology laboratory, two physicists there have been involved in a major ESP and PK research program. It was in conjunction with these scientists, Russell Targ and Harold Puthoff, that Swann first proved that 'psychic spying' might well be within the powers of a gifted psychic.

It all began in December of 1972, when Swann was first hired as a psychic-in-residence at SRI, where both his ESP and PK abilities were being examined. To say the least, he wasn't too enthusiastic about the type of psychic tasks he was asked to perform, which included trying to levitate small masses of material and psychically bending laser beams. 'I don't know how I survived,' he told *Times* reporter John Wilhelm.

'They just read too many science fiction books. They just take science fiction and superimpose it over science and say, all right, now let's try to do all the things that science fiction authors write about. It's never going to happen that way, as far as I'm concerned . . .'

It was during one of these confrontations with Targ and Puthoff that Swann proposed the idea of what he calls 'remote viewing'. He bet the physicists that, if given only the latitude and longitude co-ordinates of any location in the world, he could send his mind there and describe the area. The two physicists took him at his word, began a series of informal tests, and were amazed at the results. Swann's performances were incredible. Even if the experimenters chose the co-ordinates for tiny islands in the middle of oceans, Swann could correctly perceive the geography of the area and describe the terrain with uncanny accuracy. He rarely fouled up by describing the surrounding water instead.

As Targ and Puthoff subsequently reported in a presentation of their research which they made before the Parapsychology Foundation's 1974 International Conference on 'Parapsychology and Quantum Physics', held on 27-28 August in Geneva, Switzerland:

> In our estimation, Swann's ability to describe correctly details of buildings, roads, bridges, and the like indicated that he could perceive remote locations, sometimes in great detail, given only their geographic latitude and longitude. Thus we considered the descriptions were sufficiently accurate to warrant our setting up a research program in remote viewing.

And how does Swann view his book and its message?

I had the opportunity to discuss the threat of psychic warfare with Swann shortly after his book was published when the New York-based psychic was visiting Los Angeles as part of a promotional tour. It certainly wasn't the first time we had met, but I was a bit startled when Ingo greeted me at the door of his hotel room. I had forgotten just how imposing a figure he could be. His almost pixy-like face and his somewhat gentle mannerisms strike a note of incongruity when set against his six-foot frame. I had also forgotten that besides being a psychic and artist of note, he can also be a fascinating, and downright cynical, conversationalist. His brash outspokenness also seems discordant against his mellow and accented voice.

The first question I wanted to ask was a rather obvious one. 'How much of your novel', I queried, 'is based on your own psychic experience?'

'Almost all of it', Ingo replied, anticipating my question. 'The only really fictional thing, of course, is the plot and the people in it, and the magnitude of the psychic's powers. But there's nothing in the book that doesn't already have in science a working hypothesis behind it. It's a very well-researched book, even though it is shocking. But all the science in it is backed up by research and documentation.'

Of course, the plot of *Star Fire*, as I pointed out, concerns psychic warfare. It's not truly a unique basic storyline, since many futurologists believe that the next war may well be a psychic one, and have even written out speculative scenarios about the battle plans for such a confrontation. Could ESP-instigated mind control be successfully used as a weapon? Would psychic espionage replace the Mata Hari-like cloak-and-dagger routines of the past world wars? These are questions that many science fiction writers of the past as well as futurologists of the present have been asking. But no one has developed these themes to the degree Swann has.

'Do you personally think the next war will be fought on a psychic as well as military level?' I asked Swann, who was eager to discuss these very possibilities.

'I think we're in the advanced stages of that war right now,' he explained. 'The developments within the last year and our discovery that the Soviet Union is probably engaged in this type of research — as well as the fact that neutron and atomic bombs are no longer feasible on earth — leads us to think that the human mind becomes the appropriate target rather than buildings, bodies, armies, and their destruction. The control of populations [through mind control] is probably very much in research now and, of course, this is a stage of psychic warfare. Now the use of gifted individuals and extremely powerful psychics is probable.'

As Swann described these possibilities, I couldn't help but wonder if his warning would strike the proverbial man-in-the-street as mere science fiction. But he is not alone in thinking that we might all soon find ourselves in the midst of a psychic war. A viewpoint almost identical to his was recently outlined by Duane S. Elgin, a futurologist on the staff at SRI and himself a highly successful remote viewing subject. Elgin has predicted that, because we all seem to possess psychic abilities, by the 1990s a psychic *civil* war might break out between the military-industrial controllers of our country and a guerilla-like group of psychic radicals. These individuals would use ESP to cause selected enemy commanders to suffer mental breakdowns as well as psychokinetically sabotage computers, satellites, and weapons systems. Elgin, like Swann, has even suggested that the military might already be engaging in secret parapsychological research.

Of course, Elgin's scenario has not gone unchallenged by any means, and at least one parapsychologist of note who has read Elgin's report described is as 'utter hogwash.' He pointed out that psychic phenomena are too capricious, uncontrollable, and the effects too weak to ever be useful for military purposes.

But in any event, Elgin's predictions are pertinent to the general credibility of Swann's position and the possible role the gifted psychic will play in the next major war. And it *is* a bit ominous that two independent speculative thinkers on the psychic scene have evolved so nearly identical forecasts about our psychic future. As Swann himself explained to me:

> Another war simply can't be done on the nuclear level. The world powers are too poised, the defences too automatic. A nuclear attack launched by one country would obliterate everything as the retaliatory measures took place. So the military will have to figure out new ways of warfare. And one of these ways is mind control, which leads directly to ESP. It's that clear.

Of course, Swann's position immediately makes one wonder whether or not the US military, as Elgin suggests, is already involved in parapsychological research and especially in remote viewing. Rumours to that effect have been rife over the last few years and it's no great secret that some of Targ and Puthoff's original funding came from NASA and at least one military agency. As I pointed out earlier, even after World War II the US military contacted Dr J.B. Rhine, the founder of modern parapsychology who was still researching ESP and PK at Duke University at the time, and secretly granted him funds to see if dogs could be trained to psychically locate mines.

'Do you think our own military is interested in remote viewing?' I asked Swann.

His reply was uncertain:

> We'd have to say yes and no at this moment. There are certainly individuals here and there who are extremely interested in it. The majority of people, though, just can't believe it. The thing we've got to do is to get more people replicating remote viewing, which is being done, until it becomes real that there exists in the individual this hitherto undiscovered and unidentified level of awareness. There will be military interest in remote viewing once it becomes real that it exists. It's unthinkable that they wouldn't want to know about it. I mean, how can you say that scientists and parapsychologists should research parapsychology and the military shouldn't? Parapsychologists research it because it's *real* to them. If it becomes real to the military, they'll research it.

Despite Swann's assurances, I was far from sure that the military would become that involved in psychic research, despite the fact that the navy funded much of the SRI remote viewing research. We know that ESP is a very hard-to-control faculty. We also know that psychics often have a difficult time trying to distinguish when they are receiving genuine ESP messages from when their impressions are random sets of utter nonsense. What's more, ESP messages are often vague, fragmented, and symbolized and this limits their value (as far as I am concerned) as a cogent espionage tactic. For instance, a person 'remote viewing' a barn may indeed 'see' and describe a barn, but may perceive it in the wrong colour and in wrong perspective to nearby buildings. In many respects, ESP impressions are like dream images. They are fleeting, vague, and hard to accurately observe. And unlike Swann's superhero, Dan Merriweather, few psychics are 100 per cent — or even 80 per cent — accurate all the time.

Such a faculty doesn't strike me as that useful for the purposes of 'spying' unless a psychic could actually and *physically* project some portion of his mind and intelligence to a distant location, astral-projection-like, and view it with crystal clarity and accuracy. However, Swann was quick to disagree with me about some of the difficulties inherent in trying to harness ESP.

'Remote viewing is not much different from daydreaming,' he went on to say. 'At the time you're supposed to contact the outbound experimenter you just agree with yourself that you're going to do it. You sort of think about him and you'll start to get a flood of images starting to come in.'

'But,' I interrupted, 'do you actually feel as though some element of your mind is travelling to the distant location?'

'At times,' he replied. 'Generally, there are two forms of experience the subject reports. Sometimes you just see images which you can liken to daydreaming or something like that. But subjects often report a sense of moving to the place. They report going over streams of water or desert. They get to the places and often comment on things they would comment on when getting off an airplane — the humidity, the wind, or the cold, and so on. So we have evidence which suggests that there's probably more than one way to acquire data during remote viewing.'

Swann also challenged my contention that the imprecision of ESP communication prohibits its use as a viable communications system for military purposes.

Swann explains that, through practice, a remote viewer can actually learn how to turn off his analytical reasoning inclinations, and thus tune in on the psychic sense with no hindrances from his analytical mind.

'We've discovered,' Swann told me with a hint of pride in his voice, 'that a subject can train himself to distinguish between the two simply by trying to.'

Swann should know, since he's undoubtedly the most successful remote viewer around . . . so successful, in fact, that at least a few followers of the psychic scene have suggested that perhaps he has tried his hand at psychic espionage himself, in true *Star Fire* fashion. John Wilhelm, a former *New York Times* writer, gives an in-depth report on the SRI remote viewing work in his book *The Search for Superman*, and even reported in 1976 that Swann had done some remote viewing experiments in collaboration with the CIA. This rumour was revived recently by Henry Gris and William Dick, two *National Enquirer* reporters who repeat it in their book *The New Soviet Psychic Discoveries.*

These rumours are of constant annoyance to Swann, who seemed a bit irritated when I raised them during our talk. But just for the record, I asked him whether or not he actually had done any experiments with the CIA.

'I have not,' answered Swann almost indignantly. 'Everybody thinks that the CIA has been interested in parapsychology, but as a matter of fact it isn't true. It scares the CIA to death. They don't want to get involved with ESP because it's too controversial.'

Despite Swann's claims, though, it *is* true that independent CIA agents have, on isolated occasions, visited some of this country's leading parapsychology laboratories. So I still wondered if perhaps Swann had at least been *approached* to do a bit of psychic espionage by some federal agency.

'No,' came the invariable reply to my question. 'They aren't smart enough to ask.' Swann made his remark through a sardonic chuckle, which soon infected both of us.

Since by this time it was getting late and Swann had a plane to catch, I asked my final and more than obvious question.

'Would you say your book is a work of fiction, or more of a warning or prognostication?'

Swann had obviously given a lot of thought to this question, and his reply was carefully reasoned:

'It's certainly a work of fiction. But it's a book based on personal experience and has a high probability factor. I'm not saying a psychic war will occur like it's done in the book. It probably won't. For instance, Dan Merriweather, who's a superpsychic, has huge powers as an individual. This is unlikely to happen. There's evidence that the 'superpsychic' of the future would be a *group* of psychics working together. We have evidence to support the hypothesis that, when psychics work together, their sum result is more than the components. An individual with a lot of training, if we ever found out how to train ESP, could probably do great things. But the *real* superpsychic, I would expect to find, would be a group of people working together.'

Rumours That Won't Die

Despite the fact that *Star Fire* was written some years ago, the subject of psychic warfare is still making headlines. Even the normally staid *New York Times* raised an eyebrow when Ron McRae, a former reporter for Jack Anderson of the *Washington Post*, came out with a book in 1984 which claimed secret US military interest in parapsychology. *Mind Wars* was based in part on official US government documents and statements from officials in the know, and even reported that military officials had employed psychics to track Soviet submarines. McRae also revealed that top US intelligence agencies have been keeping up with parapsychology's latest inroads, and had even filtered considerable money to front groups to help fund the field. The use of professional psychics to help break secret codes had also been explored.

But McRae's book did not end the rumours about the military's interest in the prospects for psychic warfare. The 9 December 1985 issue of *The New American* ran a feature story on 'Will ESP be the Weapon of the Future?' which once again reported on the military's interest in remote viewing. They claimed that the military was interested in the phenomenon as an espionage (read ESPionage) tactic.

'While no one claims that ESPionage will supplant conventional techniques,' the article reported, '[remote viewing] could prove a valuable supplement to information via satellites or secret agents "in place". It could gain information in advance about enemy plans and capabilities.'

The article also pointed out that Soviet researchers are keeping their eyes on parapsychological research in the United States, and that they are actively researching remote viewing themselves.

'Significantly,' reported *The New American*, 'the Soviets are closely studying the US remote viewing experiments, replicating them, and perhaps even taking them further as a useful tool in the largest and most sophisticated espionage apparatus the world has ever known.'

These views may seem radical, but those few Western researchers who have visited the Soviet Union testify to their scientists' interest in the military applications of the sixth sense. For example, in 1983 both Russell Targ and Keith Harary were invited to the USSR, and even addressed the Soviet Academy of Sciences. The two researchers found the Soviet researchers interested in learning everything they could about remote viewing research. But their enquiries had a sinister emphasis to them. They were specifically interested in whether reseachers here in the West had found ways of screening geographical sites from being psychically probed. Targ was cynically amused by this line of questioning. Having spent so much of his career trying to prove the existence and importance of remote viewing, it was disconcerting to be asked if the sixth sense could be short-circuited! Both Targ and Harary left the Soviet Union with the realization that their colleagues in Russia weren't so much interested in the how and why of the remote viewing process. They simply wanted to know whether it had any practical application and/or limitations . . . and that spells espionage and political intrigue.

Some Personal Conclusions

All this talk about superpsychics, psychic spying, remote viewing, psychic warfare, and ESP mind control is certainly befuddling. The speculations that have been raised in this chapter are within the range of frightening possibility . . . but they nonetheless walk that thin and opaque border between science and science fiction. As a rationalist of sorts, it is hard for me to believe that ESP and PK, which most assuredly do exist, could ever be harnessed so efficiently that the military would want to rely upon them in some future war. As a parapsychologist, I have certainly never seen any empirical evidence that psychic abilities can be used for practical gain except on rare occasions and under only certain, very favourable, conditions. Even Keith Harary was only successful at his silver futures experiment before his abilities began to ebb during some follow-up studies. But as a speculator, I can in no way dismiss the possibility that someday a superpsychic might evolve with powers surpassing anything we have ever seen before, or that some researcher of the future will find a way to effectively harness ESP and PK.

All we can do is wait and see.

11.

The Psychic Power of Prayer

'The great thing is to pray, even if it be in a vague and inarticulate fashion.'

John William Strutt, third Lord
Rayleigh. Winner of the Nobel Prize
in Physics for 1904

Does prayer really help the sick? Certainly there is no lack of anecdotal evidence to this effect.

Before taking up his post as religion editor for the *Toronto Star*, Allen Spraggett was a Christian minister serving a small congregation in Feversham, Canada. He was only twenty-three years old and received his first 'break' when he was asked to give a guest sermon in nearby Collingwood, a parish of some 8000 people. Then the disaster struck. He woke up that morning so sick that he felt 'as if I had been slugged by a piece of lead pipe.' He had come down with the flu, complete with the usual fever and chills. He was so sick that he asked his landlady to call and cancel his sermon.

'While the landlady was trying to contact the outside world,' writes Spraggett in his *The Unexplained*, 'I suddenly felt an odd sensation. Mild pulsations of heat were passing through me — like gentle shocks of electricity must feel. My first thought was that I was taking a turn for the worse. Then, to my astonishment, I immediately felt much better.' He made a full recovery and was able to preach as originally scheduled, although his flu returned some three weeks later. The surprising upshot to the incident occurred when he first arrived to preach that day in Collingwood. When he showed up at the parsonage, the resident minister's wife greeted him by saying that she knew he had been sick that day.

'She said that during lunch,' continues Spraggett, 'both she and her husband were suddenly impressed that I was sick and would not be able to preach unless they prayed for my healing.'

Similar stories abound in the popular religious literature. But interest in scientifically examining the objective power of prayer dates back close to a century. Sir Francis Galton (1822-1911), the father of the science of heredity, brooded over the subject in 1883 when he wrote his *Inquiries into Human Faculty and its Development*. He noted in that work that:

It is asserted by some that men possess the faculty of obtaining results over which they have little or no direct control, by means of devout and earnest prayer, while others doubt the truth of this assertion. The question regards a matter of fact, that has to be determined by observation and not by authority. It is one that appears to be a very suitable topic for statistical enquiry.

Galton therefore decided to try answering the following question: 'Do sick people who pray or are prayed for, recover on the average more rapidly than others?'

In order to find out, the eminent scientist collected the mortality rates for people known to pray — such as ministers — and compared them to data taken from the lives of more materialistic people, such as doctors and lawyers! He found no difference in their life-expectancy rates. He became further disillusioned when he examined the mortality figures for sovereigns, for whom whole populations often pray. They had the shortest life spans of all.

The approach Galton used to study the power of prayer would hardly seem impressive or scientific today. The surprising fact remains, though, that empirical research into the power of prayer wasn't resurrected by science until the 1950s. Revd Franklin Loehr, whose original training was in chemical engineering, carried out the first scientific study on the power of prayer while director of the Religious Research Foundation in Los Angeles. For three years he tested to see whether plants grew better if they were prayed for. After making some 900 trials, with 27000 seeds, using 80000 measurements, and employing the services of 150 subjects, Revd Loehr felt he had the answer. The evidence showed that prayer could exert a physical force into the world of the six senses. With this data finding in hand, he wrote his celebrated book *The Power of Prayer on Plants* in 1959.

*   *   *   *

What about people, though? The human body is an infinitely more complex organism than a blade of grass or a seedling. Can prayer help the sick, or even those suffering the ravages of degenerative disease? It may come as a surprise to learn that research into these very questions has been undertaken by physicians as well as religious practitioners . . . and that the results of their work has been published in respectable medical publications.

The Byrd Study

The most recent of these studies has caused no little stir within the medical community. Currently a resident of the picturesque mountain town of Big Bear, California, Dr Randy Byrd is both a cardiologist and a devout Christian. (He is presently the medical director for the Fellowship of World Christians, an organization that helps prepare volunteers for missionary service.) Dr Byrd was so intrigued by the therapeutic possibilities of religious faith that he tested the power of prayer while working as a cardiologist at San Francisco General Hospital. It was the most carefully controlled and extensive study into the power of prayer ever undertaken. Dr Byrd focused his attention on cardiac patients in the hospital's coronary care unit. He programmed a computer to choose 192 patients to serve as his test subjects, for whom prayers would be said, while another 201 patients were randomly chosen to serve as the controls. The groups were matched for age and the severity of their conditions — which included heart attack, heart failure, and other cardiac difficulties.

Dr Byrd did not do the praying himself. To keep his experiment as controlled as possible, the cardiologist recruited religious practitioners of various faiths from across the country — Protestants, Christians, and Jews — to help him out. These volunteers were given the names of the people they were asked to pray for, but of course had no contact with the patients directly. Nor did any of the patients even know that the study was in progress, or that they were taking part in it.

'Each person prayed for many different patients,' reports Dr Bryd. 'But each patient had between five and seven people praying for him or her. As part of the study the people were given the name of the patient, the diagnosis, and the condition. They were asked to pray each day, but no specific amount or way of doing it was specified.'

Dr Byrd only asked that the volunteers pray for 'beneficial healing and quick recovery.' Most of the volunteers prayed privately, but some met together in order to form prayer groups.

The experiment took close to a year to complete, and the results were nothing short of astounding. Dr Byrd reported on his experiment to the 1985 meeting of the American Heart Association (which convened in Miami, Florida) where he offered the three major findings of his study. The patients for whom prayers had been said suffered fewer complications in three specific areas:

1. While sixteen of the control patients required antibiotic treatment as a result of their cardiac problems, only three of the 'prayed-for' patients had to go on them. This equals a five-fold difference.
2. Eighteen of the controls suffered pulmonary edema (water in the folds of the lungs), which contrasted sharply to the six in the experimental group who suffered this serious condition.

3. While none of the prayed-for patients required any form of intubation, twelve of the controls required artificial help with their breathing.*

Fewer of the patients who were being prayed for died during the course of the study, but this trend was not statistically significant.

Reactions to the Byrd Experiment

Dr Byrd considers his experiment an unqualified success. 'Based on this study I believe prayer is effective and beneficial,' he told the *Medical Tribune*, which reported on the study in their 8 January 1986 issue. 'This study gives scientific evidence to something Christians have believed for years — that God answers.' What is also astounding is how well many physicians have responded to Dr Byrd's study. *The Medical Tribune* spoke to several doctors across the country, and the general consensus was to commend Dr Byrd on his experiment and findings. Dr Arthur Kennel, a cardiologist at the Mayo Medical School in Rochester, Minnesota, called the Byrd study 'an intriguing probe into an intriguing question that has perplexed mankind for eons: does God answer prayer? His study appears to provide evidence that God does.'

Another physician encouraged by Dr Byrd's work is Dr John E. Merriman, who will shortly take up the reins as chief-of-staff at Doctor's Medical Center in Tulsa, Oklahoma.

'This doesn't surprise me in the least,' said Dr Merriman of his colleague's results. 'I'm quite in agreement with his study. I'm one of those doctors who pray for their patients. I believe that patients who are named in prayer do better. And that's what Dr Byrd's study shows. You can consider prayer used in this study as a treatment. And those who receive this treatment, this prayer in that fashion, did better, that's what the facts show.'

Probably the most amazing endorsement of the Byrd study, however, has come from a notorious sceptic of religious healing. Dr William Nolen of Litchfield, Minnesota, is best-known for his celebrated book *The Making of a Surgeon*. He turned his attention to the world of faith and religious healing in the early 1970s. His subsequent book *Healing: A Doctor in Search of a Miracle* was a scathing indictment of faith healing, psychic healing, psychic surgery, and unorthodox treatment of any nature. The book was so scathing that it even prompted some reviewers to accuse Dr Nolen of fudging the facts to build his case against unorthodox medicine — a charge that seemed partially borne out when one patient listed as dead in the book after receiving psychic surgery turned up alive and well. Despite his scepticism, Dr Nolen was favourably impressed by Dr Byrd's research, and even admitted so when the *Chicago Sun-Times* — picking up the story from the *Tribune* — asked him about it.

'It sounds like this study will stand up to scrutiny,' he told reporter Howard Wolinski. Dr Nolen added that perhaps doctors should write on their order sheets 'Pray three times a day' along with their regular treatment.

'If it works, it works,' concluded the physician.

So far, in fact, the only negative reaction to Dr Byrd's experiment has come from elements within the religious community. Some pastors are afraid that the results of the Byrd study will be overgeneralized and that prayers left unanswered will turn people from religion. It is interesting to note that the religious establishment was similarly wary of Revd Loehr's work on the effect of prayer on plants, feeling that God's mystery should not be placed under anything so cold as the scientific microscope.

There's an old saying, however, that one swallow doesn't make a summer. Could the Byrd data be the result of a fluke? The fact remains that the comparisons Dr Byrd made between his two subject populations consisted of responses — both negative and positive — composed of small sub-groups within the two populations. Dr Byrd has *outlined* an experimental procedure for testing the power of spiritual petition, more than he has proved anything concerning the efficacy of prayer. His experiment will have to be repeated and successfully replicated several times before the religious establishment will be able to point to prayer as a viable form of cardiac treatment. Dr Byrd is, in fact, only now formally writing up a complete report on his work.

Some Related Studies

This does not mean that Byrd's results should be held totally in reserve. For what neither the *Medical Tribune* nor the *Sun-Times* realized is that Dr Byrd's study is not the first experimental investigation into the power of prayer. It really only refined an experimental enquiry that dates back some twenty years . . . and to research that has procured curiously mixed results.

The first scientific study dates back to the early 1960s when the first double-blind experiment on the power of prayer was conducted at the London Hospital Medical College. The expriment was undertaken by Dr C.R.B. Joyce, a psychopharmacologist, who worked in collaboration with R.M.C. Welldon. They matched together several pairs of patients chosen for age, sex, and clinical diagnosis, and focused their study on patients suffering either from rheumatoid arthritis or emotional (psychological) disorders. One member of each pair was prayed for by specially chosen prayer groups located in various British cities, while the other was not. The patients were kept ignorant about the nature of the study, and their doctors reported back periodically to the researchers. They rated their patients' improvement by use of a numerical scale.

Unlike the procedures employed by Dr Byrd in the United States, the British prayer groups were given rather specific instructions on how to pray. The two researchers specifically chose a form of silent Christian prayer/meditation in which the volunteers stilled their own thoughts and focused their attention on a selected quotation from the Bible. While expressing this positive affirmation of God, the prayers then built up a mental image of the experimental patient and his name — but without making a specific petition for his/her recovery. This form of prayer is called 'the practice of the presence of God', and according to the researchers, seems to involve 'the deeper levels of consciousness.'†

The early results of the study looked encouraging. Of the first six pairs who were evaluated (as planned) after six months, five of the prayed-for patients showed better improvement than the control subjects. Chalk one up for the power of prayer! There was a delay, however, in analysing the results of six additional pairs of patients. When these subjects were evaluated a year later, it seemed that the control patients were doing better! The reason for this odd reversal effect is not known and the project came to an end on a note of uncertainty.

This British study did have one significant upshot, though, for it encouraged a researcher in the United states to replicate it in 1969. Dr Platon J. Collipp was chairman of the pediatrics department of Meadowbrook Hospital in New York when he decided to follow up on the British experiment. Dr Collipp was a little wary of the complex design his colleagues had employed, so his experiment was more straightforward. He focused his project on only one disease with a known and (at the time) usually fatal prognosis — childhood leukaemia. He therefore asked several physicians to supply him with the names, ages, and dates of diagnosis for eighteen children suffering from the disease. They were all receiving similar forms of chemotherapy. None of the doctors nor their patients knew that they were taking part in a study on the power of prayer.

The prayer groups that took part in the study consisted of ten families living in Washington state. They were given the names of ten of the children and were asked to pray for them. The experiment was conducted over a fifteen month period, and the results were fairly clear-cut. By the end of the project, eight of the ten experimental patients were still alive.

Of the eight control children, only two had been able to survive their leukaemia. This research was subsequently published in the *Medical Times*. Dr Collipp was impressed enough by his experiment to conclude that 'among the plethora of modern drugs, and the increasing ingenuity of our surgeons, it seems inappropriate that our medical literature contains so few studies on our oldest and, who knows, perhaps most successful form of therapy. Every physician has prescribed this remedy and nearly every physician has seen it succeed.'

So where do we go from here? Because of today's upsurge of interest in unorthodox and holistic healing, hopefully more research will be focused on the psychic power of prayer. The attention Dr Byrd has received because of his recent experimental research will perhaps serve as the impetus for similar studies. As far back as 1984, in fact, researchers at John F. Kennedy University — which offers a fully accredited MS degree in parapsychology — were toying with a similar idea. Research is currently being planned to see if prayer and/or distant healing can be of aid to recovering alcoholics.

On the other hand, reactions to these various studies into the power of prayer have been very simplistic. There has been a nearly universal tendency within the religious and medical establishments to see these experiments solely as tests of God's power or the efficacy of religious faith. Very few of the physicians involved realized that they might really have been studying some sort of paranormal power generated by the prayer groups themselves. C.R.B. Joyce and R.M.C. Welldon were the only researchers to take this possibility into account. When they published their paper in the *Journal of Chronic Disease*, they pointed out that their research 'was certainly not capable of distinguishing such a concept [of a spiritual force] from other psychic factors, such as extrasensory perception or psychokinesis.' They pointed to Dr J. B. Rhine's book *The Reach of the Mind*, and cited it for providing evidence that such powers could contaminate any study on the efficacy of prayers for the sick.

There are, however, cases of healing-by-prayer so dramatic that they seem virtually miraculous. Some of these healings have even been witnessed by trained physicians. They represent a form of psychic healing that goes far beyond anything seen in conventional parapsychology, or as the result of controlled clinical studies of the type conducted by Dr Byrd and other researchers before him. These cases must remain a puzzle to both science *and* parapsychology.

The Field Studies of Dr Rex Gardner
Dr Rex Gardner is currently a consultant obstetrician and gynaecologist

at Sunderland District General Hospital in Great Britain. Before taking up his practice, he was a missionary physician whose work entailed ministering to the world's poor. The chief lesson he learned during his field experiences is that religion is no foe of science and medicine. He has even collected evidence that the power of faith sometimes triumphs where science has failed.

Writing in the December 1983 issue of the *British Medical Journal*, Dr Gardner confessed to personally witnessing miracles brought about by petitionary prayer. He also explained that he has been collecting similar reports from other physicians.

The incident that sparked Dr Gardner's interest in unorthodox healing occurred in 1970. The captain of the Girl's Brigade at Enon Baptist Church in Monkwearmouth (England) was plagued by a deteriorization in a large varicose vein. The ulcer had been troubling her for several years and obstinately refused to heal. Her morning ritual entailed changing the ulcer's pus-soaked dressing, and her physician's only counsel was to tell her to give up her physical activities. The captain's faith was stronger than her doctor's, so she asked that healing prayers be said for her at the church's next prayer-meeting. A physician examined the ulcer at the meeting, but told her that the lesion would require skin grafting even if it *did* heal. The pastor of the church responded by requesting one of the women present to join him in prayer, and the captain awoke the next morning to find that the ulcer was dry. Healthy skin was covering it, but one spot continued to excrete pus. This spot remained troublesome and inexplicable until a week later, when a brigade lieutenant called on the pastor to tell him that she should have been included in the prayer group. The pastor and the young woman immediately visited the captain, prayed for her, and layed hands on her. The healing completed itself at that moment.

Of course, stories such as this commonly appear in books on charismatic healing, but Dr Gardner feels that this case deserves careful consideration.

'This story is so bizarre,' he writes, 'that it would not have been included were I not one of the doctors who examined the patient's leg at the next monthly prayer-meeting, and were not all the people who had been present available for interrogation.'

The fact that a few fortunate physicians have personally witnessed such cases remains impressive. Dr Gardner has personally collected several similar reports which he feels have no conventional explanations. Two of his cases concern victims of fatal diseases who should have died, but who miraculously recovered after petitionary prayers were said for them. The first of these was reported to the British physician from Wales in January 1975, when a general practitioner trainee became ill with meningococcal septicaemia with meningitis — an infection of the membranes encasing the brain and spinal cord. The next day she was transported to a local hospital where she received the diagnosis of Waterhouse-Friderichsen syndrome, a malignant form of epidemic cerebrospinal meningitis. Every case of this disorder ever treated at the hospital had been terminal. But that evening religious groups in four Welsh cities prayed for a healing. The petitioners requested also that the sufferer be healed totally and wholly, with no residual disabilities.

An eyewitness to the case later wrote to Dr Gardner that:

> . . . at that same time, 8.30 p.m., there was a sudden improvement in her condition, though it was four days before she regained consciousness. Physicians were unable to explain how her chest X-ray film, which had showed extensive left-side pneumonia with collapse of the middle lobe, could, forty-eight hours later, show a normal, clear chest.

But this wasn't the only miracle that resulted from the prayer-meetings. The patient's illness had caused a blind spot on the surface of her left eye, the result of an intraocular haemorrhage. The hospital opthalmologist examined and even photographed the defect, and opined that permanent and irreversible blindness would result from the problem. The healing in this case was total and whole, for the eye completely healed to the surprise of the physicians who knew of no similar case of such healing in the opthalmological literature. The hospital's only response was to suggest that perhaps their original diagnosis was in error. This was unlikely since four specialists had been asked to evaluate the case, and they had all agreed on the cause and prognosis of the illness.

A similar healing miracle was reported by two professors of medicine at the Royal Infirmary in Newcastle-upon-Tyne, England, in 1977. The recipient of the healing was a young child. The boy had been born healthy, but was disabled by measles when he was eight months old. He never recovered from the infection, and continued to deteriorate over the next three months. He lost weight, his appetite left him, and he began to experience difficulty in breathing. When he was finally admitted to the hospital, the physician there described him as 'a wasted, miserable little scrap'. A chest radiograph revealed a massive infection of the chest with an accumulation of air within the folds around the right lung. The patient was immediately started on antibiotics, but they did little good. The boy was finally diagnosed as suffering from advancing fibrosing alveolitis — a lung condition usually fatal in infants less than a year old. A biopsy confirmed the diagnosis, and the patient's condition deteriorated progressively over the next six weeks. His mother was told that the case was hopeless, and the little boy was sent home to die.

Luckily, the boy's general practitioner was open to unorthodox forms of therapy, so he suggested that perhaps the sick infant should be taken to a Pentacostal healing service. After receiving the approval of the hospital's doctors, the suggestion was acted upon. The boy was taken to a Fundamentalist service at nearby Heaton Pentacostal Church on 26 February 1978. The meeting represented a turning point in the lad's illness. Only five days later it was clear that he was recovering. Two weeks afterwards he was able to pull himself up and stand for the first time in four months, while tests undertaken at Royal Victoria Infirmary tracked his steady recovery. He never relapsed. Five years later his doctors were able to report that '. . . he was a perfectly normal boy.'

What caused these strange healings? Miracles? Coincidence? Spontaneous remission? It is hard to tell. Cases such as those collected by Dr Gardner invariably contain an element of uncertainty. For example, it is certainly true that advancing fibrosing alveolitis is usually fatal when it is contracted at an early age. But it is not *invariably* so, and remissions are known to occur. Conventional medicine simply doesn't know enough about the body's healing capacities to differentiate a miracle from a simply anomaly of healing, so the sceptic could always maintain that such cases, while anomalous, cannot be considered paranormal.

It was noted earlier that reports of paranormal cures often find their way into books on paranormal healing and charismatic religion. Case histories of sometimes wondrous healings can be read in such books as Sally Hammond's *We Are All Healers*; David St Clair's *Psychic Healers;* Father Ralph Di Orio's *A Healing to Proclaim*; or the late Kathryn Kuhlman's famous *I Believe in Miracles*. A plethora of similar books have been published over the last two decades. In fact, these books sometimes make it seem that miraculous healings occur daily by the dozens! The problem with so many of these books is that they rarely provide the reader with really necessary and technical information about the healings. This information tends to be tedious, perhaps too tedious, for the average reader, but medicine is not a simple science. An enormous amount of information has to be evaluated before a cure can be pronounced miraculous — the very information usually deleted by writers who produce popular books on healing.

Oddly, though, many cases that do find their way into the popular press are genuinely impressive — and become even more convincing once their technical backgrounds become known. Dr Gardner learned this lesson when he received a form letter from a missionary organization in Pakistan. As part of its religious message, the letter included the story of a woman healed by Jesus, who saved her from certain death. The crisis came during a caesarean, when the patient's blood refused to clot. 'This condition responds only to infusion of triple- or quadruple-strength plasma and fancy drugs in England,' the circular boldly proclaimed. It continued by saying that faith and prayer were the only treatments available to the girl, along with 'the two meagre pints of blood donated by her brothers.' Clotting finally took hold when intercessionary prayers were said for her, and she rapidly recovered.

Dr Gardner was rather appalled by the letter's naivité. He even briefly considered whether the story was a hoax, or a possible exaggeration of what really occurred during the surgery. He was also puzzled about the snide comment concerning the transfusion, since using two pints of blood is standard procedure.

Despite these (and other) misgivings, the British physician decided to track down more information on the case. He was eventually able to make contact with the physician who performed the operation, and she supplied him with the proper clinical information on its history. Dr Ruth Coggan turned out to be not only a capable doctor, but also a devout Christian. She wrote back to her colleague on 26 July 1982 to explain that she had first seen the patient on 13 May, when the woman was in her eighth month of pregnancy. She complained of continual but irregular bleeding and abdominal pain, which had been going on for the past five months. The pregnant woman entered the hospital two days later when a particularly heavy episode of bleeding frightened her. By this time her feet and abdomen were pathologically swollen, her blood-pressure was elevated, and the bleeding continued unabated. It was Dr Coggan's feeling that a caesarean was warranted. She later explained to Dr Gardner:

> Unfortunately I was completely unable to locate any cerebrospinal fluid to put in a spinal anaesthetic as I usually do, so I did the operation under local infiltration of 1% lignocaine plus intravenous pethidine, 100mg altogether. A low transverse incision in the lower uterine segment went right through the placenta which was found to be extremely adherent to the lower uterine flap and was raggedly removed. Copious dark blood was released on entering the uterus. A 2-3kg female child — who thrived. (I'm afraid I have no note about the absence or presence of retroplacental clot, but the placenta was pretty chewed up by the time I had incised it and removed the adherent bits.) Heavy blood loss at time of operation and profuse loss post-operatively — not clotting. Deep pools of unclotted blood between the patient's thighs

and pad — heavy and prolonged trickling. Oxytocin was added to the dextrose saline drip, and then we prayed with the patient after explaining to her about Jesus in whose name we had prayed for her before the operation, and who was a great healer. I also told her that we were not going to worry. I had seen Jesus heal this condition before and was sure He was going to heal her. We then managed to get 2 pints blood for her — brisk bleeding continued. First clot was seen 48 hours after operation. Heavy loss had continued till then but her general condition gave no cause for concern after the initial post-operative examination at two hours. We prayed again with her on the night of the operation and then to thank Jesus for her healing when she went home with her baby on the tenth day.

Dr Gardner's own opinion is that the patient probably lost in excess of her total blood volume during the crucial forty-eight hours before the clotting began. He therefore shares Dr Coggan's opinion that the healing was probably miraculous. 'The story, which the normal techniques of historical scholarship would almost certainly have caused us to dismiss,' he writes, 'has become impressive because we are in a position to question the person concerned.'

Sometimes these miracles seem even to overcome death itself. Tobin Talbot and his wife served as Christian missionaries to the Mong people in Thailand in the 1960s. Some years later they told a remarkable story to Dr Gardner, to which they had been eyewitnesses. The first villager to convert had been a fifty-year-old woman named Mrs Ling, whom the other villagers ostracized for her commitment. They publicly jeered at her and warned her of the dire consequences resulting from her act. The threats took their toll, and in the tradition of the hex death, she became ill and rapidly deteriorated. The villagers continued to jeer while the local missionaries recited petitionary prayers for her recovery. Mrs Ling did, in fact, die . . . but she spontenously revived twenty minutes later, whereupon she reported a classic near-death experience, explaining that she had gone to the next world where she met Christ. She claimed that He had sent her back to Earth with several messages. She then called forth the villagers who had previously laughed at her, telling each of them secrets from their pasts. These secrets, she claimed, had been given to her during her spiritual sojourn.

'So accurate and devastating were these,' Talbot wrote to Dr Gardner, 'that the village priest's son fled, to return half an hour later and announce that he wished to become a Christian. He is now an elder of the village church.'

The woman seemed transformed by her experience, and exhibited a sudden and uncanny knowledge of religious thought. She subsequently learned to read in an inexplicably short period of time, shorter than the missionaries had ever seen before.

Dr Gardner, of course, realizes that this case, fascinating though it is, was never properly documented. There is certainly no objective evidence that the villager really died, but it is clear that Mrs Ling must have been very ill. Both the villagers *and* the local missionaries thought she really had died, while her instantaneous recovery seems rather inexplicable. It is for this reason that Dr Gardner includes it in his short codex of properly documented religious miracles.

The sceptic could remain unimpressed by even these cases, though. Recovery from severe illness, spontaneous remission, the return from the jaws of death — such phenomena may represent little understood, though perfectly normal, properties of the body's own healing capacities. Today's cities are filled with former hospital patients who were proclaimed incurable, but who somehow survived their afflictions and ordeals. It is for this reason that writers and clinicians interested in unorthodox healing like to focus on a different kind of case — the spontaneous healings of physical injuries such as bone fractures or wounds. Such injuries heal in a conventional and predictable manner, so the physicians treating them should be in a perfect position to determine whether any unusual factors complicated the process. Sure enough, Dr Gardner has collected two instances in which paranormal forces served to accelerate the healing process.

One of these cases was reported to him by a group of Lutheran nuns residing in Darmstadt, Germany. The Evangelical Sisters of Mary were building their mother house and chapel in 1951 when the accident occurred. One of the nuns fell on to a freshly cemented floor, broke through it, and fell on to a wooden beam. She was rushed to a local hospital where X-rays revealed a compound pelvic fracture. The other nuns responded to the crisis by holding a prayer vigil for their stricken sister. They were told by hospital officials that the injured sister would be in traction for several weeks, but to the extreme consternation of the physicians, the other sisters took her home two days later so that they could heal her through prayer. She was administered laying-on-of-hands as well, and the results were spectacular.

'The sister stood up from her bed,' one of the eyewitnesses told Dr Gardner. 'She had not been able to move on her bed without excruciating pain, and now she could actually stand on her feet. We looked at her, and for some moments could hardly take our eyes from her . . . Within two weeks the sister was completely healed and presented herself to the doctor. The story spread throughout the country like wildfire.'

Dr Gardner followed up the case by collecting corroborative statements from the other nuns of the order, which included their eyewitness testimony. He learned that the healing was complete and that the fortunate sister later walked without so much as a limp.

A similar case was collected by Dr Gardner in 1976. The miraculous nature of this healing speaks for itself:

> In 1976 a group of four Christians, three expatriate missionaries and a national carpenter, travelled to a remote part of Nepal to start a new leprosy clinic. While erecting a chimney stack, the missionary builder fell on to a metal pipe on the upper verandah and then rolled off and fell 10 feet on to a concrete parapet. The missionary doctor was with him. Mr P had obviously hurt his left side and at first was thought to have fractured his ribs. His blood-pressure fell, his pulse rose, his abdomen became rigid and silent, and it became obvious that he was suffering from intra-abdominal haemorrhage from a ruptured spleen. The party had just arrived, the medical supplies were as yet unpacked, and in any case did not contain surgical equipment. The doctor was able to give him morphine and set up a saline intravenous infusion. They sent a police message for help which never got through and there were no human resources left.
>
> After two hours the patient asked for prayer and anointing with oil. The four Christians gathered round. They read the Biblical injunction together. 'Is any sick among you? Let him call for the elders of the church; and let them pray over him, anointing him with oil in the name of the Lord: and the prayer of faith shall save the sick, and the Lord shall raise him up.' Cooking oil was employed for anointing. Though the drip soon stopped, his pulse and blood-pressure rapidly improved.

The worker's condition rapidly improved, and soon his body was functioning normally although inexplicably. Today he is still working as a builder in Nepal.

Some Conclusions

In conclusion, what can we make of these purportedly miraculous healings? The point emphasized by Dr Gardner is that these cures represent nothing new. A scholar as well as a physician, he presented these cases in 1983 side-by-side with similar stories extracted from the writings of the Venerable Bede (AD 673–735), the great English historian and theologian. The miracle of healing is therefore not a legend left over from Biblical days, but a force that has been present throughout the rise of religious belief. Since he is personally a devout Christian, Dr Gardner believes that these healings point to the existence of spiritual forces in the universe that sometimes focus on us. Secularized students of the paranormal will perhaps challenge this view, seeing in these cases evidence of a psychokinetic force capable of being liberated through faith and prayer.

It really doesn't matter which of these two explanations is the correct one. The essential point is that the bare existence of the healing force no longer seems in question. Both science and religion should be working to harness this power for the benefit of all mankind.

End-Notes for Chapter Eleven

* These findings are all statistically significant. The odds against the first two findings occurring by chance are 100 to 1. The third result would only occur by chance once every twenty times the experiment was run.

† This form of healing is currently taught in a much revised version by psychologist Lawrence LeShan, who teaches workshops on paranormal healing. See his book *The Medium, The Mystic and the Physicist*.

12.

Psychic Healing by Touch

'Therapeutic touch' is the clinical term for a practice known to mankind for centuries. The laying-on-of-hands has been practised by several primitive cultures, while its contemporary roots date back to the ministry of the early Christian church. Something resembling therapeutic touch was also popular during the eighteenth century, when Dr Franz Anton Mesmer (1733-1815) and his followers discovered that they could cure their patients by running either their hands or magnets up and down the body. Their belief was that the body represented a bioenergetic system, somehow linked to the cosmos, which sometimes becomes unbalanced or clogged. Patients who were duly 'mesmerized' certainly reported feeling better after receiving these stroking procedures, although the sceptics claimed that these feelings were purely imaginary. Several psychic healers practising today employ a similar technique while helping their own patients forget their pain and recover from their illnesses.

Despite the fact that conventional science places little stock in the phenomenon, the practice of therapeutic touch has been making a comeback ever since the 1970s. This renaissance of interest has resulted primarily from the work of Dr Dolores Krieger, who started using the procedure in her own nursing work in 1969. She discovered the technique after learning that she could help remove her patients' pain and discomfort by touching them. This led her to write her book *Therapeutic Touch: How to Use Your Hands to Help and Heal* in 1975 in which she publicly described the procedure.

Therapeutic touch is, according to Dr Krieger, a rather complicated practice. So to properly implement the healing, the nurse or practitioner follows a fairly rigid ritual by slowly moving his/her hands up and down the patient while looking for places where the body's energy-field is blocked. This diagnostic procedure is, however, conducted only when the practitioner has first entered a state of relaxed concentration. The healer's hands do not touch the body during this phase of the healing, but remain a few inches above it. When a site of disturbance is 'felt' or subjectively 'sensed', the practitioner then places his hands on the spot and works with the location by sending some of his own energy to it. Dislodging the blockage by working solely with the body's energy-field is an alternative procedure, though the practitioner does not touch the body while performing this operation (which is called non-contact healing).

Dr Krieger is emphatic that therapeutic touch cannot be performed casually. 'Therapeutic touch is not just putting your hands over a painful area', she states, 'nor is it a massage to loosen muscles. You have to be taught to concentrate and direct your healthy energy to get proper results'.

The specific mechanisms behind the efficacy of therapeutic touch is not known, even though Dr Krieger and her colleagues claim that some sort of energy is genuinely transferred as part of the interaction.

'Basic to therapeutic touch', she wrote in 1979, 'is the concept that the human body has an excess of energy. The person who administers therapeutic touch engages in an effort to direct his own excess energies for the use of an ill person, who can be thought of as being in less than an optimal energy state'.

This all sounds great, but does therapeutic touch really work? The answer will depend on whether you speak with a believer or a sceptic, for a debate over the efficacy of the practice has been raging in several nursing publications ever since Dr Krieger's book was issued.

Therapeutic Touch Enters the Lab

Research on the beneficial effects of therapeutic touch was, in fact, spearheaded by Dr Krieger herself. Beginning in the early 1970s, she began reporting the results of several laboratory experiments exploring the biochemical effects of the practice. Her principal research was conducted at New York University, where she is currently a professor of nursing, while her main research entailed measuring the haemoglobin levels of several patients undergoing therapeutic touch therapy. Since haemoglobin is the respiratory pigment in red corpuscles, this level is essential to a person's health.

Dr Krieger eventually conducted three separate studies to explore this possible response to healing touch. The therapeutic touch for these studies was applied by Oskar Estabany, a retired Hungarian military officer from Canada who is well known for his psychic healings. The results for each of the studies was the same. Those subjects treated with therapeutic touch for between six to fourteen days invariably showed greater haemoglobin counts than a group of control patients. Dr Krieger followed up on her experiment several months later by contacting those patients who had participated in the therapeutic touch sessions. Most of them reported back that they were continuing to enjoy good health, normal blood-pressure and excellent appetite.

The outcome of these early studies seemed impessive; certainly impressive enough for Dr Krieger to go forward with her work by training other nurses in the procedure. They, in turn, have been contributing their own research to the growing literature on therapeutic touch, both by way of personal reports and by conducting rigid experimental research.

One of these gifted first-generation practitioners is Janet Macrae, who consulted with Dr Krieger while working towards her Phd in New York. Since she was (then) a staff nurse specializing in pediatrics, she immediately took an interest in whether therapeutic touch could be used with small children. Dr Macrae does not believe, though, that physical touch is necessary while practising this form of healing. She therefore prefers to work directly with the body's energy-field — i.e., the invisible radiations which psychics and practitioners of the laying-on-of-hands believe extend into the space surrounding the body.

'A casual observer might think we are dealing with nothing' she reported in 1979 to the *American Journal of Nursing.* 'However, if the observer took some time to practise she would soon find her hands becoming sensitive to these finer energies.'

Dr Macrae should know, since she credits herself with helping several children by working with these energy-systems. One of the cases she reported to the *Journal* concerned a four-year-old boy who complained of considerable pain after some surgery.

'I ran my hands through his energy-field — about four to six inches beyond his body,' she reports. 'I literally found the pain . . . and directed it out of his field, using a stroking motion. The little boy stopped crying and feel asleep after about three or four minutes of therapeutic touch.'

The effects of therapeutic touch can be specific and localized too. Dr Macrae discovered this fact while working with a ten-year-old leukaemia patient. The boy was suffering from localized pain in his jaw, which was probably being caused by his chemotherapy. Since conventional analgesic drugs were not working on the pain effectively, the concerned nurse decided to use therapeutic touch.

Dr Macrae writes:

One day, I asked him if I could put my hands on the place where it hurt. He said yes, so I centered myself quickly and passed my hands through his field. Above the right side of his jaw I felt a fine tingling sensation. I brushed it away. However, it reappeared above the left side of his jaw. I then cleared off both sides simultaneously, and Paul informed me that his jaw was fine but that his upper chest had begun to hurt. I put my hands over his chest and the pain went back to his right jaw. At that point I stopped to re-evaluate the situation. I realized that I was not treating the patient's energy-field as a whole, so I changed my method. I put my left hand over his jaw where the pain was, and with my right hand, I directed the area of tingling through his whole field and out past his feet.

The boy spontaneously responded by telling the nurse that he could feel the pain moving down his chest, travelling through his abdomen, and leaving through his feet!

The New York-based nurse found, too, that therapeutic touch can be beneficial even when no perceptible *physical* change can be seen in the patient's condition. For example, Dr Macrae likes to use therapeutic touch to relieve lung congestion in the children she cares for. She treats this specific problem by using stroking movements to disburse the congestion, and then she directs the problem out of the patient's body through the feet. Sometimes the patient will respond positively to this form of treatment, even though the congestion often remains biologically present in the body.

The problem with reports such as these, however, rests with their purely anecdotal nature. Such reports would never impress the sceptic or even the sympathetic scientist looking for formal 'proof' of the healing touch. And these concerns take us right back to Dolores Krieger.

Dr Krieger is not unsympathetic to the sceptic's position, which was her primary reason for conducting her original blood-haemoglobin studies in the early 1970s. But practitioners of therapeutic touch like to point to some rather subjective effects of the skill, effects that are extremely difficult to properly evaluate. These practitioners claim that patients receiving therapeutic touch seem to become extremely relaxed and less prone to anxiety during the sessions. But could there be any way to test such an observation experimentally? This is the very issue Dr Krieger and some of her colleagues began considering in 1978. The result was a rather sophisticated study which focused on *both* the healer *and* her clients during the practice of therapeutic touch.

This specific study was first contemplated while Dr Krieger was visiting the Langley Porter Neuropsychiatric Institute in San Francisco. She spent part of her stay discussing therapeutic touch with Dr Joe Kamiya — one of the US's leading authorities on psychophysiology. Dr Kamiya and several of his graduate students were intrigued by the specific physiological effects conceivably induced by therapeutic touch, while they were equally curious about the brain state the practitioner enters during the transaction. It didn't take long for Dr Krieger to volunteer her services when Dr Kamiya and one of his students decided to find out. She ended up taking part in a two-day study that still remains a classic in the literature.

During this experiment, Dr Krieger took part in the therapeutic touch sessions with three patients, while she was simultaneously linked to an EEG (which constantly recorded her brain waves). Several other psychophysiological readings were taken from Dr Krieger as well, including her pulse rate, galvanic skin response, skin temperature, and so on. Each of the patients chosen to receive the treatments was participating in the hospital's pain and stress reduction programme. The first patient was an elderly gentleman who had become partially crippled after receiving a spinal injection. The second patient was a woman suffering with fibroid tumours, and the final patient was being treated by the staff for persistent recurring migraine.

During the first day of the study, only Dr Krieger's psychophysiology was monitored. The patients' readings were taken as part of the second day's work.

The end results of the study were fascinating. The experimenters found that while engaged in her healing, Dr Krieger's brain produced an unusual amount of beta waves — fast waves that occur when a person is concentrating on an intellectual task. She also seemed to tense up during the therapeutic session, but her rapid brain waves seemed to be independent of this state. Her eyes tended to shift relatively little, even though she sometimes opened them partially during the sessions. These readings, taken together, indicated to the researchers that their subject was entering into a state of steady concentration while treating her patients, but that this concentration was relatively unfocused. The readings taken from the three patients were, however, less striking. While they tended to enter a state of relative relaxation while undergoing therapeutic touch, their levels did not shift significantly from the beginning to the end of the sessions.

But even if the patients didn't exhibit striking psychophysiological changes while being touched, their symptoms certainly improved. The elderly gentleman dispensed with his crutches for the first time in months, tucked them under his arm, and walked out of the hospital. The second patient's tumours suddenly vanished, while the third patient testified that the severity of her migraines diminished after the completion of the treatment. Dr Kamiya and his colleagues played down these secondary results in a report published in the *American Journal of Nursing* by writing that these improvements '. . . may not be related to the therapeutic touch experience and no claims can be made.' But it is difficult *not* to credit these sensational results either to therapeutic touch or to Dr Krieger's psychic abilities. Dr Kamiya and his collaborators do report (in a brilliant display of scientific understatement) that 'the experience was important to the patients'!

Dr Kamiya has not been the only researcher interested in the psychological effects of therapeutic touch, however. Shortly after the San Francisco researcher worked with Dr Krieger, a roughly similar experiment was conducted by Dr Patricia Heidt, a psychotherapist in private practice in New York. She, too, had long been intrigued by the claim that patients receiving therapeutic touch became unusually relaxed during the procedure. Her carefully designed experiment was conducted at St Vincent's Medical Center in New York, and her extensive protocol employed the services of ninety patients. Both men and women were used for the project and they were all being treated by the hospital's coronary care unit.

In order to focus on the effects of therapeutic touch, Dr Heidt — who was first trained in the skill by Dr Krieger — broke down her patients into three large groups. She treated the first group by performing formal therapeutic touch with them. The second group were not so lucky, since they only received casual touchings during which Dr Heidt undertook no procedures to really heal them. The third group served as a second control group, and Dr Heidt simply sat next to their beds and spoke softly with them for the same period of time it takes to perform therapeutic touch. Every one of the patients rated their level of anxiety both before and after their private sessions by filling out a special form. (This questionnaire was administered by a research assistant, and asked them whether they felt jittery, relaxed, and so forth.) To keep the conditions of the experiment as uniform as possible, each of the subjects was 'treated' in his/her own hospital room, and they were all tested during the same time of day.

And the results?

Based on the claims being made for the therapeutic touch by Dr Krieger and others, they were right in keeping with the psychotherapist's expectations. The patients treated with the formal procedure showed a significant post-session reduction of their anxieties, which was a reduction considerably greater than that reported by either set of control patients. These results demonstrated, in Dr Heidt's opinion, that the effects of therapeutic touch represent a genuine phenomenon, and cannot be due purely to the psychological effects of the practitioner's presence.

In her report to *Nursing Research*, Dr Heidt concludes:

Research on therapeutic touch documents and lends support to the effect of interpersonal relationships on patient care. For a long time this aspect of care has been less appreciated and acknowledged for its healing functions than objective scientific data. For example, early behavioral research so clearly demonstrated the power of human contact that it became important for scientific investigators to control carefully for its effects and isolate the object of study from the investigator. Before the scientific era of health care, helping persons relied on their own presence as a source of helping and/or healing. The history of health care since that time has been increasingly less mindful of the effect of the bedside manner of human contact, and more dependent on the effect of drugs, instrumentation, and technological advances to aid recovery. Therapeutic touch offers a framework for understanding the potency of the human organism as a resource in healing and recovery care.

The Renewed Debate over Therapeutic Touch

By 1981, the case for the power of therapeutic touch certainly seemed impressive. But then in 1983 two psychiatric nurses from Georgia re-ignited the controversy over the benefits of therapeutic touch by soundly criticizing the research we've been summarizing — and sometimes their points were irrefutable.

This extremely important critique was the work of Philip E. Clark of the Dwight David Eisenhower Army Center in Fort Gordon, and Mary Jo Clark, currently an assistant professor of nursing at the Medical College of Georgia in Augusta. When they published the results of their findings in the January–February 1984 issue of *Nursing Research*, they picked holes in or raised objections to every published study of therapeutic touch they could find. For example, they found several problems even with Dr Krieger's original haemoglobin experiments, which they singled out for extensive comment. Dr Krieger had been rather sketchy about the criteria she used when choosing her subjects for these experiments. Could she have been biased to select subjects she *knew* would respond to the treatment psychologically? This is certainly a possibility that can't be overlooked. The Clarks also feel that she used improper statistics when evaluating her final results. But their biggest gripe rests with the fact that Dr Krieger had encouraged her patients to practise meditation while the study was still in progress. The Georgia researchers rightfully point out that this practice could have contributed to the rise in some of the subjects' haemoglobin levels.

The Clarks ended their critique by commenting on a final and inexplicable phenomenon they found by examining Dr Krieger's experimental results. It seems that in her final study, even the subjects in the control group exhibited extremely elevated haemoglobin counts! While this increase was not nearly as significant as that exhibited by the experimental subjects, the Clarks feel that Dr Krieger's research cannot be properly evaluated until this puzzling rise can be explained. It may have represented some overlooked factor that complicated the entire experiment.

If we dismiss the findings of Dr Krieger's biochemical studies, this still leaves the results of Dr Kamiya's project to be explained. Unfortunately, Dr Kamiya's published report particularly focused on the readings taken from Dr Krieger while it merely summarized the results obtained from the three patients. The Clark report criticizes Dr Kamiya for this reporting error, pointing out that his experiment simply can't be evaluated until these data are supplied to the scientific community. (The two researchers did not, however, try to explain the surprising healings which resulted from Dr Krieger's touch!)

While the research undertaken by Dr Patricia Heidt is probably the most sophisticated in the literature, the Clarks found a problem with that study, too, which they feel severely compromises its findings. They point out that the practice of therapeutic touch entails a formalized 'ritual' during which the practitioner works over the patient's body. This impressive (and perhaps psychologically important) ritual was not included in the procedures experienced by the patients receiving casual touch. The two sceptics therefore posit that the reduced tension seen in the test subjects was really a placebo effect. They were probably psychologically responding to the ritual of healing, rather than to some sort of energy transfer from the practitioner.

The Clarks go on to suggest that Dr Heidt's study could have been easily designed to bypass the placebo effect. The psychologist could have shammed the therepeutic touch ritual by passing her hands near her control subjects, while not really trying to send any energy to them. If any of the therapeutic touch group still showed significant effects under these conditions, the possibility of a confounding placebo effect would thereby be eliminated.

It is difficult to read the report published by the Clarks without being impressed by it. Their insightful comments show that the case for therapeutic touch isn't nearly as convincing as Dr Krieger and her followers would like to think. It is hard to argue with the Clarks when they conclude their report by writing that,

the current research base supporting continued nursing practice of therapeutic touch is, at best, weak . . . Therapeutic touch as a modality does excite interest. However, without a broader research base, it may be presumptuous to teach the art or to seriously discuss the use of this practice in the treatment of illness. The practice of therapeutic touch by nurses will never gain professional credibility without clear, objective evidence to support it . . .'

It would be easy to end this discussion of therapeutic touch with this pessimistic outlook. Sceptics who refuse to believe in the efficacy of psychic healing will probably consider the Clarks' report the last word on the subject. This would be rather rash, though. For in the same month the Clarks issued their report, a researcher from South Carolina published the results of an experiment seemingly designed to counter each and every objection raised by the two Georgia sceptics. The results of this study were so startling that it made headlines in the science section of *The New York Times*.

This research was the brainchild of Dr Janet Quinn, who currently directs the Department of Medical-Surgical Nursing at the University of South Carolina's College of Nursing in Columbia.

Dr Quinn can claim both a personal and professional interest in the practice of therapeutic touch. She took her BA in nursing and subsequently worked both in emergency rooms and intensive care units before turning her knowledge to teaching. She became interested in the psychological dimensions of her profession while teaching in New York, and eventually met Dr Krieger, who introduced her to the field of therapeutic touch in 1976. Dr Krieger especially urged the younger woman to experiment with the procedure while practising her own nursing skills.

'I was sceptical,' commented Dr Quinn to the *American Journal of Nursing* in 1979, 'but somehow I sensed that what was happening was important.'

This sense of importance led Dr Quinn to participate in a workshop on therapeutic touch conducted by Dr Krieger. It was during this workshop that she was enthusiastically converted to the promise of therapeutic touch. The catalysing incident took place while she was practising the technique under the guidance of a more experienced practitioner.

'My hands somehow seemed to know what needed to be done,' she writes, 'and I let them lead me. I felt the energy of the client balance, and even out . . . My interaction had finally been therapeutic and beneficial. It was a miraculous day, which I shall never forget.'

Dr Quinn has been studying the power of therapeutic touch ever since, but it wasn't until the early 1980s that she put her experience to the test.

The research that recently brought considerable publicity from the press was not truly original, since it was primarily a replication of the work reported in 1981 by Dr Patricia Heidt.

Dr Quinn was nothing if not fastidious, and she even conducted her research in the same coronary wards in New York where Dr Heidt previously worked. The experimental subjects she chose to participate in the study included twenty-three women and forty-seven men at St Vincent's Medical Center. Since Dr Quinn decided not to perform the therapeutic touch procedure herself, she enlisted four nurses familiar with the skill to serve as the practitioners. Three other nurses were recruited for the experiment and were taught to *imitate* the therapeutic touch ritual while counting backwards (instead of focusing their 'energies' on the patients). Before receiving the therapeutic touch or taking part in a related session, each subject was given a self-evaluation form which asked him/her about their anxiety levels. The subject then received either several minutes of non-contact therapeutic touch, or received the faked demonstration. When each of the sessions was concluded, Dr Quinn asked the patients to evaluate their sense of tension and/or anxiety once again. There's where she found exactly what she was looking and hoping for. The patients who had just finished receiving therapeutic touch reported a significant reduction in their fears, a reduction that was *not* experienced by the control subjects.

But Dr Quinn decided to be extra-cautious before publicizing these strong and impressive findings. She considered the possibility that the *behaviour* exhibited by the four nurses trained in therapeutic touch might have differed from the performances of their role-playing counterparts. If such behavioural differences were contaminating the study, the sceptic could rightfully posit that these differences contributed to the results. So to test for this possibility, Dr Quinn filmed the seven nurses performing their respective (genuine versus fake) procedures. These videotapes were later shown to a panel composed of fifteen judges, who tried to guess which of the films depicted the bogus operations. These evaluators, much to Dr Quinn's relief, were incapable of determining the real from the role-playing practitioners. So whatever effect the South Carolina researcher found in her studies, it can't be explained as a placebo very easily.

Dr Quinn currently hopes to replicate and extend her studies, and she recently received a three-year grant to continue her work. If she is successful in replicating her research it will serve as impressive evidence that each of us possess the power to heal . . . a power science has ignored for too long.

But for now, the debate over therapeutic touch is still raging on.

13.

Science Investigates the 'Flight of the Soul'

Few people are aware just how completely chained we are within our physical bodies. We are virtually enslaved by the prison of our sensory organs. We can only make physical contact with our universe through them, and each is extremely limited. They are easily hallucinated, subject to illusion, and often malfunction or give way completely. We can only 'see' part of the visible spectrum between infra-red and ultraviolet and our sense of hearing is rather primitive. It is certainly much weaker than the auditory perception of many animals. Not only are our sense perceptions limited, but what we see and hear may not actually be very objective at all, but coloured by our own thoughts and expectations.

The crux of the matter is that, over many generations, we have been programming ourselves — or have been programmed by our culture — to perceive the world in only one slender way along the secure boundaries of three-dimensional reality. We never stop to think that we may only be experiencing a limited frequency of the universe just as our sight only perceives limited points within the visual spectrum. Would it be possible to transcend our reliance on our sense perceptions and actually disregard the body completely? Some people have had that exact experience.

The Out-of-body Experience: Some Historical Perspectives
Travelling psychically over time and space is an ancient phenomenon known as the out-of-body experience. It was reported by the ancient shamans, by the Greek philosophers, and by the mediaeval alchemists. Yet it is an experience that many people still have today. Usually the experiencer has the vivid sensation that his mind has physically detached itself from the body and can perceive, travel and exist completely independently of it. It is not a rare experience either, and people report it all the time. For instance, the following account is from my own files:

About two years ago I had read in a book about inducing sleep by relaxing each part of your body at a time. I decided to try this. That night about 1 a.m. I went to bed. I started to concentrate on each limb. It was starting to work. I found my limbs impossible to move . . . I began to get a little dizzy, as if I could not draw a breath. All of a sudden I felt my body rise off the bed. I felt myself 'floating' in the air over my bed. I reached down with my hands to grip the bed, and saw my own body there in the bed. I turned my head to look at the bed and saw myself still there in the bed. I started to wave my arms and legs about and was back upon the bed, sitting up.

Until only recently few people would ever think of discussing this type of experience in public. Derision, ridicule, even charges of mental illness were their usual rewards if they did. In the past, only a few adventurers in different parts of the world dared report their out-of-body travels in any detail. Among them were Sylvan Muldoon in the United States, Hugh Callaway in Great Britain (who wrote under the name Oliver Fox) and Marcel Louis Forhan in France (who wrote under the name Yram). To the general public, these men must have seemed either masters of the occult capable of exploring dimensions beyond the reach of the everyday layman, or simply madmen or liars. The writings of these habitual projectors served as the public's first source of information on the subject, and their autobiographies still make for gripping reading.

In 1919, for instance, the noted American psychical investigator Hereward Carrington wrote a chapter in his book *Modern Psychical Phenomena* about the experiences of a French researcher who had investigated the phenomenon. This volume eventually came into the hands of a sickly mid-Western youth named Sylvan Muldoon. Muldoon had been having OBEs since childhood, and when he read Carrington's book, he wrote to the famous investigator claiming that *he* could write a book on what the French 'authorities' *didn't* know about the experience! A correspondence ensued, which resulted in Carrington and Muldoon — then just over twenty-years-old and confined to bed — producing their joint *The Projection of the Astral Body*, which appeared in 1929.

Muldoon had his first experience when he was 12. While visiting a spiritualist camp in the mid-West, he awoke one night only to find himself paralyzed. The catalepsy finally gave way to curious floating sensations. When he finally opened his eyes and his vision cleared, Muldoon found himself hovering over his own body and he saw a slender silver cord connecting his phantom self to his physical body. Muldoon was shocked, but hardly realized that his experience heralded what would be years of chronic OBEs.

Dozens upon dozens of these incidents are chronicled in Muldoon's autobiography. He was eventually able to control and even willfully induce the experience. His attempts, successes, and partial failures are all recounted. On one occasion, for example, he fell asleep thirsty, only to find himself awake and out-of-body in his kitchen. He was apparently trying to turn on a tap to get a drink. On yet another occasion Muldoon describes how he touched a power line and was immediately catapulted out-of-body. He calmly watched as his body writhed in agony. He also noted that dreams of flying would herald an OBE. This led the young experimenter to develop methods of dream control. He would go to bed and give himself suggestions, right up to the moment he fell asleep, that he would have specific dreams that related to his OBEs. When these dreams manifested, Muldoon could then wake himself and would find himself out-of-body. He also discovered that he could consciously leave the body by calming himself through relaxation exercises and by slowing his heartbeat.

Muldoon ended his career as a scholar as well as a psychic. He and Carrington began collecting accounts written by others who had experienced the OBE. These accounts represented the first evidence that the OBE was not a rare experience. They placed these cases in their book *The Phenomenon of Astral Projection*, while Muldoon published another casebook, *The Case for Astral Projection*, himself some years later.

As his health improved, though, his uncanny abilities waned and disappeared. Muldoon lost most of his active interest in the field and spent the rest of his life running a beauty shop in the town of Darlington, Wisconsin. He died in 1972 but left behind several notebooks reporting his observations and experiences. These were, unfortunately, destroyed by his over-zealous relatives, who felt that Muldoon's experiences violated their religious tenets.

While Muldoon was undergoing his strange adventures in the United States, an Englishman was discovering his own abilities at astral travel. Hugh Callaway was a London occultist who also discovered that he possessed a phantom double locked within himself. Callaway related his experiences in two articles which appeared in the *Occult Review* and finally authored a book titled *Astral Projection*, which has become yet another classic in the field. Fox (Hugh Callaway) discovered his OBEs through the inner world of dreams. He learned that if he could figure out he was dreaming *while* he was dreaming, he could wake himself in the out-of-body state. This allowed him to experience almost nightly out-of-body experiences, during which he not only visited friends, but even had many strange adventures in unseen dimensions. He often met the inhabitants of these other worlds.

One of Fox's most curious stories concerns his girlfriend Elsie. One day he began bragging to her about his experiences, and she, too, announced that she could leave her body. She promised to project to him that very night. And she made good on her claim. While Fox was in bed at home, he suddenly saw Elsie's figure appear mysteriously in the room. The phantom walked about as though examining the place. The next day, she was able to accurately describe the layout of the room to a most astonished young man.

Could it be that, while most people remain invisible during their OBEs, on occasion a person undergoing the experience might actually be seen by others? There is a rich collection of cases on hand indicating that this is possible.

A series of such cases have been placed on record by S.H. Beard, a London businessman and a friend of Edmund Gurney, one of the founders of the Society for Psychical Research in England. Gurney was so impressed by Beard's records that he placed them in his co-authored two-volume study *Phantasms of the Living*, one of the great classics of early parapsychology. Beard began his experiments in November 1881. After reading about the power of the will, he decided it might be interesting to project himself to the home of his fiancée, Miss Verity. He began his experiments that very night. He sat at home willing himself to her London home but soon feel asleep. But the next day he learned that, at the time of his attempt, his apparition had indeed appeared in his fiancée's bedroom. Not only had Miss Verity seen him, but her sister had awoken at the critical moment and she, too, had seen the phantom. Beard eventually repeated his experiment and actually felt himself parading around the Verity home at the same time his apparition was seen.

The Changing Image of the Out-of-body Experience
Despite the unusualness of Beard's experiences, and the occult glamour that imbued the writings of Muldoon, Fox, and other astral voyagers, we know now that the out-of-body experience is a rather common one. Many people undergo such experiences in the course of their daily lives who would not ordinarily consider themselves psychics or mystics. Celia Green polled large groups of people about the OBE while working at the Oxford-based Institute of Psychophysical Research in the 1960s. She found that nearly 20 per cent of the 380 individuals she questioned had experienced the phenomenon. Since that time, similar surveys have been conducted in England, the United States, Australia and in Iceland. The results indicate that within any group of people, between 10–20 per cent of them will report at least one out-of-body experience. This means that *millions* of people have undergone the experience.

It wasn't until the work of Dr Robert Crookall in the 1960s, however, that we really learned how common these incidents seem to be, and how the experience is typified by a highly specific phenomenology.

Crookall, who died in 1981, had achieved an eminent career in science before turning to parapsychology. A holder of doctorates both in geology and general science, he was formerly a faculty member at the University of Aberdeen and a member of HM Geological Survey. His concern over whether man survives bodily death ignited his interest in mediumship and later prompted him to study the out-of-body experience. Crookall was struck by the fact that so many OBE reports seem to describe an identical experience, so to check out his impression, he began collecting as many cases as he could find. His main plan was to make a critical analysis of his data in hopes of learning a little about the exact nature of the experience. He eventually collected close to 1000 reports, which have appeared in such books as *The Study and Practice of Astral Projection, More Astral Projections,* and *A Casebook of Astral Projection.*

Crookall analysed his data over and over again and published several highly original analyses of his survey. His first goal was to determine if people undergoing the OBE tend to experience a similar phenomenology, as he had suspected when he first undertook his project. He believed that if distinct patterns were to arise in his data, this fact alone would prove the OBE to be a genuine phenomenon and one certainly worthy of scientific attention. After making a content analysis of over 300 cases, Crookall did find that certain experiential features crop up time after time in these accounts. Six primary features in particular stood out: the percipient often felt that he left the body by being drawn out through the head; a black-out occurred at the moment of separation; the phantom 'double' initially hovered directly over the physical body, then resumed this same position before re-entering the body; a black-out again occurred upon re-entry; and a rapid return to the body caused physical repercussion.

Crookall also discovered that people undergoing OBEs tend to see apparitions of the dead, are capable of exhibiting ESP, are sometimes either projected to a beautiful 'Paradise' world, or find themselves in a misty, hellish environment. Many of Crookall's correspondents also saw a cord connection between their out-of-body selves and their physical bodies.

Crookall's second analysis was even more interesting. In 1964 he showed that while all OBEs fit into general patterns, there seem to be qualitative differences between two different *types* of out-of-body experiences. For this analysis, he broke down his cases into two large

It was Dr Robert Crookall who discovered that out-of-body experiences are more common than had previously been thought. (Mary Evans/Psychic News)

groups. In the first he placed those OBEs which had occurred naturally — when the percipient was near sleep, ill, exhausted, or simply spontaneously. The other category consisted of those cases that were 'forced' by the use of anaesthetics or resulted from shock, suffocation, hypnosis, willful attempts at projection or any other artificial means. After making a content analysis of the two groups, he found that the natural OBEs were much more vivid and have different overall characteristics from those which are enforced. Such experiences as leaving through the head, seeing the silver cord, and demonstrating ESP were consistently more common to the natural group than in the enforced cases. Unfortunately, Crookall did not have enough material for these differences to be statistically significant, but they did represent strong qualitative trends in his data.

Crookall re-analysed his data once again a few years later in 1970. This time he compared those OBEs reported by famous psychics to those reported by everyday sorts of individuals. Once again he found a difference. Psychics tend to report OBEs resembling enforced projections, while most of us common folk have much more vivid and natural experiences.

It is interesting that other researchers have confirmed Crookall's discoveries about many of the experiential aspects of the OBE. Working in England at roughly the same time, Celia Green found her data revealing similar patterns about the OBE — how the phantom double hovers over the body upon release, how the experience can be induced through anaesthetics or during illness, how the experiencer can demonstrate ESP during the incident, and so on. But her data did show some differences from Crookall's as well. Green found that many of her correspondents did *not* project in the form of a phantom double. Many of them perceived themselves instead as balls of light, amorphous shadowy forms, or merely disembodied specks of consciousness. She also found very few people who actually saw anything like the famous 'silver cord' of occult fame, about which Muldoon wrote so often.

If anything, Celia Green's work demonstrated that, important as Crookall's work was, the OBE might not be as pat an experience as he had believed. It was beginning to look as if the OBE is a multifaceted experience which constantly avoids any clear analysis. But it wasn't until a few pioneering researchers began studying the OBE in the laboratory that our knowledge about the experience really began to advance.

The OBE Enters the Lab
The experimental exploration of the OBE was the brainchild of Dr Charles Tart, who is currently a psychologist at the University of California, Davis.

A long-time student of the psychic field, Tart conducted his first experiments in the late 1960s.

He designed his most significant experiment around the claims of a young woman, whom he called Miss Z in his report, who had reported to him that she would often find herself out-of-body during each night's sleep. Tart suggested to the young woman that she try to 'prove' this experience to herself by placing numbers on slips of paper and placing one of them, without looking at it, on a shelf at a vantage point above her head. Then she could validate her experience by trying to read it. A few days later Miss Z informed Tart that she had carried out the task successfully. The researcher was so excited by this news that he invited her to his laboratory to see if she could replicate the experiment under controlled conditions.

For the actual experiment, Miss Z was instructed to fall asleep in a sleep chamber at the University of California at Davis, float up in the OB state, and read off a randomly-determined five digit number placed on a shelf above the bed. She was also hooked up to a polygraph so that Tart could monitor her brain waves, skin resistance, and other psychophysiology from an adjoining room.

The experiment was run for four nights, but while Miss Z often reported leaving the body, it wasn't until the fourth night that the results that Tart was waiting for were forthcoming. That morning at 5.57 a.m. Miss Z appeared to be in a light sleep, but her electroencephalographic (brainwave) records started recording a bizarre pattern of activity. Tart could not determine if she were actually asleep or awake. By 6.04 a.m. Miss Z seemed to be more fully alert and called out over the intercom that she had seen the number during an OBE she had just undergone. She called it off — 25132. This was entirely correct and the odds against guessing it by chance were astronomical.

The odd brain wave patterns that accompanied the OBE also fascinated Tart. They indicated that Miss Z was in a poorly developed sleep state that was being disrupted by moments of apparent wakefulness. Yet the records didn't show that Miss Z was having rapid eye movements, which invariably accompany dreams. Tart was so puzzled by these read-outs that he showed them to Dr William Dement of Stanford University, who is one of the world's leading authorities on dream research. Tart notes in his report on this experiment that Dement 'agreed with me that they could not very well be classified into any of the known sleep stages, nor could they even be classified unambiguously as waking or drowsing patterns.'

Miss Z was not the only subject Tart was able to recruit into the laboratory. Robert Monroe, who has since written his autobiographical *Journeys Out of the Body*, also stayed at the lab for several nights. The experiments performed with him were similar in design to those formerly conducted with Miss Z, although the results were nowhere near as striking. While Monroe was not able to read a five digit number placed in an adjoining room, on one occasion he did visit and accurately report what was doing on in the hallway outside! During that night's experimentation, Monroe reported that he had left the body and had travelled about the lab rooms. He correctly saw that the lab technician, who was supposed to be monitoring the experiment, was out of the room where she had been posted and was talking to a man in the corridor. Since the technician had violated her part of the experimental protocol by unexpectedly leaving her post, Monroe's observations were doubly striking. Tart also studied the psychophysiology of Monroe's OBEs. They tended to occur in a brain state akin to dreaming, and corresponded to a sudden drop in blood-pressure.

While Tart's work was a pioneering attempt, it really did not tell us very much about the nature of the OBE. His experiments validated the 'reality' of the experience, but didn't help us in getting to the core of the OB enigma. What really is happening during OBE? Is some element of the consciousness *physically* detaching itself from the body?

OBE Research at the ASPR

Other investigators have tried to more thoroughly isolate exactly what is happening during the experience. A series of such attempts were made by Dr Karlis Osis of the American Society for Psychical Research in New York during the 1970s. Osis's work can be divided into three stages. First he held a 'fly-in' which was a screening project to see if he could find good OB subjects. People from all over the United States were invited to induce an OBE and 'fly-in' to New York. They merely had to report back to him what objects they saw which were specially placed on a table in his office. The second phase of the research comprised a lengthy project with New York artist and psychic Ingo Swann, who can voluntarily induce OBEs from a waking state. A third approach to the OBE was developed which made use of optical illusion viewing boxes. These experiments were designed to determine if physical sight and OBE vision are comparable phenomena. If OBE vision is similar to physical sight, believed Dr Osis, this would indicate that a person who has left his body really *has* left his body and is not seeing-at-a-distance through simple ESP.

During the initial fly-in experiments, however, Osis and his colleagues found that they were facing a much more complicated phenomenon than they had anticipated. About 100 persons attempted the fly-in to the ASPR between 1972 and 1973 and Dr Osis later calculated that fifteen of them showed some success at describing the objects. Some described exactly what was on the table, but things were not just that simple! Weird anomalies kept cropping up in the reports. For example, when Dr Alex Tanous, a well-known psychic from Maine, 'flew-in', he saw objects positioned on the table that were only placed there days *later!* The same thing happened when yet another psychic attempted the experiment. She became disoriented while out-of-body and, although she never made it to Osis' office, she gave a striking description of what was transpiring in another ASPR room at the time of her visit!

Some of the fly-in results were as bizarre as they were unexpected. For one series of experiments, Dr Osis wanted to see if his fly-in subjects could be psychically detected. So he asked Christine Whiting — a psychic from New York — to hold vigil in his office and try to describe any projector she might 'see' visiting there. Dr Tanous 'flew in' for a short visit during one of these sessions, and Miss Whiting — who of course never knew just *when* an attempt would be made — saw his apparition in the room. She described him as wearing brown corduroy pants and a white cotton shirt. This was indeed the apparel Dr Tanous was wearing in Maine at the time of his attempt.

During another experiment, though, she saw *two* apparitions. This result was unexpected but turned out to be extremely evidential. Miss Whiting began by giving Osis a good general description of Mrs Claudette Kiely, a psychic from out of town who was attempting a fly-in at the time. But then she described the phantom of a boy on roller skates! This just didn't make sense to Osis — who only later learned that Ms Kiely's son had fallen asleep at his mother's home while watching a television show depicting waitresses on roller skates. This was at the same time his mother was flying-in to the ASPR.

These reports forced Osis to realize that trying to divorce OB vision from ESP was no simple matter, and so a more formal OB study was initiated. This led Dr Osis right to Ingo Swann, who can project his mind from a waking state rather than while asleep, and can do it at will . . . any time, any place. Since he can describe what he's seeing while floating out-of-body, Osis and his assistant (Janet Mitchell) invited him to the ASPR for a series of tests.

For these experiments, a free-floating shelf was constructed and hung near the ceiling of a specially prepared room. Colourful targets were then placed in the box, two at a time, although they were isolated from one another by a barrier. For each experiment Swann was hooked to a polygraph, and was then asked to project his mind to the box, see what was there, and report back what he saw. Several such tests were run between January and April 1972 before this project was concluded.

Swann was indeed successful at the task and would sketch what he 'saw'. These drawings were often almost exact replicas of the targets. One target, for example, was a flat red heart with a black knife-like object placed over it. Swann diagrammed a large oval, designated it as red, and then drew a pointed object superimposed over it. He said that the pointed object was black. On the other side of the shelf was a bull's-eye with a pie-slice cut from it. Swann was able to draw a precise depiction of this as well. His only error was in designating the correct colours of the concentric circles. He placed them in inverted order. Other tests were just as impressive.

In their never-ending desire to find a way of isolating OB vision from simple ESP, Osis's colleagues went on to develop several ingenious optical devices to test the nature of OB vision. They eventually built a contraption that created an 'illusion' which could be seen only by looking into the box.

This apparatus consisted of a box, the background of which was divided into four quadrants. Two wheels were included inside, one made up of several colours, while the other contained a number of simple pictures. When the box was activated, it randomly selected one background colour, one picture, and one of the segments. This operation produced an optical illusion which could only be seen by standing in front of, and looking into, the box through a window. Only by physically positioning oneself in this way could the target be seen correctly. Dr Osis hoped to find gifted OB subjects who could induce the experience, travel to the next room, look through the box window and correctly report what they saw.

Both Alex Tanous and Ingo Swann were successful at this little game and chalked up many successes with the box. But they produced some fringe benefits as well. One one occasion the experimenters got a rather unusual surprise when Dr Tanous reported that he could not see the target because the inside of the box was dark. The experimenters couldn't understand what he was complaining about. Then they checked and found that the bulb illuminating the box had burned out. Needless to say, Dr Tanous could have had no normal way of knowing that something was wrong with the light.

OBE Research at the Psychical Research Foundation

An altogether different approach to the OB problem was being made at the same time at the Psychical Research Foundation in Durham, North

Carolina. The PRF is funded specifically to study those psychic phenomena which indicate that man survives death. And when they found a young man who could induce OBEs at will, they spent the next two years studying this strange phenomenon.

The subject used for this entire research project was a Duke University psychology undergraduate, S. Keith ('Blue') Harary, who originally hailed from New York. It was these experiments that gave Harary his first start in parapsychology, which would eventually led him to SRI and beyond. (See, for instance, chapters three and four in the present book).

Harary was a polite young man sporting a short-cropped beard surrounding an impish grin. He had previously been one of Dr Osis's successful fly-in subjects. His talents at wilful projection were not studied in any depth, though, until he moved to Durham. Harary does not need to go to sleep before having an OBE, so this makes him an ideal experimental subject. He merely puts himself into a deeply relaxed state and then frees himself from the body while still half awake. This procedure places him in a drastically altered state of consciousness during his projections, after which he is dazed, disoriented, staggering and sometimes even in physical pain.

The first tests with Harary were designed by Dr Robert Morris, who was the PRF's director of research at the time. He systematically worked with Harary to find some tests that would give consistent results. For their pilot tests together in 1972-73, Harary would usually be placed in one of the PRF's two adjoining buildings. He would then try to leave the body, go to the other building, and read off an alphabet letter prominently displayed on a door. Sometimes he was successful, but at other times, he failed. Since these experiments didn't seem to suit Harary too well, Dr Morris decided to change the design of the experiment. For the next phase of the research, Harary was placed in a booth in the main building of the Foundation. His job was to project to the building situated behind it where several members of the PRF staff were stationed. Dr Morris was hoping that his subject would be able to see who was there and report his observations back to him.

Harary was stunningly successful at first, but just as with the target studies, his ability to see clearly soon slackened off.

Despite these sporadic failures, some curious incidents occurred that simply couldn't be explained normally. During some of these early visitation experiments, some of the staff members — who were just idly sitting around waiting for Harary's visit — began having strange feelings when he was with them. They could feel his presence and, on one occasion, his fleeting apparition was seen by one of the volunteers. These detection experiences always occurred at the precise times Harary was projecting to the back building — times the staff couldn't possibly have second-guessed. This phenomenon piqued Dr Morris' interest, especially when the psychologist experienced one of the 'visitations' himself. So he and Harary developed a complex project to see if animals could reliably detect OB visitations. Harary's pet kitten Spirit was recruited for the tests.

These tests were quite ingenious. The PRF staff first constructed a shuffleboard-like apparatus (with raised sides) which was marked off into twenty-four squares. Spirit was placed on the board in one building while Harary was sequestered in his booth at the other PRF building. He then tried to project to his pet. Spirit, like any kitten, would run around the board rambunctiously while trying to escape from it. He would also mew profusely and pitiously as soon as he was placed in it. But when Harary projected to him, the kitten would suddenly settle down and just purr contently. This experiment was run several times, and the kitten reacted consistently each time — so much so that the experimenters could easily tell when Harary was present.

When Dr Morris left Durham in 1974 to take a position at the University of California at Santa Barbara, the remaining PRF staff members continued on with the research and devised several variations on the successful kitten work. One experimenter, for example, wanted to see if Spirit would orient himself and *walk towards* Harary if he projected to the kitten in an empty room. So a room at Duke University was cleared of all its furniture for the test, and a closed-circuit television monitor was hooked up so that the cat's movements could be seen from an outlying area. Harary projected to the room several times, but Spirit never consistently moved towards him. But there was a surprise in store for Dr John Hartwell, who was watching the test on the television monitor. He began having strong 'detection' experiences when Harary was projecting to the isolated room. This would have been uncanny enough, but then on one fateful occasion, he looked up at the monitor and actually saw Harary's apparition standing in the room!

Psychological Research on the Out-of-body Experience
Research into the nature of the OBE unfortunately declined in the mid-1970s. The primary reason for this was that both the ASPR and the PRF — which had spearheaded this research — soon used up the funds they had been able to obtain for their projects. There was very little experimental research of any note conducted into the strange byways of the OBE after the conclusion of these two major projects.

There is today, however, an upsurge of interest in the OBE. But this research has been of a very different kind. Experimenters are beginning to realize that since it is not a rare nor unique experience, the OBE may be something just about anyone can undergo. Perhaps even non-psychic subjects could learn to leave their bodies, and this has led to what might be called the 'human potentials' approach to the experience.

Some of the most pertinent experimental research confirming this view has been that of Dr John Palmer, formerly of John F. Kennedy University in Orinda, California and currently a researcher at the Institute for Parapsychology in Durham, North Carolina. Dr Palmer began experimentally studying the OBE during the mid-1970s when he was a research associate at the University of Virginia. He has long argued that *if* the OBE is a human potential, it should be possible to induce the experience in volunteer subjects by having them follow certain 'training' procedures. Palmer was impressed by the fact that many of those very special people who can voluntarily undergo OBEs did so by relaxing, entering into an inwardly-focused state of consciousness and would then often 'imagine' themselves leaving the body before actually inducing the experience. So the young psychologist began training individuals in these techniques.

His first experiment was conducted at the University of Virginia and employed sixty volunteer students who claimed no particular psychic ability. He met with the students individually, briefed them about the developability of the OBE and then recruited them for the experiment. The idea behind this initial meeting was to encourage the students to believe that they *could* induce the experience by following certain training procedures. Each subject was then taken to a lab room where he/she was shown a table upon which a picture would be placed during the forthcoming test. The student was asked to familiarize himself with the room since he would later be asked to journey there while out-of-body. Then the volunteer was taken to another room where he/she was placed in a chair and taught how to relax completely by progressively tensing and releasing each muscle group of the body. Then the student was subjected to a state of mild disorientation. A monotonous sine-wave tone was played into the subject's ears through headphones while he/she was made to stare into a rotating spiral vortex disc. The volunteer was then asked to imagine himself leaving the body and entering into the spiral.

If the student succeeded in inducing an OBE, he/she was then asked to visit the adjoining lab room and take a look at the picture which had been placed on the table. This part of the test was designed to 'prove' that the subject actually had been out-of-body.

This technique for inducing OBEs was very successful. Some 42 per cent of the students answered affirmatively when asked if, at any time during the experiment, it seemed that they were *literally* out-of-body. Unfortunately though, few of them were successful at correctly describing the target picture. This was particularly odd, since many of the subjects felt that they *had* seen it.

Dr Palmer soon replicated his experiment by testing forty additional subjects. This test was designed along the same lines as the first experiment, but several revisions were introduced in order to refine it. The subjects for this test were first relaxed through the use of progressive muscle relaxation, but Dr Palmer did away with the use of the spiral disc. Instead he taped halved ping-pong balls over each student's eyes and then had him/her stare into a red light. 'White noise' was played into the subject's ears through headphones as well. This setting, as we discussed in chapter two, produces slight disorientation and considerable daydream-like imagery. Dr Palmer felt that this state of sensory isolation might be more powerful than the spiral disc in helping his subjects feel as if they were 'leaving the body'. Just as he had done during his first experiment, Dr Palmer again instructed his volunteers to 'visit' an adjoining room and see what picture had been placed there on a table.

As an added part of the experiment, however, Dr Palmer only instructed twenty of his subjects to actually leave the body during the test. The others were merely asked to 'image' about the picture in the next room. This precaution was taken in order to discover the relative roles out-of-body travel and 'normal' ESP might be playing in the experiment.

The results of the test were more straightforward than Dr Palmer obtained from his first experiment. No less than thirteen of the twenty subjects who were specially *told* to leave their bodies during the ganzfeld stimulation reported OBEs. However, four of the 'control' subjects reported spontaneous OBEs. Those who reported the OBEs tended to describe the target pictures with some degree of accuracy and more consistently than did the other volunteers. This would, of course, indicate that during the test these people really had been able to leave their bodies in order to visit the adjoining room.

Dr Palmer conducted yet a third experiment in which he used a vibrating chair along with ganzfeld stimulation during the induction procedures. Since many people report that their bodies 'vibrate' during the initial phases of the OBE, the experimenter thought that producing this sensation artificially might help induce the experience. He was correct. When he tested forty subjects with this new technique, nearly half of them reported OBEs.

Dr Palmer has come to several conclusions about the nature of the

OBE as a result of his project. He certainly believes that it is possible to induce the experience experimentally by the use of sensory isolation and relaxation techniques. But he also feels that there are psychological factors which help people to experience out-of-body travel, and that these components are more important than anything else. He was struck by the fact that those subjects who were specifically *told* to have or expect an OBE during the experiments had them more frequently than those subjects who were not so instructed. (This finding was quite clear in his second major project.) This led the psychologist to conclude that *psychological expectation is a key factor in helping people to induce OBEs*. In other words, if you believe a certain technique will work, it probably will!

Despite the fact that Dr Palmer believes that the OBE may be more psychological than parapsychological, he doesn't close his eyes to the possibility that the OBE might eventually be found to be a genuine mind–body separation. The major finding of his research, however, is that the OBE is actually a human potential and not a psychic gift.

This fact has also been recently confirmed by a team of researchers in Kansas.

Added Light on the Psychology of the Out-of-body Experience

Dr Stuart Twemlow, Dr Glen Gabbard and Dr Fowler Jones are all either practising psychiatrists or educators in the field of mental health. They are affiliated with such prestigious institutions as the Topeka Veterans Administration Medical Center and the University of Kansas, and have been studying the out-of-body experience since 1976.

This project began when Dr Twemlow granted an interview about his interest in the OBE to the *National Enquirer.* When the psychiatrist found himself flooded with letters from people who had undergone the experience, he and his colleagues began making an in-depth study of the phenomenon. The three researchers were primarily interested in determining whether or not people who undergo OBEs are in any way psychologically different from those who do not. So to implement their study, which was partially supported by the University of Kansas Medical Center and the Topeka-based Menninger Foundation, the team contacted 339 individuals throughout the country who had experienced an OBE at some point in their lives. This selection was made on the basis of the letters which Dr Twemlow had originally received. These individuals were then invited to undergo a battery of psychological tests which gauge such personality factors as the ability to create mental images, a willingness to seek out dangerous experiences, potentials towards hysterical and psychotic behaviour, attitudes towards death, psychological adjustment, and a host of other characteristics. The results of these data were then computed and compared to a similar set of data drawn from eighty people who had written to Dr Twemlow about their interest in the OBE but who had *not* actually had one.

If the ability to leave the body is a rare psychic talent, one might expect that only certain *types* of individuals would be capable of experiencing the phenomenon. If the OBE is a human potential, however, you would not expect to find any specific personality characteristics differentiating people who experience the phenomenon from those who do not. The Kansas team found the latter to be the case, for they could discern no discrete 'psychological profile' of the OBE-prone individual from their data.

But if the OBE *is* a potential, then why doesn't everyone experience it? Why do only 10--20 per cent of the population report such experiences? Certainly there must be *some* hidden factor that distinguishes or characterizes people who experience out-of-body travel.

One possible solution to this puzzle has recently come to light and was made public by Dr Palmer in 1978 when he addressed a convention of parapsychologists who met at Washington University in St Louis, Missouri. He reported that towards the end of his project he had started monitoring the brain waves of his volunteers at the University of Virginia. He was hoping to discover if any changes occurred when a person experienced an OBE. It was during this phase of his research that he made a surprising discovery. He found that those subjects whose brain wave patterns showed an abundance of 'theta' waves while they were *preparing* for the experiment invariably reported OBEs during the forthcoming test. He went on to explain that, during the course of his work, he had come across three subjects who showed over 30 per cent 'theta' in their resting parietal EEG. All three subsequently had OBEs as a result of his induction procedures. It was too much of a coincidence to overlook.

But just what is so special about theta waves?

Theta waves are perhaps the most mysterious of the brain's rhythms.* They are rather uncommon and seem to manifest when a person is involved in a deep alteration of consciousness. Intense creative exercises or yogic meditation seem to induce them. They also occur when a person attempts to create intense mental imagery or when deliberately inducing an altered state of consciousness.

Dr Palmer's discovery suggests that an individual who is naturally relaxed and meditative may be particularly prone to undergoing out-of-body experiences. It may be that people who have a natural ability to clear their minds and alter their attention *away* from the outside world might also possess the ability to leave the body.

The possible discovery of a link between theta waves and the OBE also holds out a very special promise to people who wish to develop the ability to induce the experience. Since it is possible to learn how to generate theta waves through biofeedback, nurturing such a capability could lead to the development of out-of-body skills.

The discovery that the out-of-body experience could be possibly related to specific brain wave rhythms is one of the most exciting avenues of potential research on the subject. Future research is obviously needed to further explore this issue, and it is a shame that no one has yet followed up on Dr Palmer's provocative finding. So to date, psychologists, parapsychologists and even philosophers are *still* arguing over the nature of the out-of-body experience . . . whose perennial mystery still seems to be evading us.

End-Notes for Chapter Thirteen

* The brain constantly produces small electrical pulsations that can be monitored by placing electrodes on the scalp. The resulting tracings are then graphed out as an electroencephalogram. These waves are grouped into four categories. The most predominant wave is the beta wave, which registers between fourteen and thirty cycles per second and which accompanies any sort of intellectual activity, such as problem solving. When we relax and clear our minds, our brain waves slow down to between eight to twelve cycles. These are called alpha waves. Delta waves are even lower, registering between a half and three cycles, and usually appear during deep sleep. They indicate brain pathology when they occur in a waking EEG. Theta waves come between alpha and delta waves at four to seven cycles.

14.

New Evidence for
Life After Death

The belief that we will survive bodily death is as old as mankind itself. Despite this fact, research into the nature of the soul is a new frontier within both science and psychology. It was not until the close of the Victorian Age that serious research on the subject was initiated when the Society for Psychical Research was founded in England in 1882. The SPR researchers were preoccupied with studying the phenomena of spiritualism with its darkened seances, spirit mediums and tilting tables. The evidence for life after death has been steadily accumulating ever since, and today, few parapsychologists would argue that there is *no* case for survival. But the issue is no longer whether survival is a reasonable explanation for such psychic phenomena as apparitions, death-bed visions, or the communications received through trance mediums. The real issue facing researchers today is whether the survival theory is the only or even the best explanation for these phenomena.

The Historical Problem
This is a problem that researchers studying the issue have long faced. Research into the phenomenon of trance mediumship represents a good case in point. The original founders of the SPR were fascinated by the subject, since they were constantly discovering psychics of extraordinary talent. Most of them were capable of entering trance, during which they seemed to 'bring through' spirits of the dead. The SPR researchers were sceptical of this phenomenon, but their subsequent research proved that something truly extraordinary was going on. Some of these mediums were socially prominent people who were wary of their gifts and never became professional spiritualists. The SPR founders were even more surprised when they began communicating with their deceased friends and relatives through them. They even began introducing their friends and colleagues to the seances anonymously, but that posed no problems for the psychics, who easily brought through evidential communications for these sitters too. They even succeeded when they were shipped off

to foreign countries to sit for complete strangers.

But the early parapsychologists were plagued by constant doubts. They soon realized that two mutually exclusive theories could explain these brilliant psychic displays: either they were really speaking with the dead, or somehow the psychics were extracting this information from the sitters' own minds.

This second possibility even explained some of the trance communications better than the spirit-communication theory. It certainly explained, for instance, why the SPR's favourite psychics often produced a mixture of correct, incorrect, and vague information during their seances. These researchers soon rejected the simple telepathy theory, though. For the more cases they investigated, the more obvious it became that some psychics could bring through information that was unknown previously to those present at the sittings. (This information usually concerned the client's deceased relatives, and was only corroborated when the sitter checked old family records.) Sometimes these psychics would deliver messages from the dead that the sitter *knew* was wrong, only to discover that the information was really correct. So in other words, sometimes the SPR's psychics knew more about the 'communicators' controlling them than their own relatives!

The more sceptical members of the SPR stuck to their telepathic theory, though. They posited that, while entranced, a gifted psychic could use his or her ESP to collect information from any person who ever knew the sitter or his/her relatives — or perhaps even by clairvoyantly scanning printed sources of relevant information concerning them.

This theory might strike you as awfully far-fetched, but even today, we simply have no idea whether the sixth sense is restrained by any limits, or what feats it is really capable of accomplishing. The theory that a psychic can employ such unlimited powers of ESP to help impersonate a 'spirit' is called the super-ESP hypothesis. The problem posed by this theory will come to haunt the remainder of this chapter.

Researchers interested in the survival issue have been debating the relative strengths and problems of the super-ESP theory for decades. There is little disagreement whether the early SPR founders collected impressive evidence for survival. Most parapsychologists today agree that they did. But no unequivocal evidence proving survival ever emerged from these early studies, simply because the first parapsychologists could never get around the impasse posed by the super-ESP hypothesis.

The telepathic, clairvoyant, and even precognitive powers of the medium could always be invoked — even if theoretically — by the sceptic to explain away the evidence. This super-psi theory even gained some guarded support when, in 1925, Dr S. G. Soal reported on his (now famous) sittings with Blanche Cooper, a trance medium in London. Soal reported on a series of crucial sittings in which he conversed with an old friend of his, Gordon Davis. They were able to reminisce about their old friendship through the entranced psychic, and the personation was perfect. Dr Soal even testified that the psychic's voice forcefully reminded him of his old friend's. It came as a shock when Soal learned that Gordon Davis was still alive and living happily in London!

Despite these problems, contemporary parapsychologists interested in the survival controversy are continually on the look-out for ways of overcoming the super-ESP theory. New cases, new categories of evidence, and new ways of conceptualizing the survival issue have been making a comeback within parapsychology ever since the 1970s. Though still the occupation of only a few parapsychologists working in the field today, their efforts have resulted in new evidence pertinent to the survival question.

Contemporary survival research has been proceeding on two broad fronts:

1.   research to see if we, the living, are capable of surviving death;
2.   research on direct contact with the deceased.

We'll look at each of these approaches in turn.

Survival Research with the Living

Research on the out-of-body experience became the focus for considerable survival research during the 1970s. If the self can extend beyond the body during life, as this enigmatic experience suggests, then it could be argued that the 'self' is not permanently tied to the body and its fate at all. In other words, such a phenomenon would represent an *a priori* case for survival. Researchers at both the American Society for Psychical Research in New York and the Psychical Research Foundation in Durham, North Carolina became interested in this question when they received funding for survival research in the 1970s. This research was outlined in the last chapter, so we'll only briefly review it again.

Dr Karlis Osis was in charge of research at the ASPR. His approach was to see if there existed some *perceptual element* within us capable of leaving the body. This led him to work with his fly-in experiments, and also with Ingo Swann, for whom he designed a number of out-of-body perceptual tests.

Research conducted at the Psychical Research Foundation in Durham proceeded in different directions, since Dr Robert Morris, who was in charge of research activities there, was more interested in finding some aspect of the self that could leave the body and be *detected*. This led him to initiate his successful 'detection' experiments with Keith Harary, then a Duke University undergraduate. The most famous and successful series of experiments concerned his little kitten Spirit, whose behaviour significantly altered when Keith projected to it.

Both Dr Osis and Dr Morris came to believe that their experiments were consistent with the survival hypothesis, but not proof of it. Dr Morris drew a particular blank when it came to determining what his experimental results really implied, and to this day he remains neutral about what conclusions can be drawn from his research.

Parapsychologists today, however, are looking for more than merely *a priori* evidence for survival. For a while it did seem that the best approach to the issue would be by way of the out-of-the-body experience, but this approach did not end up as helpful as many parapsychologists had hoped. The out-of-body experience turned out to be too psychologically, as well as parapsychologically, complex to work with, and to date it still remains a total puzzle to many researchers who have explored its mystery. For example, even with his remarkable talents, Keith Harary was extremely inconsistent when performing target OBE experiments of the sort Dr Osis employed with Ingo Swann. And even Dr Osis had to admit ultimately that he could find only one other subject capable of performing successfully on his tests.

The relevance of the out-of-body experience to survival research continues, however, to interest some investigators. For, in the long run, some evidence was collected during the 1970s which indicated that, in certain cases at least, something physically detectable is leaving the body during the out-of-body experience. But this conclusion must remain provisional, for many other parapsychologists prefer to believe that ESP and PK-at-a-distance can explain even Swann's and Harary's laboratory successes.

Research on Near-death Phenomena

Research on the out-of-body experience brings us to two other areas that are currently occupying the interest of some survival researchers: These include the study of the near-death experience (which often incorporates an OBE) and the study of apparitions.

Certainly the readers of this book are familiar with the phenomenon of the near-death experience, which first came to wide public attention when Dr Raymond Moody's book *Life after Life* was published in 1975.

His book chronicled the accounts of many people who had clinically died, but who survived to tell their tales. They invariably spoke of out-of-body travels, meeting their deceased relatives, and visiting the 'spirit' world. Research on the NDE was placed on a more scientific footing when Dr Kenneth Ring in Connecticut and Dr Michael Sabom in Georgia, eschewing the anecdotal approach used by Moody, used proper sampling procedures to poll near-death survivors. They, too, found that NDEs are commonly reported by those who survive clinical death.

Dr Sabom took his research a step further by investigating several cases in which his informants correctly described the procedures used to resuscitate them. The medical and technical knowledge displayed by these respondents was remarkable, and led Dr Sabom to conclude that his informants had genuinely left their bodies and were somehow *watching* the procedures.

Nor has Dr Sabom been alone in his findings. One well-documented case, similar in some respects to those collected by Dr Sabom, was recently placed on file by Ms Kimberly Clark of Harborview Medical Center in Seattle, Washington. The case came to light when she was counselling a woman recovering from a heart attack. The woman was very agitated because of an experience she had undergone while seemingly unconscious. She explained to Ms Clark that she had left her body while being resuscitated. She subsequently left the room and found herself on the ledge of another storey of the hospital, where she spotted a tennis shoe with a worn toe. The woman beseeched Ms Clark to check out the ledge, which she did. And there, with some travail, she spotted the tennis shoe. What particularly impressed the researcher was the *way* the patient had described the shoe. 'The only way she would have had such a perspective,' she writes, 'was if she had been floating right outside and at very close range to the tennis shoe.'

Researchers interested in this phenomenon like to focus even more intensely on 'core' or 'transcendental' NDEs. These are reports that go beyond simple out-of-body experiences, in that the dying person seems to travel to a spiritual realm. This journey is usually experienced by travelling through a tunnel or void while separated from the body. These reports are no less common than simple OBEs:

> I had a heart attack, and I found myself in a black void, and I knew that I had left my physical body behind. I knew I was dying, and I thought, 'God, I did the best I knew how at the time I did it. Please help me.' Immediately, I was moved out of that blackness, through a pale gray, and I just went on, gliding and moving swiftly, and in front of me, in the distance, I could see a gray mist, and I was rushing toward it. It seemed that I just couldn't get

to it fast enough to satisfy me, and as I got closer to it I could see through it. Beyond the mist, I could see people, and their forms were just like they are on the earth, and I could also see something which one could take to be buildings. The whole thing was permeated with the most gorgeous light — a living, golden yellow glow, a pale color, not like the harsh gold color we know on earth.

As I approached more closely, I felt certain that I was going through that mist. It was such a wonderful; joyous feeling; there are just no words in human language to describe it. Yet, it wasn't my time to go through the mist, because instantly from the other side appeared my Uncle Carl, who had died many years earlier. He blocked my path, saying, 'Go back. Your work on earth has not been completed. Go back now.' I didn't want to go back, but I had no choice, and immediately I was back in my body. I felt that horrible pain in my chest, and I heard my little boy crying, 'God, bring my mommy back to me.'

Yet other people who report the experience of dying have more spiritual encounters:

I got up and walked into the hall to go get a drink, and it was at that point, as they found out later, that my appendix ruptured. I became very weak, and I fell down. I began to feel a sort of drifting, a movement of my real being in and out of my body, and to hear beautiful music. I floated on down the hall and out the door onto the screened-in porch. There, it almost seemed that clouds, a pink mist really, began to gather around me, and then I floated right straight on through the screen, just as though it weren't there, and up into this pure crystal clear light, an illuminating white light. It was beautiful and so bright, so radiant, but it didn't hurt my eyes. It's not any kind of light you can describe on earth. I didn't actually see a person in this light, and yet it has a special identity, it definitely does. It is a light of perfect understanding and perfect love.

The thought came to my mind, 'Lovest thou me?' This was not exactly in the form of a question, but I guess the connotation of what the light said was, 'If you do love me, go back and complete what you began in your life.' And all during this time, I felt as though I were surrounded by an overwhelming love and compassion.

The widespread nature of the NDE has been further confirmed by work with other selected populations. Dr Bruce Greyson, originally working at the University of Virginia, collected a number of NDE accounts from suicide survivors. Nancy Bush at the International Association for Near-Death Studies in Connecticut found several cases reported by children who almost died — a remarkable finding since recent research shows that children between the ages five and twelve rarely experience conventional OBEs.

Certainly these experiences are consistent with the survival hypothesis. In other words, they are the kinds of experiences that might be *expected* to occur if we really do survive death. But by themselves, there is little direct evidence that the near-death experience represents a literal journey into the beyond. Researchers who promote the NDE as *proof* of survival still need to address or clarify a number of thorny issues:

1. The NDE 'syndrome' is *not* limited to people at or near the point of death. They occur while some individuals are undergoing classical 'mystical' experiences; while using a variety of hallucinogenic drugs; or while under the influence of certainly commonly used anaesthetics. The experience, in other words, can occur in situations where the prospect of death is not a direct threat. This fact alone eliminates using the NDE as specific evidence that we will ultimately survive death.

2. A second reason for doubting whether NDEs represent a real journey into death is that the phenomenon sometimes seems to be influenced by cultural beliefs, teachings, and artifacts. Some older accounts, for instance, contain references to angels with wings. Those occurring in non-Christian cultures sometimes differ even more dramatically from the type of experiences reported today in the West. Take the story of Er as told by Plato in his celebrated *The Republic*. Er experienced a near-death incident in which he saw the souls of the dead choosing their reincarnations, a perspective rarely *ever* mentioned in current NDE accounts.

So in short, some sceptics argue that the NDE lacks the kind of consistency we would expect if it were a genuine glimpse of the mysterious beyond. It should be noted, however, that survival-oriented researchers disagree with these criticisms. They rightly point out that NDEs possess an unusually large number of universal features. This has suggested to them that the experience transcends cultural conditions and teachings. In this respect, the NDE is very similar to a related class of near-death occurrences — so-called death-bed visions, where the dying person will see welcoming figures (often deceased relatives) guiding them into death. Critical research on this subject was undertaken by Dr Karlis Osis back in the 1950s and '60s when he first discovered how widespread the phenomenon is. After surveying hundreds of doctors and nurses who have attended the dying, he published his celebrated monograph *Deathbed Observations by Physicians and Nurses* in 1961. Dr Osis could find no medically viable explanation for these cases. Such simple 'solutions' as oxygen starvation to the brain or the hallucinatory side-effects of the patients' medication was ruled out in a number of cases. During the 1970s Dr Osis conducted a similar study in India, and found that the cases reported from that culture were little different from those collected in the West. (He reported on this subsequent research in his book *At the Hour of Death*, which he co-authored with Dr Erlendur Haraldsson of Iceland.)

These findings are certainly consistent with the survival theory — i.e., that such experiences represent a prevision of a future life. But alternate (and just as logically consistent) theories can also account for death-bed visions *and* near-death experiences. The most commonly promoted theory of this type posits that these experiences are broadly uniform because, in the long run, we all feel and react pretty much the same when we confront death and dying. In other words, experiences such as the NDE and death-bed visions are archetypal. They are built-in patterns of response that come to our aid when we confront the trauma of our imminent death. The recurrent types of imagery recorded during these experiences — such as seeing our deceased loved ones, marvellous landscapes, religious and mythical figures, etc. — are universal symbols drawn from our unconscious minds. They provide us with a perfect psychological defence against the very situation that threatens to overwhelm us.

Some students of the near-death experience believe that this explanation can also explain cases such as those collected by Dr Sabom and Kimberly Clark. They suggest that the person experiencing an NDE or death-bed vision may use ESP to bolster the experience and give it added credence. So despite the importance of the NDE to survival research, researchers are hopelessly deadlocked over its nature and meaning.

Survival research conducted with living subjects can only take us so far. Many people will continue to leave their bodies and people on the threshold of death will continue to report visions of the world beyond death. But none of these phenomena really tell us what — if anything — will happen to us after the purely *biological* death of the body. OBEs, NDEs and kindred phenomena are important to survival research in the same way the phenomena of parapsychology are important in general. They show that there exists some component within the mind that science and psychology cannot explain . . . at least not in strictly physiological terms. Unfortunately, there is no way of knowing whether this component of the mind really survives death or whether it merely 'dies' along with the biological demise of the body.

So if research with the living cannot provide us with concrete proof of survival, where does this state of affairs leave us? It leaves us right back with the phenomena which excited the interest of the first psychical researchers close to 100 years ago: cases that suggest direct contact with the dead.

The Renewed Debate about the Super-ESP Theory

Not all contemporary parapsychologists have been impressed with the super-ESP theory, a theory that rather put an end to survival research by 1940. While most parapsychologists believe that this form of expanded ESP is a theoretical possibility, some researchers argue that we have no right to invoke such a theory as though it were a proven fact. They point out — and rightly so — that ESP is a comparatively weak effect when we see it operating in the laboratory. It is so weak, in fact, that we only know it is manifesting by applying statistics to our experiments. This certainly doesn't look like the faculty needed to explain many of the impressive cases of 'spirit return' already placed in the literature by the turn of the century. While there is some tentative evidence that something akin to super-ESP probably best explains cases such as Dr Soal's Gordon Davis communications, there is really no evidence that this faculty can explain all cases of post-mortem return. So far as is known, for example, ESP — whatever its range and capacity — cannot suddenly enable a person to speak in a foreign language he never learned normally.

Xenoglossy and the Problem of Drop-in Communicators

The subject of xenoglossy, speaking a language the subject has never learned or heard, is the special interest of Dr Ian Stevenson of the University of Virginia. He has recently published three cases reporting the phenomenon, the first of which was issued in 1974. The subject of this first investigation was a Philadelphia, Pennsylvania housewife identified by Dr Stevenson only as Mrs T. E. During several hypnotic sessions conducted by her husband, an entity began to communicate in a strange language which was later identified as Swedish. The communicator, who called himself 'Jensen Jacoby', claimed that he had been a peasant who died during a battle. Several Swedish-speaking witnesses interacted with the entity, whose vocabulary genuinely seemed restricted to that of the sixteenth and seventeenth centuries. 'He' was even able to correctly identify old Swedish artifacts borrowed from a local museum when they were presented to him through his 'channel'. Dr Stevenson undertook an extensive search into the woman's background but failed to uncover any evidence that she had ever studied — or had even been exposed to — the language.

Dr Stevenson also recruited a specialist on the language to aid him in his investigation. Dr Nils Sahlin, a Philadelphia resident who teaches Swedish, testified to the psychiatrist that 'most remarkable to me was the medium's pronunciation of the words she used, whether ours or her own. She did not speak her Scandinavian as an American would. She had absolutely no difficulty with the umlaut sounds or other peculiar Scandinavian sounds and accents . . .'

The Rev Carroll Jay of Greenbush, Ohio, reported a curiously similar case in his book *Gretchen, I Am*. This book tells how Mrs Jay started undergoing strange sleep fits in 1970 in which she would speak in German. Revd Jay was able to make contact with the entity through hypnosis, and several sessions with a communicator who called herself 'Gretchen' resulted. Dr Stevenson was called in to investigate the case by the Jays, and since he speaks fluent German, the psychiatrist was able to interview the entity directly. 'Gretchen' told of her life in nineteenth-century Germany in some detail, although most of her claims could not be verified. Dr Stevenson, nonetheless, felt that the entity was capable of making intelligent and creative use of the German language, although she often spoke it badly. He also undertook an investigation into Mrs Jay's background and could find no evidence that she had ever studied the language.

The only problem with both these cases is that each subject resorted to fraud on at least one occasion. But it is Dr Stevenson's feeling that these rudimentary incidents of bad faith cannot account for the linguistic complexities of the cases.

The most recent of Dr Stevenson's xenoglossy cases comes from India and concerns an educated woman in Nagpur who keeps entering strange trances. During these periods she 'becomes' a woman who died years ago in another part of the country. The subject of this on-going investigation is Uttara Huddar, who speaks Marathi, English, and some Hindi and who works in the field of education. Yet when she is spontaneously entranced, she becomes a girl who calls herself Sharada, who speaks only Bengali — a language distinct from any known to Uttara. It is also impressive that she has offered many obscure details about her life which have invariably turned out to be true. Some of these incidents could only be verified by checking previously unpublished documents. The Sharada case is probably the strongest case of xenoglossy collected so far.

Of course, the critical problem with these xenoglossy cases is trying to figure out exactly *what* we are dealing with, since it is not clear whether these cases represent genuine post-mortem return, spirit possession, or reincarnation. In the long run, though, each of these possibilities still points to survival after death.

A second form of mediumistic phenomenon that is very difficult to explain by the super-ESP theory is the 'drop-in' communicator. Drop-ins are entities who are previously unknown to either the medium or any of the sitters. They tend to show up suddenly and unannounced at seances, and they typically offer considerable information about themselves which very often turns out to be correct. These communicators seem to mastermind their own appearances, and they often give credible reasons for their appearances — such as wishing to deliver an important message to some relative who is still alive. Communications from drop-in entities can be fairly easy to fake, since the information they sometimes offer has, in some instances, been traced to previously published sources (such as obituaries) the psychics probably consulted or accidentally came across and memorized. But a number of cases exist in the literature that cannot be accounted for so easily. For example, in some recorded instances the facts offered by the drop-ins proved correct . . . but had been inaccurately reported in the only printed sources of information available to the psychics.

A series of exceptionally interesting drop-in communicators was examined in 1972 by Dr Alan Gauld, a psychologist at the University of Nottingham. His investigation focused on a ouija board circle operated by a small group of people in Cambridge. They had formed the group during the Second World War and continued their sittings for many years afterwards. Communications were received from over two hundred entities during that time, of whom most were deceased friends and relatives of the sitters. Eleven of these communicators, however, had been drop-ins, but the group had made little effort to verify their earthly existences. These were the cases that Dr Gauld began focusing upon many years later when he examined the group's records.

Between 1950 and 1952, for example, a communicator named Harry Stockbridge* offered several bits of information about himself. No one in the group knew him, but the entity explained in halting terms that he had been connected to the Northumberland Fusiliers as a second lieutenant. He had died on 14 July 1916. He also said he was 'Tyneside Scottish', tall, dark, thin, and that his special feature was his large brown eyes. He told the group that he hung out in Leicester and that records about him could be found there. He also added some comments on his likes and dislikes.

The original Cambridge group had done very little to investigate the communicator's story when Dr Gauld took it up in 1965 — fifteen years or so after the reception of the messages. But by checking military records, the British psychologist was able to discover that a Second Lieutenant

H. Stockbridge of the Northumberland Fusiliers had in fact existed. He was killed in action on 19 July 1916. Dr Gauld at first thought that the communicator had erred about the date of his death, but when Stockbridge's actual death certificate was examined, Gauld discovered that the communicator had been correct and the official military records wrong. His death had occurred on 14 July. The death certificate also noted that the officer had been born in Leicester (in 1896). Further detailed research by way of unpublished military archives showed that before his death, Stockbridge had been transferred to a Tyneside Scottish battalion. Dr Gauld was also able to track down some of Stockbridge's surviving relatives, who kindly verified the physical description the entity gave of himself.

Dr Gauld carefully notes in his report on this case that only two members of the Cambridge group were operating the ouija board when the Stockbridge communications were received. According to the psychologist, neither of them '. . . had any contacts in Leicester or had ever visited it, and I could trace no likely line of contact between either of them or any member of the Stockbridge family.' Nor could Dr Gauld find any published records (such as newspaper obituaries) that offered *all* of the information given to the Cambridge group.

Researchers other than Dr Gauld have also been attracted to the study of drop-in communicators. Dr Ian Stevenson has especially studied the talents of the late Hafsteinn Bjornsson, a trance medium in Iceland who was also often bothered by drop-ins at his seances. Two of them offered enough information for Dr Stevenson to verify their identities by exploring old records . . . records that were probably unavailable to the psychic. (He published his reports on the psychic and his drop-ins in 1975 in the *Journal of the American Society for Psychical Research.*)

It is up to the sceptic to explain how super-ESP can lock-in on such a personality, an entity completely unknown to either the psychic or his/her sitters. It seems to me that the super-ESP theory cannot account for the highly specific nature of the information they tend to deliver. Nor can the theory explain why a particular communicator was latched on to telepathically or clairvoyantly. My own opinion is that the most facile explanation for the drop-in communicator phenomenon is that these entities are exactly what they claim to be — i.e., self-conscious entities who have survived death and are seeking to make contact with the living.

Summing up the Evidence for Survival Today

Many parapsychologists today are hopelessly divided about the nature of the evidence. It was, as I mentioned previously, just this impasse that caused the field to withdraw from survival research from the 1930s through to the 1960s. Researchers such as Dr Karlis Osis are currently suggesting that our research efforts should be continued and intensified in order to break down this impasse. These researchers, who would also include the indefatigable Dr Ian Stevenson, believe that special effort should be given to studying those cases and categories of evidence that cannot be explained away by any extension of the super-ESP theory. Still other researchers are recommending specific strategies which, if successful, would certainly put a hitch in the super-ESP theory.

The most current of these are what are called 'cipher' tests. First proposed by the late Dr Robert Thouless of Cambridge University, the test requires that a person who plans to communicate to us after his/her death graph out a cipher. Psychics would then be asked to break the code through ESP while its creator is still alive. If this proves impossible, the cipher-maker could then reveal the code after his/her death — ostensibly through a medium. Dr Thouless felt that a successful communication of the code, under these special conditions, could prove survival. Since he first made his suggestion, other parapsychologists have gone on to elaborate on them. Dr Stevenson has suggested that the potential 'communicator' set a combination lock that could be opened through a verbal message translatable into a digital code. The person who prepares the lock could then, after finding himself surviving death, communicate the verbal code through a medium.†

Dr Thouless prepared his own cipher before his recent death in 1985. Dr J. G. Pratt — a close colleague of Dr Stevenson's — left his friend a lock when he died in 1979. These researchers were very interested in the survival problem, and they should make excellent communicators. But so far, their ciphers remain unbroken. And unfortunately, new inroads in computer technology now make it much easier to break the codes by conventional means.

The evidence, as it stands today, cannot definitively tell us whether or not we will survive death. Each person's leap to conviction will be long or short, depending primarily on how he/she evaluates not only the evidence, but the *a priori* possibility of survival. Both of these factors will colour how each student of parapsychology evaluates the considerable evidence the field has collected on the subject.

As for myself, over the years I have found myself vacillating on the issue. I certainly believe that, based on the published evidence, a belief in life after death is a logical one. The evidence strikes me personally as being almost persuasive. But then problems always seem to crop up in even the best evidence. A good example of such a problem was recently

Dr Robert Thouless of the University of Cambridge devised 'cipher' tests to prove the case either for or against life after death. (Mary Evans/Society for Psychical Research)

reported by Judith Skutch and her daughter in their book *Double Vision,* which chronicles their psychic adventurings together. Mrs Skutch's own grandmother set a combination lock for Dr Stevenson, and based her digits on a single word to be used as a code after her death. Shortly after the elderly woman died, Mrs Skutch received a psychic impression to visit the late Ena Twigg, who was then London's reigning trance medium. Mrs Twigg held a sitting with Mrs Skutch, ostensibly made contact with the recently deceased woman, and communicated a number of evidential bits of information to the sitter. But when the communicator tried to give the code word, the experiment failed.

So here we have a case in which the psychic was on sure footing while communicating information possibly 'lifted' psychically from the sitter's own mind. But when she tried to produce the ultimate proof of survival, she failed.

With problems such as these cropping up in so many cases, it is no wonder that many parapsychologists remain agnostic on the survival issue. So while I remain optimistic about our prospects for survival, my belief in life after death is probably based 85 per cent on the empirical evidence. The remaining 15 per cent probably derives from my spiritual values and religious faith. And faith, unfortunately, is not a phenomenon that can be shared with others.

End-Notes for Chapter Fourteen

* A pseudonym used by Gauld to protect the surviving family's privacy.

† Dr Stevenson did not really originate this type of test. He refined it from a couple of cases reported from the early history of spiritualism. There were a few incidents reported then in which 'communicators', speaking through mediums, correctly gave the combinations of safes once in their possession.

15.

Searching for Proof of Reincarnation

Belief in reincarnation is usually nothing more than a matter of personal conviction. There are, in fact, several ways by which you can justify accepting the doctrine. Most people rely on philosophical justifications — i.e., that reincarnation explains the inequities and injustices of life; that it is a more reasonable cosmological scheme than any other conception of the after-life; and that a majority of the world's peoples accept and teach the doctrine. Millions of people simply can't be wrong! These are all undoubtedly valid observations, but they hardly prove the objective truth of the reincarnation belief. They are but lines of speculation that one can either entertain or reject.

We live today in a scientific and technological world, a world that has long placed more stock in hard data than philosophical speculation. Can belief in reincarnation ever become a scientific rather than religious matter? Just how well *does* the reincarnation doctrine fare when the hardcore evidence for its legitimacy is critically examined? Does such evidence even exist in the first place?

These are the questions that only recently have come within parapsychology's purview. For the past fifteen years searching for evidence proving life after death has been in the forefront of parapsychology. That search has been summarized in the previous chapter. Since the survival issue is one of the field's most central points of concern, it has gradually and reluctantly forced parapsychologists to confront the reincarnation question. I say 'reluctantly' because many parapsychologists tend to think that reincarnation doesn't fall within the central concerns of parapsychology. Studying the evidence for life after death has been difficult enough . . . but reincarnation? In fact, to date only one parapsychologist actively working in the field has ever studied the reincarnation issue in any depth. Dr Ian Stevenson of the University of Virginia has made a career out of tracking down and studying cases of children who spontaneously remember their past lives. Until very recently, most other researchers have felt that the scientific investigation of reincarnation was in good hands . . . and that they could best busy themselves elsewhere and with other projects.

I came to realize that this attitude was extremely biased in 1978, when I first saw the movie *Audrey Rose*. This adaptation of the singularly striking novel tells the story of a young girl terrified by vivid memories of her past-life death in a flaming car accident. Seeing such a case presented on the screen — a case no different from many that appear in the growing literature on reincarnation — made me realize my own previous bias. It also made me realize that any parapsychologist interested in the survival question has a responsibility to examine the reincarnation issue in depth. The evidence bearing on this question is actually surprisingly extensive. It is a mixture of good, bad, and even absurd research.

Spontaneous Past-life Recall

Cases of spontaneous past-life recall is one of the more intriguing aspects of the evidence. Many people claim that they have suddenly recalled scenes or fleeting memories of a past life. These experiences tend to come by way of dreams, mental imagery, waking visions, or *déjà vu* sensations. Dr Frederick Lenz, a one-time San Diego psychologist, has written a book devoted to such first-hand accounts. *Lifetimes* not only contains several interesting cases, but Dr Lenz also claims that such experiences arise from within the context of a specific phenomenological 'incubation' syndrome. People undergoing spontaneous past-life recall, he claims, first feel their bodies getting lighter. They then see vivid colours dancing before their eyes, the room will begin to vibrate, the experiencer will become euphoric, and then the past-life scene or memory will burst into consciousness. Dr Lenz's research was the first time I had read about this past-life memory syndrome, so I decided to explore the phenomenon further.

I began collecting similar cases in 1981 and was able to round up twenty hitherto unpublished accounts.* They closely matched the type of cases Lenz had published in his book. The data were unusual to say the least. I was never able to confirm the existence of Dr Lenz's 'incubation' syndrome, but what *was* truly impressive was that some of my correspondents claimed that the experience had brought with it utter conviction in the truth of reincarnation. (Many of them had been uninterested or sceptical of reincarnation before their paranormal incidents.) But the most important aspect of my cases was that a few of them could be corroborated — in other words, pieces of information cropped up in the accounts that the experiences could not have come by normally. This feature most commonly highlighted past-life memories which came by way of dreams.

One lady from California, for instance, wrote to me about a vivid dream she had as a young woman. She saw herself as the wife of a Norse leader killed by invaders. The most distinctive aspect of the dream was a cameo signet ring she had seen her 'husband' wearing and which designated his rank. Many years later, my correspondent discovered that cameos were originally a Scandinavian art form, and she uncovered several photographs of ancient rings that matched the one she had seen in her dream.

This type of information cropped up in enough of my cases to suggest that my contacts had been tapping into some source of information beyond the reach of their day-to-day minds. Sometimes these cases also profoundly affected my correspondents' lives.

For example, another obviously intelligent and articulate woman wrote to me about a curious recurrent dream she had as a child. She would find herself crossing a bridge situated high above an expanse of water. The bridge could only be reached by ladder, and it tended to sway in the wind. She could never reach the other side of the bridge in her dream, which she found curiously troubling. Some thirty years later she found the source of her information while perusing a copy of *Life* magazine. It turned out that the bridge represented in her dream was the first cat-walk bridge over New York's East River. It pre-dated the building of the Brooklyn Bridge by several years. It was a very narrow and treacherous makeshift construction, and more than one person was known to have fallen to his/her death from it.

But my correspondent's story didn't end there by any means. She also wrote to me that, 'I am convinced that I was one of those [who fell from the bridge] because I have never had that particular dream again, and because a lifelong fear that I would meet my death falling from a great height was dispelled with the recognition of the bridge.' This reaction is similar to the testimony of those fortunate people who claim that they have been cured of their phobias through 'past-life' therapy — i.e., through remembering under hypnosis the past life causes of their present problems.

Cases such as the two I have just discussed point to reincarnation, but they hardly prove it. Veridical features only seem to crop up in a few cases of spontaneous past-life memory, and these cases tend to get bound up in a morass of weak or non-evidential ones. You have to take the good cases along with the bad, and any theory posited to explain the past-life memory phenomenon must be capable of explaining both sets. To prove the case for reincarnation, the sceptic would have to be presented with more elaborate kinds of cases.

Extra-cerebral Memory and the Case for Reincarnation

The research of Dr Ian Stevenson represents just this sort of more elaborate data. For the past two decades, he has been specifically collecting reports of children who literally seem born with memories of their past lives intact. These reports tend to come from cultures where belief in reincarnation is a religious tenet, such as in India, Sri Lanka (Ceylon), Turkey, and among some tribes of Alaskan Eskimos. It is here where we run into both problems and possibilities, however. For the study of extra-cerebral memory cases is not as clear-cut as many believers are prone to think. The collected evidence is actually annoyingly contradictory.

To be fair, some of Dr Stevenson's cases are very good and totally consistent with belief in reincarnation. The fascinating case of Ravi Shankar is typical, and Dr Stevenson included it in his seminal *Twenty Cases Suggestive of Reincarnation*. Ravi was born in Kanauj, India in 1951 with an unusual birthmark under his chin. It looked like a two-inch long serrated mark that somewhat resembled a knife wound. From the time he first began to speak, Ravi claimed that he had lived a past life in another district of Kanauj where he had been murdered. He even gave the proper name of his former father. Ravi talked so incessantly about his past life that his present father tried beating him to get him to stop, but the boy's memories kept on flowing into his mind. The truth of the matter was that on 19 July 1951 the young son of Sri Jagewash Prasad (the man identified by Ravi) *had* been murdered while playing near his house. The boy's throat had been slashed and he was then beheaded by a relative and an accomplice. Two suspects were apprehended by the local police. They confessed, but had to be released on a technicality. Jagewash Prasad later talked with Ravi at length, and became convinced that the boy was familiar with details of his son's death about which he alone was knowledgeable. Ravi even recognized his accused past-life murderer when he saw him walking down a street. The boy literally panicked.

This case is fairly representative of extra-cerebral memory cases at their best. Dr Stevenson has collected over 2000 such reports, and has published detailed analyses of about sixty-five of them. There are three features that crop up in these cases that point specifically to reincarnation:

1. The children usually possess paranormally-derived information about the 'donor' personalities;
2. They sometimes bear birthmarks or other marks seemingly inherited from their previous lives, and
3. Quirks in their behaviour can often be traced back to idiosyncratic behaviour patterns typical of the deceased.

The following case is fairly representative of these sorts of reports. Dr Stevenson has pointed to it himself, since it includes typical strengths and weaknesses found in cases of extra-cerebral memory.

The subject of the investigation was a Lebanese member of the Druse religion, which openly teaches reincarnation. Kemal Andawar (a pseudonym employed by Dr Stevenson) was born on 17 May 1966 in the small town of El Kalaa, which is located fifteen miles outside of Beirut. He was one of seven children and his father, Fuad Andawar, was a pine-cone seller of extremely modest means. Kemal's reincarnation memories surfaced when he was two years old, when he spontaneously heard the name of Dr Arif Eldary mentioned in his presence. He immediately claimed that the gentleman was his brother. More past-life recollections were brought forth when he grew a year older. The boy explained that his name had been Abu Naef (which means the father of a son named Naef), that his family name was Eldary, and that he had lived in a neighbouring town five miles away. He also eventually remembered the names of his (past-life) wife, two other sons, a brother and a sister. Kemal also complained about his present family's poverty, comparing it and their house unfavourably with the relative luxury of his previous life in Hammara and elsewhere. His death occurred, he explained, while he was visiting the Lebanese resort of the Cedars after his emigration from the country. He and his wife were involved in an automobile accident in which they struck a wall of concrete bricks. One of the blocks fell on him while he was trying to escape from the vehicle.

Kemal's parents readily identified their son's past-life identity, since they were passingly familiar with the family he was describing. They realized that their son was talking about the life of Faruq Eldary, who had been the eldest of four brothers living in Hammara. Faruq had been a businessman and an honorary consul in Portuguese Guinea, who had died as a result of an automobile accident during a visit to his homeland in 1965.

Kemal's father took his son to Hammara on a field trip during which they tried to verify some of the boy's statements. They tried to make contact with the Eldary family, but the family's reception to the visit and Kemal's reincarnation story was cool and rather distrustful. So the two Andawars left and did not pursue further enquiries until Dr Stevenson undertook his investigation of the case in March 1972.

When the psychiatrist first visited El Kalaa, Kemal was six years old and he was still talking about his previous life. Dr Stevenson eventually paid three visits to the family in 1972 and 1973 during which he interviewed two important witnesses to the case — a neighbour and a distant relative of the family. They corroborated the story of Kemal's emerging past-life memories and recollected some of the claims he had made during the germinal phases of the case. Dr Stevenson and his translator were also able to talk with the surviving family of Faruq Eldary as well as with a few peripheral witnesses and informants. Because the Eldary and Andawar families had casually met, Dr Stevenson did not consider the case as strong as many others in his files. There is little evidence that the families knew each other intimately. They had no social connections and lived in different cities and within different social classes. Despite these facts, Dr Stevenson found that all the names given by Kemal when he was a small child were correct. His description of the accident in which Faruq was killed was also reasonably accurate, though it appears that the businessman was *not* killed by a falling brick. His family was under the impression that he died while *en route* to the hospital from a heart attack precipitated by the crash. Kemal's parents claimed no knowledge concerning any of this information.

Aside from the purely informational aspects of the case, Dr Stevenson also points out that Kemal's childhood behaviour also seemed linked to his reincarnation claims. He was arrogant towards his present (and to his mind socially and economically inferior) family, and he was obsessed with cleanliness. This trait is rare in small children, although during his life Faruq had likewise been plagued by such a concern. (This fact was discovered only *after* Kemal was actively displaying this idiosyncratic behaviour.) The young boy was also phobic about automobiles, which seems reasonable had he genuinely died during his previous life as a result of a car accident.

Dr Stevenson himself sums up the evidence in this case — both pro and con — fairly and cogently:

> The main weakness of this case lies in the fact that the two families concerned had some prior acquaintance, although it is certain that they were not close friends. It is best to assume, however, that few if any of Kemal's statements about the previous life were of matters completely unknown (or unknowable) to his parents . . . On the other hand, the different circumstances of the two families concerned give the case one of its main strengths. Kemal gained nothing from claiming to be a member of a well-known family, and the claim alienated him somewhat from his own family. They had made no effort to exploit the case in seeking publicity or in any other way, and they had tried to discourage Kemal from talking about the previous life. His expressions of superiority to them would alone have justified this, but his parents were, in addition, afraid of unjust charges on the part of the Eldarys who might have thought them guilty of exploiting Kemal's claims. And as for the Eldarys

themselves, Kemal certainly gained nothing from them by his claims to be one of them. They either rebuffed or ignored him, and none of them had taken the trouble to visit him until the case was investigated.

The fascinating case of Kemal Andawar is certainly not a 'test' case for the reincarnation doctrine. Other cases in the literature are much stronger, but this report represents what can be considered a 'typical' case of extra-cerebral memory.

With so many cases of this quality (and many much better) in hand, you might be thinking that the case for reincarnation would be considered 'proved'. But it isn't . . . and not by a long shot. To begin with, these impressive and veridical cases of past-life recall are actually relatively rare. They turn up now and again in a huge body of cases that are mostly worthless. Many of these less-than-impressive cases prove to be the result of fantasy and play-acting on the part of the child, yet they read identically in pattern to those cases that turn out verifiable. So what we may be dealing with is a psychological phenomenon that, on rare occasion, becomes reinforced with paranormally-derived information. Some scholars have suggested that perhaps the child creates the fantasy, and then uses his/her psychic powers to gather up information genuinely pertinent to a once-living individual.

This theory might strike you as pretty far-fetched, but even cases of genuine extra-cerebral memory conceivably point somewhat in this direction. Dr Stevenson has published at least one truly anomalous case from India in which the child recalled living a previous life in a neighbouring town. The problem with this case was that the 'donor' individual was still alive when the child was born! He had died when the child was three years old. The child began talking about his 'past life' after almost dying from a near-fatal illness that overtook him at that time, perhaps indicating a phenomenon akin to 'possession' rather than reincarnation. On the other hand, Dr Stevenson's most elaborate case was his detailed investigation of an even more curious report that came from Lebanon. This one was problematic since Dr Stevenson discovered that two children, at different times, recalled the *same* past life. If that weren't enough, one of the children seemed to be recalling his past life by moulding together information drawn from the lives of two people who had been relatives. Certainly this case doesn't conform to the idea of *simple* reincarnation.

Supporters of the reincarnation belief who point to Dr Stevenson's research like to call attention to his birthmark cases (such as Ravi's) as representing the best proof of reincarnation. But even within this body of cases there exist problems with which we have to contend. For example, cases are occasionally reported from India in which young children claim past lives as popular deities or legendary heroes. They will sometimes be born with peculiar birthmarks that will match ones easily discernible on public statues of these imaginary personalities! We dare not suggest that these cases represent genuine examples of reincarnation, yet they conform to the same pattern — *avec* birthmarks — as do most other cases of extra-cerebral memory. Sometimes these children will even display sophisticated and precocious information about the gods and heroes they claim to have been!

It should be obvious by now that the phenomenon of extra-cerebral memory cannot in itself serve as proof of reincarnation. Some of the cases in the literature point in that direction. But a careful examination of the published evidence suggests that these cases may be resulting from a complex set of dynamics other than straightforward rebirth.

So when studying the evidence for reincarnation, it starts becoming clear that what is generally considered the 'best evidence' really isn't. This fact places the student of the survival question in somewhat of a quandary, and it forced me, personally, to start looking in other directions for proof of reincarnation.

Hypnosis and Past-life Regression

Hypnosis has long been a tool some researchers and 'new-age' psychologists have used to trace their subjects' past lives. Unfortunately, the topic of past-life regression is not considered too kindly by critical students of the reincarnation issue, nor by parapsychologists in general. The poor reputation that hypnosis has earned as a tool in reincarnation research has probably been best summed up by Dr Leonard Zusne and Dr Warren H. Jones in their text *Anomalistic Psychology*. They write that:

> . . . because suggestion is part of hypnosis, suggesting that the subject go back beyond the point of his or her own birth and examine his or her previous lives achieves precisely that result — the subject all too willingly proceeds to do just that. This, however, is no proof of reincarnation. The cases that have been thoroughly investigated show beyond the shadow of a doubt that one is dealing with hypnotic hypermnesia [improved recall] coupled with the subject's unconscious wish for exhibition, for romance to liven up a drab life, for fantasy as an ego defense mechanism, and similar psychological needs, all reinforced by the hypnotist's own beliefs in the reincarnation doctrine.

Few psychologists and parapsychologists would disagree with this assessment. The main problem with regression work is that people undergoing hypnosis are prone to exhibit a curious phenomenon called *cryptomnesia,* or 'hidden memory'. They will tend to weave together stories based on all sorts of information they have picked up over the years but have consciously forgotten. These stories will therefore be filled with obscure but accurate pieces of information, but this information can usually be traced to books previously read by the subject.

This is the 'official' explanation for the fascinating stories some hypnotized subjects come up with. There also exists some excellent evidence that it is a cogent interpretation of many cases. This research has come primarily through the efforts of Dr Reima Kampman, a Finnish psychiatrist at the University of Oulu. Dr Kampman has published a number of papers showing that some people can come up with all sorts of strong and impressive bits of information when taken back to a 'past life'. But when these same subjects are rehypnotized, they can often explain where they first came across this information during the course of their *current* lives. This information was apparently imprisoned in their minds but consciously forgotten until it was drawn upon during the hypnotic trance.

Despite such findings, some cases can be found in the literature on past-life regression that simply can't be explained by the theory of cryptomnesia. These cases are rare, and only a handful exist. But just because they *are* rare does not mean we have the right to overlook them.

The case of George Field is somewhat of a classic, and it is fairly representative of these exceptional cases. George was a teenager from New Hampshire who was first regressed in 1975 by the late Loring G. Williams, an amateur hypnotist and teacher. Each time he was hypnotized, George would become a Civil War farmer from Jefferson, North Carolina named 'Jonathan Powell'. George proved himself familiar with both the history and the geography of North Carolina while hypnotized, and most of his information proved to be accurate. The climax of the case, however, came only when Williams took him down to Jefferson and hypnotized him in the presence of the town historian. She questioned him in detail about his life and about some of the prominent townsfolk of the 1860s. George, speaking as 'Jonathan Powell', was totally conversant with the lives of these people, where they lived, and their financial status. Since the historian was discussing historically obscure people who lived over a century ago, it is unlikely that George Field could ever have picked up his information normally.

Even more impressive is a case published in 1984. It was brought to public attention by Dr Linda Tarazi, a clinical psychologist from Glenview, Illinois. Dr Tarazi called her subject 'Jane Doe' in the report she sent to *Fate* magazine, since she wanted to ensure her privacy. Dr Tarazi initiated her hypnotic work with Jane in the 1970s. The young woman turned out to be an excellent subject, and invariably became 'Antonia Micaela Ruiz de Prado' while entranced. This trance personality claimed that she had been the daughter of a Spanish military officer who lived in the sixteenth century. The story she told was certainly colourful, and extended over her life in England, Germany and Spain — where she became a prisoner of the Inquisition. Dr Tarazi's initial reaction to the story was that it was '. . . interesting and romantic but it was not unduly impressive.' She became more intrigued with the case, however, when she realized how accurate her subject's information turned out to be. Jane offered the names of several Spanish churchmen and officers of the Inquisition during her trance sessions, and especially while reliving her life in the city of Cuenca. Dr Tarazi was finally able to verify much of this information by learning Spanish, going to Cuenca, and consulting sixteenth-century town documents! The subject did not speak Spanish nor had she ever been to Spain.

Can these cases, then, be considered the ultimate evidence of reincarnation? To some people they probably will be, but they tend to fall short of being any sort of magical proof. For the study of cases of past-life regression is complicated by the same problems that hinder the study of extra-cerebral memory cases. Some weird anomalies crop up that simply can't be explained by any theory of simple reincarnation. For example, there are some cases in which the hypnotic subjects constructed their past-life stories by *combining* incidents drawn from the lives of more than one once-living person.

Such a phenomenon occurred in 1977 when Dr Eugene Jussek, a physician in Los Angeles, California began work with a particularly fascinating hypnotic subject.

Dr Jussek practises holistic medicine and was treating Charles Roberts for his strange outbursts of temper and aggression. Roberts was thirty-nine years old and originally trained to become an electrical engineer, although he ended up working in a brewery. While he had done some travelling in Europe, he had never visited Great Britain, which would later turn out to play a major role in his past-life revelations. Dr Jussek was able to trace several of his subject's purported past lives, but his patient's most vivid recollections concerned a life in nineteenth-century England as a banker. He gave his name as 'James Edward Stewart' who was born in 1801 and lived at seventeen Yorkshire Road in Northampton. His other recollections included the fact that his father owned a bank, that he went to school at a place called Creighton, and that he also attended a 'Draidon' school. Some of his more colourful memories concerned a visit he paid to London when he was seventeen, and stayed (while *en route*) at the Wayside Inn and at the All Man's Club in London where his father was a member.

This information was given during a single session, which also resulted in a wealth of additional details. 'James Stewart' certainly liked to talk, and he went on to tell Dr Jussek that his father's business was located on Canterbury or Canterby Street where he himself worked as a teller. He explained how much he disliked banking, and didn't like the fact that he had to take over the bank when his father died. 'Stewart' finally disclosed that he died in 1861 from pneumonia. He offered the name of his attending physician, and he was presumably buried at St James Church in Northampton.

Dr Jussek decided to explore the earthly life of 'James Stewart' when he next travelled to Europe. The physician and his family visited both London and Northampton after collecting the Stewart material, and the results of their visit were a curious mixture of success, failure, and sheer perplexity. Most of the names, location and streets given by the entranced Charles Roberts turned out to be correct. Dr Jussek even documented the existence of the schools that his subject had mentioned. They were no longer in operation, but they were listed in local commercial directories published in 1862 and 1871. It is highly unlikely that Roberts could have come by this information normally. The Jusseks also located the bank in which Stewart had presumably worked.

The whole case seemed to be corroborating nicely until Dr Jussek tried to trace the earthly existence of Stewart himself. That's when an important complexity in the case came to light. He discovered that a *John* Stewart once lived in Northampton even though it was a rare family name in the area. This gentleman indeed died from pneumonia in 1861. This seemed to be Dr Jussek's man, but *this* Mr Stewart had been a wine-merchant! So it seems that Charles Roberts had tapped into the life of a banker named Stewart but *also* into the terrestrial life of a wine-merchant of the same or similar name who lived in the same general area.

And yes . . . the California physician did locate a London tavern called the Old Man's Club. It no longer exists, but during the nineteenth century it especially catered for bankers![†]

Cases such as these are puzzling and it is difficult to determine how they come about. Cryptomnesia really can't explain them very well, but then neither can reincarnation as we normally conceptualize it. Yet any cohesive explanation for past-life regression cases must be able to explain both the best cases as well as these curiosities.

The Continuing Search

So just where does the search for proof of reincarnation eventually lead us? There seems to exist a large and impressive body of evidence that points, as a whole, to something akin to reincarnation. Certainly something of cosmic importance is being revealed in the cases reviewed in this chapter that should be of interest and importance to us. The fundamental problem with evaluating cases of so-called past-life memory is that the entire way in which we usually conceptualize reincarnation may be fundamentally in error. We here in the West take a rather simplistic approach to the subject, often based on a rather naive understanding of Eastern thought — the very cradle of the reincarnation doctrine. Few of us ever take into consideration the simple fact that many world religions offer competing and contradictory doctrines of rebirth. For example, some schools of Hindu thought talk about the reincarnation of the soul, while Buddhism rejects the very existence of a permanent self. This religion talks only of rebirth of a person's cravings and personality patterns. Even within Hindu thought there exists competing schools of reincarnation belief. Some philosophical doctrines preach that reincarnation is a process of spiritual purification, while this idea is actively decried by other Hindu traditions. Some world religions even teach that only part of the personality reincarnates, while the rest does not.

Rebirth of some sort can probably best explain the evidence parapsychology has collected on the reincarnation issue. But it is difficult to determine just what *specific* concept of rebirth the evidence tends to document.

So when all is said and done, the evidence remains both intriguing and puzzling . . . but with no final solution in sight.

End-Notes for Chapter Fifteen

* For a complete report on these cases, see my book *The Search for Yesterday* (Englewood Cliffs, NJ: Prentice Hall, 1985).

† Dr Jussek has never published a full account of this case. Several years ago, however, he turned over to me transcripts of the critical hypnotic sessions, a private account of his research in England, and copies of several corroborating documents. A full account of the case appears in my *The Search for Yesterday.*

16.

Do the Planets Influence Us?

Back in 1951 the noted French astronomer Dr Paul Couderc wrote that:

> . . . if the stars are an important factor in the personality of each individual,
> and played a part, *however small*, in the formation of bodily and spiritual
> character, along with all the thousands of other factors which shape his destiny
> . . . then it would be an incalculably valuable property. One could try and
> apply it for the good of humanity.

It seems certain that Dr Couderc really didn't believe that any such evidence would ever be forthcoming; but he was wrong. For in the very year he wrote these words, a French psychologist had just finished the first phase of a project that would eventually prove that at least a speck of truth lay behind the claims of astrology. Michel Gauquelin has since published dozens of studies relating planetary positions to the careers and personalities of those born under their influence. His work has been replicated both in continental Europe and in England as well as in the United States — and often by scientists who were determined to prove him wrong. It is no understatement to suggest that the Sorbonne-trained researcher has almost single-handedly taken the basic concepts of astrology out of the quagmire of occultism and into the firm hands of science.

Probably the most notable discovery M. Gauquelin has made is the so-called 'Mars effect'. Many years ago the French psychologist became obsessed with cataloguing the exact hours of birth when people of note and achievement came into the world. Luckily, birth certificates in France include this vital information, and by 1951, Gauquelin had collected the birth times for 576 notable French physicians. He then charted the planetary positions and astrological houses at their times of birth. The distribution was not random. The doctors were born more often in the two hours after the rise and culmination of Mars and Saturn than could be explained by chance. They also tended to be born before the rise and culmination of Jupiter. These findings so intrigued Gauquelin that he replicated his research using the birth times of sports champions for his data base. Here he found one of his strongest effects. The champions tended to be born specifically after the rise and culmination of Mars.

The case for the Mars effect is probably M. Gauquelin's most important finding. It has been replicated twice by other researchers and in 1981 it caused a storm of controversy when a group in the United States tried to disprove it. This fiasco came about when the New York-based Committee for the Scientific Investigation of Claims of the Paranormal decided to replicate the Gauquelin work and prove it false. (The Committee is, by the way, hardly scientific and it rarely investigates anything. It is actually a debunking group dedicated to criticizing and exposing any claims that run counter to their nineteenth-century understanding of conventional science.) CSICOP doled out the responsibility of replicating the Mars effect to Dennis Rawlins, a scientist and CSICOP advisor in San Diego, California. He worked in collaboration with several other CSICOP advisors and members throughout 1977, having become interested in the Mars effect two years earlier. Rawlins was sceptical of the effect and expected to refute it by using what he considered to be better sampling techniques and statistical tests. The Mars effect turned out to be more tenacious than he originally expected, and he later reported back to CSICOP that their collaborative efforts were verifying Gauquelin's discovery.

CSICOP couldn't have that! So they held a series of meetings in which they discussed the matter, reanalysed the statistics, and then reworked them falsely until they fell below the level of significance. Then they went to press with these rather 'creative' findings as if they constituted the original data. Rawlins of course tried to stop this disaster from occurring, but he was rebuffed and then thrown off the Committee for his efforts. Luckily, the San Diego researcher had the integrity to publish the inside story in 1981 by way of a huge report he wrote for *Fate* magazine. The result caused considerable embarrassment for CSICOP, especially when some of their own advisors resigned in protest of the cover-up. The best defence CSICOP could come up with was to claim that the Mars project had never *really* been their project in the first place!

The vestigial discovery of the Mars effect led M. Gauquelin to explore what was soon to become his life work — discovering the inter-relationships between birth times, personality, and career choices later in life. To date he has collected strong statistical evidence that Mars predominates in the birth charts of sports champions and exceptional military leaders. Jupiter tends to appear in the sectors following its rise and culmination in the charts of famous actors and politicians. Prominent scientists are apparently born under the similar influence of Saturn, while artists and musicians tend to be born when the Moon is on the rise. What is particularly fascinating is how the nature of these occupations have been popularly linked with the 'dispositions' of the corresponding planets. We tend to think of Mars as aggressive and war-like, while we habitually link Jupiter with extroversion, since the word 'jovial' comes from the Greek analogue Jove. The moon has long been a symbol of mystery and romance (not to mention insanity!) which commonly typifies writers. All of these discoveries are discussed by Michel Gauquelin in his latest book *Birthtimes*, which is a fascinating and eminently readable autobiographical account of his discoveries, how he made them, and the reaction of conventional science to his work.

The Expanding Nature of the Gauquelin Work

I had the good fortune to meet with the eminent researcher when he visited the Los Angeles area in October 1983. I had just read his book and was eager to discuss many of the implications of his findings. Sitting with him in his Beverly Hills hotel room, I found him to be a charming and analytical man who takes a real joy in his work and critically discussing it with those interested in his discoveries.

I was, of course, interested in learning how he had become involved in astrology in the first place.

'As far as I know,' he explained, 'I have always been interested in astrology. I don't know why. My father was interested in astrology, but just for fun. He was a dentist. I learned to calculate a chart, but when I was sixteen I began to wonder if maybe the whole subject was rubbish. So what could I do? I discovered some books by French astrologers who had tried to put astrology on a scientific and statistical basis. So the first thing I did was replicate their work, but I failed. I was still so interested that I tried many tests with the zodiac and other claims of astrology but with no positive results. Then one day I decided to look into birth times.'

M. Gauquelin didn't have to go any further. I knew from his book that he had collected the birth times of well-known French physicians and how this had led to the discovery that the exact time of our births and various planetary configurations seem to correspond to our later career choices — especially if we end up excelling in them. This discovery may seem to validate the claims of popular astrology with its zodiacs, horoscopes and predictions; but it really doesn't. In fact, the research M. Gauquelin has conducted over the last several years has done much to disprove our normal conception of astrology.

'I am relatively far from popular astrology,' Gauquelin reminded me. 'If I am right in my research, I can say that there is something true in the *idea* of astrology. But the horoscopes they are using today are not valid.'

M. Gauquelin should know, since he has personally investigated whether zodiac signs have any relationship to personality. He conducted this research with the same care he used while studying the relationship of career excellence to planetary positions, but to no avail. He even tested several French astrologers by providing each of them with the horoscopes for twenty subjects, half of whom possessed one set of striking characteristics while the others were typified by the opposite profiles. Their job was to differentiate the two sets of horoscopes on the basis of their art. 'I have to admit that astrologers regularly fail these tests,' he writes in *Birthtimes*, 'and are sometimes so disillusioned that they accuse me of rigging the cases.'

But what M. Gauquelin *has* discovered is more complex and more challenging than anything most astrologers would ever dare dream.

The primary significance of his work is not that birth times seem linked to later career choices, but to a more basic principle. Birth times seem linked to our basic personality development. M. Gauquelin began moving toward this idea when he realized that there is a hereditary factor involved in the time we 'choose' to be born. By computer analysing the birth times for over 60,000 people, Gauquelin and his wife discovered that we are often born when the planets are in the same configuration as when our parents were born. This effect is a lawful one, since the effect is doubled if both our parents were born under the same planetary influence. The effect disappears, however, if a child is born by Caesarean or any other form of unnatural birth. This astounding finding led Gauquelin to realize that planetary influences alone do not affect us, but work in conjunction with several other underlying factors. And this led him, in turn, to search out what similar underlying factors might cause people born under the influence of certain planets to excel in certain occupations later in life — which brought him right back to his home discipline of psychology.

The next phase of his research was obvious but painstaking. He read through the biographies of the famous people he had already studied and charted out what character traits they were known to possess. Then he correlated his data to a detailed list of possible character traits he had drawn up, which consisted of dozens of adjectives that could be used to describe a person's basic temperament. The next step in his project was to group people who had excelled in similar occupations into groups of opposites — i.e., he would group famous sports champions into those who were 'strong willed' and those who were described as 'weak willed.' He similarly compared actors who were described as 'outgoing' to those who were, according to their biographers, introverted.

The results were pretty much in line with what Gauquelin was expecting. There was a significant difference between the two groups of data for each set of occupations. The iron-willed champions were more often born under the influence of Mars than were the weak-willed ones, while outgoing actors were born when Jupiter was positioned in key sectors of their charts more commonly than when introverted actors were examined. These discoveries even applied to writers. Those writers described by their biographers as 'sensitive' were often born when the Moon was on the rise or at its culmination. So it would appear that the correlation between planetary position and excellence in later career choice is not a direct one. Planetary configurations apparently indicate our basic temperaments, which in turn lead us to choose those careers where these characteristics can work to our advantage. The planets do not actually dictate nor directly influence our later career choices.

What is truly bizarre, however, is these planetary correlations only seem related to superstars and not to the ordinary man nor for those who have failed in life. Gauquelin has demonstrated this in a unique way. In the 1960s, he conducted an experiment in which 300 subjects at the Societé Francaise de Psychotechnique in Paris were asked to record the occupations to which they felt drawn when provided with a special list. Their choices, which indicated their career predilections and their basic temperaments, did not relate at all to the planetary configurations that had accompanied their births. Gauquelin later asked the readers of his books to mail him subjective evaluations of their own personalities along with their birth times. He subsequently broke down the respondents into groups based on basic personality types; such as extroversion versus introversion, neuroticism versus stability, and tough-mindedness versus tender-mindedness. But once again he could not find any interrelationships between their personality traits, birth times, and planetary positions.

So what Gauquelin has discovered are predilections which mildly influence our personality development and not laws that predict how a child will eventually turn out.

'If the birth is natural,' M. Gauquelin explained as we discussed these very issues, 'we can assume that a baby born when Mars is rising has more *chance* to display some trait such as aggressiveness later in life. But this prediction should be mixed with many other factors such as education, luck, environment and so on.'

When I asked just *why* only the superstars in their respective fields

— and especially in sports — showed this planetary influence, M. Gauquelin was very cautious in his response.

'I am glad you asked that,' he continued, 'because I think the Mars effect controversy emphasized this too much.* The better the champion is, the stronger the effect seems to be. But this does not mean that, on the other hand, there is no planetary influence at all for the others. It only means that the best of the best, the cream of the crop, more often display the model personality which is needed to become a great superstar in sports. The same could be said of actors with Jupiter as well as scientists with Saturn.'

M. Gauquelin continually emphasized that his data do not imply any sort of fatalism, but only constitute one factor among many that help to shape a person's future personality. I suggested that perhaps his research implies that a superstar in *any* field is produced only when a delicate balance between talent and personality (as reflected in his planetary configuration at birth) combine.

'There are many things that mould a superstar,' he replied, 'including talent and personality. But the point involved with planetary correlations only seems to be personality. So another person, say an otherwise ordinary athlete who does not display the Mars effect, could excel due to another factor. When I looked into the biographies of famous people, the Mars effect does not appear only for sports champions. It could apply to actors or for scientists or for writers. But the fact remains that *most* sports champions are born with Mars predominating. I think this effect is relatively strong. If you are looking just at character traits and comparing them with planetary positions at birth the effect is very clear. But you can be successful in any profession with several types of temperament.'

The Parapsychology Connection

But how does *any* of this really bear on the science of parapsychology and its primary problems? You might be asking yourself this question by now. M. Gauquelin's research is certainly off-beat and fascinating, but parapsychologists have never considered astrology (or anything even remotely connected to it) to be of importance to their field. This attitude has, however, begun to slowly change. This change is not coming because parapsychologists are becoming more interested in other disciplines bordering conventional science. It is due to some theoretical changes the field is undergoing. One old explanation for ESP is that it represents something akin to mental 'radio'. During a typical ESP experiment, for example, we tend to view the agent as 'sending' his impressions — perhaps wave-like — to the percipient, who then 'receives' the information and brings it up into his consciousness. (This is roughly the theory reviewed in chapter two, and it is called the cybernetic model.) This is certainly a logical way of viewing the telepathic process, but it has recently come in for some harsh reappraisal by theoretically-oriented parapsychologists. These researchers argue that the cybernetic model cannot explain many facts of extrasensory perception — for example, that complex information can be 'transmitted' and 'received' as readily and successfully as simple information.

Researchers critical of the cybernetic model prefer to posit 'conformance' or 'correspondence' theories for extrasensory perception which posit that nothing is really 'transmitted' during ESP. In other words, when the agent thinks of a symbol or picture during a telepathic experiment, his intentions directly and automatically influence the contents of the receiver's mind. The receiver's thoughts and memories thereupon rearrange themselves so that they correspond or conform to the contents of the agent's mind. There is no causative connection between the sender and his receiver, though, and this curious correspondence occurs without any direct transference of information. This process might be roughly compared to C. G. Jung's concept of synchronicity — i.e., the result of a series of acausal but meaningful coincidences.

Dr John Palmer is one of the few parapsychologists who has seen the relevance of such theorizing to a possible connection between parapsychology, astrology and Gauquelin's work. He broached this subject as part of his presidential address to the Parapsychological Association in 1979 at St Mary's College in California. During his talk Dr Palmer pointed out that 'the recent growth of scientific astrology is a development we cannot afford to ignore.' He then specifically commented on a possible future *rapprochement* between parapsychology and astrology:

Parallels also exist between the two fields in the ways they conceptualize their phenomena. Most scientific astrologers take a rather empiricist and a theoretical approach to their subject matter, not unlike the parapsychologists of the 1930s. However, one can still distinguish paradigms in astrology, two of which seem to coincide with the transmission and correspondence paradigms of parapsychology. Prototypical of the transmission paradigm in astrology is the theory that the planets and stars influence human behaviour by direct 'geocosmic' forces. Such an approach seems analogous to the ELF wave and bio-energy theories of ESP and PK, the most extreme manifestations of the transmission paradigm in parapsychology. The correspondence paradigm in astrology has the same origin as its counterpart in parapsychology — the writings of Carl Jung, who as you know, treated astrology as a prime example of synchronicity. According to this view, cosmic events and events on earth coincide because of an ordering principle inherent in nature and represented as archetypes of the collective unconscious.

It is my sense that scientific astrologers at the present time seem to function from the transmission paradigm more so than from the correspondence paradigm. But that could change. If it does, and if parapsychology continues to move toward the correspondence paradigm, we could find ourselves in a situation where parapsychology and astrology are applying comparable theories to explain classes of phenomena whose boundaries become increasingly indistinct. Even if the transmission-paradigm continues to dominate astrology, the relationships they uncover — if they are reliable — are still relevant to and probably explainable by parapsychological theories arising from the correspondence paradigm.

Dr Palmer cautioned his colleagues that he was not proposing a 'shotgun wedding' between astrology and parapsychology, since he did not feel the field was ready for such a move. But he ended his comments by saying:

. . . as the correspondence paradigm becomes more and more dominant in parapsychology, it will become increasingly difficult (for us, at least) to justify intellectually the separation of the two fields. The time may soon be coming when an article by Gauquelin on the birth charts of athletes would be considered appropriate for a parapsychological journal.

Exploring the Nature of the Planetary Influence

Of course, M. Gauquelin has not excelled only in collecting and publishing all this data. He, too, is interested in discovering *why* these various correlations exist. But he is more interested in finding a causal rather than an acausal or parapsychological explanation for his discoveries. It is obvious how personality could relate to an individual's future success in a particular professional field. Certainly an athlete is going to excel better if he is aggressive than if he is placid, just as a 'sensitive' writer is going to have an edge over an insensitive one. But why should we 'choose' to be born under the specific influence of a certain planet and not another? And how could a distant celestial body act as an indicator of our future personality? M. Gauquelin thinks he has some partial answers.

He explains in *Birthtimes* that his germinal idea was that planetary positions may act as a trigger factor which helps dictate the time a baby enters the world. The child's sensitivity to the planetary position is probably, he further suggests, inherited since babies tend to be born under the same planetary influences as were their parents. He writes:

The foetus at term would be endowed with a 'planetary sensibility', which would stimulate its entry into the world at a given moment in the daily course of this or that planet, rather than at some other time. This planetary sensibility would be of genetic origin, and the planet itself would not modify the organism of the newborn child. Instead, it would act as the 'trigger', the 'activator' in parturition, while its position in the sky would simply reflect the psychobiological temperament of the child.

Gauquelin rejects the idea that the planets could actually directly affect a foetus or baby at birth on both scientific and mathematical grounds. He has discovered, however, a complicating factor in his data that bears on the explanatory models he has been developing. He had found earlier that the sun — unlike Mars, Jupiter, Saturn or the Moon — does not have an affect on birth time or personality. But when he began to chart the history of solar disturbances over the last several years, he found a most unusual effect. The hereditary similarities between the birth times of children and their parents increased on those days marked by solar geomagnetic disturbances when compared to births that had occurred on relatively quiet solar days. 'The discovery of this "facilitation" marks an important step in understanding the nature, if not the mechanism of the planetary effect,' writes Gauquelin in his book. 'It also alters my explanatory model.'

Luckily, the French psychologist did not have to reject his original theory; he only had to modify it taking his new discovery into account. Gauquelin is now theorizing that perhaps the sun acts like a sort of motor or generator with the solar field acting as a medium. He has gone on to posit that the Moon and those planets that are either close to Earth or of great mass may cause disturbances in this field. When especially strong, perhaps these can be felt by the unborn child, who is already sensitive to these planetary disturbances — or the perturbations of one specific planet — by way of his or her heredity. This idea could account, explains Gauquelin in his recent book, for why the more distant planets do not seem to exert an observable influence on our lives. They may be simply too far away and/or too small for the disturbances they make to exert any influence over us.

M. Gauquelin has suggested this rather complex explanation because he feels that the relationship between birth time and planetary position must rely on a causal, though not a direct, mechanism.

'If you take a metaphysical position,' he told me, 'you can say that these correlations have no causal effect and that it is all synchronicity or something like that. I think that we have to look for a causal effect first. If we fail, well . . .'

He paused before going on.

'It should be clear,' he continued, 'that, as far as I am concerned, the planet does not modify anything at the time of birth. It is just a trigger when the time of birth has arrived. According to his genetic temperament, the foetus could react more likely to the rising of one planet than another.'

When I suggested that he was proposing a sort of genetically-determined set of coincidences, M. Gauquelin took exception with this idea.

'The idea is that when the baby is ready to be born,' he replied, 'we cannot change the genes of the foetus. We have to take this into account. We cannot say, as the astrologers claim, that the planet adds something to the baby. We can just imagine that there is something — some signal from the planet — which could provoke or unsettle the labour and activate it. That's why I am also trying out some experiments with the onset of labour and not the time of birth.'

These ideas have, of course, revolutionary implications for psychology in general. It may be, for instance, that our basic temperaments are inherited in some way from our parents — which would explain why we are sensitive to the same planetary influences and why certain planets have become associated, through history, with certain temperaments. Certain *birth times* in themselves are linked to basic temperaments. This is perhaps why Professor Hans Eysenck, an eminent British psychologist at the University of London, has been taking such an interest in Gauquelin's work and has replicated much of it. Dr Eysenck has long championed the view that heredity is more important in personality development than environment, and Gauquelin's work may be pointing in that same direction. The French researcher's work may also be a partial explanation why infants at birth already seem endowed with their own individual personalities — a fact most behavioural psychologists eschew but which every mother knows from experience.

It should be clear by now that Michel Gauquelin is one of the most important figures in the new field of astrobiology. But he is not willing to simply rest on his laurels and is now actively looking toward the future. He told me, as we came to the end of our discussion, about the plans he has to extend his basic findings. He explained that he would especially like to explore how planetary influences affect everyday sorts of people. This was a subject he began to investigate several years ago, but with rather poor results. Gauquelin feels that these tests failed because people are notoriously biased about how they perceive themselves. This is certainly a very valid point, as any psychologist will tell you. I can well remember, for instance, how a good friend and I were filling out a personality questionnaire one day out of pure boredom. My friend was appalled by how I was answering the questions. When the phone rang and I went to answer it, he used the interruption to engage in a little mischief. 'While you're on the phone,' he yelled to me, 'I'm going to change all your damn answers!'

So much for personal objectivity!

What M. Gauquelin would now like to do is collect descriptions of people based on how *other* people who know them very well describe them. When a consensus has been reached among these friends and he has collected several hundred such profiles, the French psychologist will once again sort them according to basic temperament and then see what the planets would have predicted. He expects significant patterns to emerge. Forms for participating in this study are included in *Birthtimes*.

Of course, M. Gauquelin is at present facing a problem he didn't have to worry about when he began his research over three decades ago. Ever since the 1950s, more and more women have opted for artificially-induced labour or Caesarean section, which totally upsets the patterns he has been finding. It will also make it harder for him to collect his data in the future.

'If I am right,' he concluded about his research, '[my research] demonstrates that there is something right in the old ideas of astrology. So we have to take into account that the universe may be a little bit astrological. For some people this conclusion may be the end of the end. But for me, it's just a little thing to add to the knowledge of science. The most important thing should be the applications, the practical applications. Here I have to face another problem — the mechanization of birth. If a birth remains natural, I think I have a very good practical tool for already predicting the basic temperament of the child. This is just what astrology has been claiming.'

He smiled at this point and added a little coda to his last remarks.

'I'm just speaking about the Gauquelin kind of astrology,' he said, 'not the whole of astrology.'

End-Notes for Chapter Sixteen

* M. Gauquelin was referring to the experiment conducted by the Committee for the Scientific Investigation of Claims of the Paranormal, summarized earlier in this chapter.

17.

The Failure of Scepticism

By this time, the reader of this volume should have a good grasp of parapsychology's accomplishments over the last fifteen years. Its future progress seems assured, and there seems to be an ever-growing number of scientists taking up its mantle. Parapsychology has become *the* science of the 1980s, a field that — after its long history of painful struggles — is finally receiving not only the recognition, but the respect of the scientific community.

Before concluding this book, however, we're going to be revisiting the subject that opened it. This is the subject of the sceptic and his dilemma.

Several of the sceptic's primary criticisms were outlined in the opening chapter. The goal of that chapter was to offer the reader some idea of the 'best' case for the existence of psi. This was accomplished by way of some of the field's better experimental research, which is the most common way parapsychologists reply to their critics: they keep refining their experiments, controlling them against error in every way they can, and by presenting their final results to the scientific community. Despite what the sceptic will tell you, the results of experimental psi research do not begin to ebb when more and more controls are instituted in the parapsychology laboratory. While it is true that many, many pioneering ESP and PK experiments did not replicate well, that is an entirely different matter. But the criticisms we examined earlier represent only a slim part of the sceptic's case against parapsychology. So in this closing chapter we'll be looking at the response some of the field's most vocal sceptics have made in the face of our actual findings — the type of experimental results we've been describing during the course of the last dozen chapters or so. Can a case be made against these results? Does the sceptic still have a leg to stand on, even if his balance seems shaky and easily tripped?

Before beginning this final evaluation of the sceptic's dilemma, however, you might be asking yourself a question. *Why* should we be ending this book by studying the critic's case? The answer is simple. Parapsychology's findings are controversial. Don't for a minute think that they aren't. So the case for parapsychology cannot result solely from the best evidence we can offer for the existence of psi — we must also examine the best case against it. For if we cannot answer the specific charges the critics are making against the field's most important findings, then even the 'best' case for psi will ultimately fail.

This is the very reason so many parapsychologists like to argue with our critics. It's not only that we feel a moral and scientific obligation to defend our science against its detractors, it's also because, in the long run, the sceptic's case usually collapses so completely. When you are arguing with the debunkers, you begin to realize something that is very, very important. Their case is so bad that, if psi *doesn't* exist, it's a wonder the sceptics can't come up with something better! So for the purposes of this chapter, the writings of two celebrated sceptics of the paranormal will be examined. The first represents the reasonings of a famous scientist who, though passingly familiar with the field, can't seem to get his facts straight. Our second sceptic has a more dubious reputation. He is a professional debunker who is willing to misrepresent and even distort the field in order to 'expose' it.

If parapsychology represents the Western scientific ethic at its best, then the writings of these commentators represent it at its worst.

Carl Sagan's Case Against the Paranormal

Dr Carl Sagan represents a phenomenon unique to our time. On the one hand, he is a well-trained and well-disciplined scientist. This is obvious from the fact that he holds the position of David Duncan Professor of Astronomy and Space Sciences at Cornell University in New York. On the other hand, Dr Sagan has also taken up a second occupation as a professional celebrity. His book on the evolution of human intelligence, *The Dragons of Eden*, was a bestseller and a Pulitzer Prize winner, while his easy going mannerisms and mellifluous voice have made him a television talk-show mogul. Little wonder then that Sagan's *Broca's Brain* became a nationwide bestseller after it was released in 1979. It's an eclectic work, since it covers a myriad of scientific topics, and it includes several subjects pertinent to the study of the paranormal. These writings are contained within a single chapter of the book, where some twenty-three pages are devoted to a series of topics ranging from astral projection to UFOs. The chapter is typically Saganesque in that it is witty, entertaining, and full of object lessons. It also is typical of Sagan in another way as well: it contains a greater concern for cuteness than accuracy.

Sagan's attitude towards the paranormal might be described as 'open-minded pessimism'. He does not condemn the *a priori* notion that paranormal phenomena may exist in the world, for he correctly realizes that their existence is an empirical issue that must be experimentally investigated. But he has become pessimistic about the results of these empirical investigations. The reason for his attitude may not be too clear to the casual reader of Sagan's book. It is not because (as Sagan thinks) the evidence for the paranormal is weak. It is because Sagan himself isn't aware of most of it.

To explain why he is sceptical of the paranormal, he devotes several pages of his book to a series of object lessons, in which he demonstrates that the case for the paranormal rests on:

(a) fraud;
(b) the acceptance of claims for which there is little experimental evidence;
(c) the existence of uncanny phenomena which only *appear* to be mystifying until scientists take a closer (and more 'scientific') look at them; and
(d) coincidences reported and evaluated out of context.

The specific subjects Sagan singles out for special comment are astral projection, 'communicating' animals, and precognitive dreams. There is strong evidence that each of these phenomena actually exist, but no mention of this evidence is mentioned by Dr Sagan in his haste to dismiss the paranormal. It's not that Sagan has underhandedly ignored the evidence; it seems more as if he didn't do his homework before cranking out his comments on these subjects.

His views on astral projection represent a perfect case in point. The subject serves as Sagan's first object lesson — i.e., that many claims of the paranormal have never been backed up with experimental evidence. He opens his comments by telling his readers that astral projection often occurs during 'religious ecstasy or hypnagogic sleep, or sometimes under the influence of an hallucinogen.' These points are rather debatable since, according to several surveys of the people who have reported the experience, out-of-body experiences do not seem to be particularly related to drug use or 'ecstasy'. Nor does Sagan apparently have any idea what the hypnagogic state is. While it is true that many people have OBEs when entering or coming out of sleep, there is simply no such thing as 'hypnagogic sleep'. By definition, the hypnagogic state is that phase of awareness *before* sleep onset, typified by fleeting mental imagery. (These usually stop at the point when the dozer enters actual sleep.) The term hypnagogic sleep is a contradition of terms, akin to referring to a stuffed coyote as a 'real live, dead dog'. This may seem like a minor point, but it shows that Dr Sagan, despite being a scientist, is not familiar with even the basic terminology used in a scientific field (sleep research) alien to his own.

Of course, Dr Sagan has a very pragmatic approach to the subject of astral projection, for he writes:

> There is a simple way to test astral projection. In your absence, a friend places a book face up on a high and inaccessible shelf in the library. Then if you ever have an astral projection experience, float to the book and read the title. When your body reawakens and you correctly announce what you have read, you will have provided some evidence for the physical reality of astral projection. But, of course, there must be no other way for you to know the title of the book, such as sneaking a peek when no one else is around, or being told by the friend or by someone your friend tells. To avoid the latter possibility, the experiment should be done 'double blind'; that is, someone quite unknown to you who is entirely unaware of your existence must select and place the book and judge whether your answer is correct.

Sagan's design represents a good and valid scientific experiment. What he does not tell his readers, though, is that *just this type of experiment has been successfully conducted*, even though he writes that 'to the best of my knowledge no demonstration of astral projection has ever been reported under controlled circumstances with sceptics in attendance.'

Had Sagan read even one book on the out-of-body experience, he would have known better than to make such a statement. The research of Dr Charles Tart — which was outlined in chapter thirteen — is well known to just about any student of the paranormal and precisely fits Sagan's outline. The research Dr Morris conducted with Keith Harary was even better controlled, but its shade never comes to haunt the pages of *Broca's Brain*.

Dr Sagan might, of course, object that Dr Tart was not a 'sceptic'. But just what is Sagan's definition of the term? Is he talking about a sceptic of psychic phenomena in general? A sceptic of some specific claim being investigated? Or of the specific psychic or subject being tested? No parapsychologist would merely *assume* that a subject he is testing is automatically telling the objective truth concerning his psychic abilities. Parapsychologists are taught to be sceptical. That's why we conduct controlled experiments.

Dr Sagan's second object lesson is that many psychic mysteries have normal solutions when they are examined critically. To make this point, he cites the case of Clever Hans, the famous 'communicating horse' of

Wilhelm von Osten from Berlin in Germany with Clever Hans, his famous counting horse. (Mary Evans Picture Library)

Elberfeld, Germany. I'm glad Sagan brings up this famous and much quoted case, since I've always had a rather soft spot in my heart for Clever Hans. I studied most of the important literature on this case years ago and to this day, I have never met anyone sceptical of the case who has actually studied all of the original documents. Sagan is no different, and he makes an object lesson out of himself in this section of his book. He proves that many sceptical scientists are perfectly willing to parrot what other debunkers have said or written about a case, but without bothering to check out the story for themselves.

Before proceeding further, though, let me summarize the story of Clever Hans the way Dr Sagan tells it. Then we'll take a look at the *real* story, and one you'll never find in Dr Sagan's book:

Back in the 1890s a horse trainer named Wilhelm von Osten of Berlin, Germany began training his horse Hans to 'communicate' by spelling out and answering questions with his hoof. His most singular ability was his penchant for solving mathematical puzzles the same way. Clever Hans soon became a celebrity and the rage of Europe, and von Osten was celebrated for proving that animals can reason and communicate meaningfully with us. This was an astonishing claim, so the Prussian

Academy of Science sent out a commission, headed by Oskar Pfungst, to study Hans. Through a series of ingenious experiments Pfungst discovered that Hans really could not solve the mathematical puzzles himself, but that he would watch his onlookers as he tapped out the answers. When he reached the correct answer, he simply responded to the observers who would unintentionally nod or make some subtle sign which would cause him to stop. The mystery was solved, Clever Hans was exposed, while von Osten became the laughing stock of Europe and finally died a broken man in 1909.

Now this is all true to a somewhat limited degree. Dr Sagan, like most sceptics, obviously believes that the Pfungst work permanently disproves the whole notion that animal prodigies may exist, since he writes that 'despite the unambiguous nature of Pfungst's evidence similar stories of counting, reading, and politically sage horses, pigs, and geese have continued to plague the gullible of many nations.'

Yet had Dr Sagan studied the case of Clever Hans for himself, instead of merely borrowing the story from what other authors have written, he would know that his statement is a flagrant bit of nonsense.

Here then is the whole (though much abbreviated) story of the Clever Hans affair:

When poor von Osten died, Clever Hans passed into the possession of Karl Krall, a wealthy merchant and a talented amateur parapsychologist and inventor in Elberfeld. Krall long believed that Clever Hans had not been given a fair shake, and that horses *could* be trained to communicate by using von Osten's training methods. He was very familiar with the Pfungst work, and spent considerable time training his other horses, as well as Clever Hans, to respond to mathematical puzzles under conditions where visual cueing was impossible. Krall even successfully trained a blind horse and a blind-folded horse. He then invited some of Europe's greatest minds to Elberfeld so they could test the horses themselves. Clever Hans was quite old by this time, but was included in the tests. These savants — who eventually included Professor E. Clamparède of the University of Geneva, and Dr A. Beredka of the Pasteur Institute — were also familiar with the Pfungst investigations. They were allowed to test the horses any way they wished, and they, too, devised their experiments to control against visual cues — as well as against other sources of sensory cueing.

Perhaps the most tightly controlled experiments they instituted made use of a telephone receiver which was placed by the ear of the particular horse they were testing. The experimenters would then pose mathematical equations to the horse while remaining in another room altogether. None of the witnesses could hear the problems as they were spoken to the horses. They merely watched the horse and recorded its response. Krall's horses often answered correctly even under these extraordinary conditions, despite the fact that no one in the horse's presence knew the questions or the answers. Nor could the questioner cue the horse over the phone, since he could not watch the horse while it was responding. Since Krall didn't attend many of these tests, the horses' responses couldn't be the result of a carefully planned fraud on his part, either.

Maurice Maeterlinck, the great Belgian author and playwright (1862–1949), also visited Elberfeld and worked with the horses, sometimes alone and sometimes in collaboration with several European scientists. In his book *The Unknown Guest* he, too, reports some remarkable results which cannot be explained as the result of sensory cueing. Sometimes Maeterlinck and his colleagues would ask the horses to answer mathematical problems so complex that they had to be worked out laboriously on paper. Yet the horses would usually respond correctly, even before the examiners could calculate the proper answer for themselves! Maeterlinck also took part in some tests for which the mathematical problems were written on posters. They were presented to the horses randomly, and no one was allowed to see what the problem under consideration was. This procedure didn't seem to bother the horses one bit.*

I could go on and on discussing the Elberfeld horse. No one knows for sure what the solution to this mystery will turn out to be, but it certainly isn't the one Dr Sagan — or other sceptics like him — suggests.

The problem of coincidence is Dr Sagan's final major object lesson. He brings up this issue as part of a brief discussion concerning precognitive dreaming. He parrots the cliché that people dream about the deaths of close friends or accidents all the time. By coincidence, some of these are bound to be true, and those dreams that happen to come true by pure coincidence tend to get reported while the hundreds of failures do not. The 'precognitive' dreams you read about in books on extrasensory perception in everyday life are just lucky hits taken way out of context.

Dr Sagan is certainly not the first sceptic to raise this issue. The question of chance coincidence is a problem with which researchers in the field have been grappling for years. In fact, compare Dr Sagan's account to the following passage written by an astute student of the paranormal: 'Before estimating the value of the fact that a person has dreamt of the sudden death of a friend on the night when the death took place, we should have to ascertain that that person is not in the habit of dreaming of distressing or horrible events.'

These words were not written by a critic of parapsychology. It was written in 1886 by Edmund Gurney, one of the first scholars to study psychic phenomena scientifically. It appears in his co-authored *Phantasms of the Living*, which was one of the first major books that tried to critically evaluate the evidence for spontaneous ESP. The important point to remember is that Sagan's concern about the problem of coincidence is a very old one. But even the first parapsychologists had little trouble showing the fallacy in this line of argumentation. In fact, how the first parapsychologists overcame the coincidence problem represents a fascinating chapter in the field's history.

While they were collecting cases of spontaneous ESP, Gurney and his colleagues discovered that many of their informants reported 'dreams' or other types of psychic experiences which seemed to foretell or inform them about the deaths of close friends or relatives. So these scholars immediately set forth to demonstrate that these 'death coincidences', as they called them, were not the result of simple coincidence, which was one of the first objections raised about their study when it was finally published. Gurney and his fellow founders of the Society for Psychical Research went on to design a new survey which would address this thorny issue, by asking people all over England to describe their 'hallucinations' and psychic experiences. Their final report, published in 1894 by the Society for Psychical Research, was called the *Report on the Census of Hallucinations* and represents a classic piece of parapsychological literature. The SPR investigators confirmed the pattern they had first uncovered in *Phantasms* — i.e., that people tend to have dreams and other psychic experiences that focus on the deaths of friends or relatives. These deaths were often unexpected and/or sudden. With this new survey in hand, they compared the *rate* of these reported death coincidences to the probability that a given person in England would die at any specific moment. (This rate was calculated on the basis of statistics made by the Registrar-General.) They found that the preponderance of the accurate death coincidences they had collected was 440 times greater than chance could account for.

Of course, today, these statistical procedures might seem rather simplistic. But the logic behind them was certainly not flawed. It also shows that Dr Sagan's criticism was addressed by parapsychologists in some detail even before the turn of the century.

Of course, Dr Sagan's argument is so self-evidently simplistic that one might be tempted to bypass it altogether. The critical issue parapsychologists face when studying precognitive dreams has little to do solely with the problem of coincidence, since researchers are more interested in the *amount* and *quality* of the information encoded within the experiences they collect. Let me explain this comment by using a hypothetical example: say that one night you dreamt that your old Aunt Hatty had died, only to learn the next day that your dream was correct. That could be a coincidence. But what if you correctly dreamt that your Aunt Hatty died in an automobile accident while wearing a red dress? And because she swerved to miss hitting an animal crossing the road? Case reports rich in such detail are being placed on record all the time. They cannot be explained on the 'coincidence' theory simply because they *are* too detailed.

Dr Sagan is a scientist, of course. He wants to see hard evidence for the existence of psi and no one can blame him for that. But if Dr Sagan were as familiar with parapsychology as he pretends to be, he would know that the phenomenon of precognitive dreaming has been studied in the laboratory under controlled conditions. They were included as part of the Maimondes Medical Center's famous explorations into the world of dream ESP that we reviewed in chapter two. During some of these experiments, the subjects were asked to dream about target pictures that were only chosen randomly the next day. Some of the subjects had no difficulty succeeding at this task, and precognition seemed as easy for them as telepathy.

What is so especially annoying about Dr Sagan's criticisms is that I haven't cited any secret information or unpublished reports in this response to him and his *Broca's Brain*. The studies I've been citing in this chapter have been fully reported in such publications as the *Journal of the American Society for Psychical Research*. They have also been summarized in most serious books on the paranormal. Had Dr Sagan familiarized himself with the scientific literature on the paranormal freely available to him, he would certainly have come across these experiments and reports.

But enough of Dr Sagan. Now let's turn to another sceptic and critic of parapsychology. This is a sceptic who *is* familiar with the field.

A Magician's Crusade Against the Paranormal

One of parapsychology's more recent attackers is James ('the Amazing') Randi, a magician-turned-debunker from Rumson, New Jersey. As a former escape artist and mentalist, Randi has been waging a holy war against psychics and parapsychologists for several years. Randi's most complete challenge to the field comes by way of his recent book *Flim-*

Flam! It was originally published in 1980 and was subtitled 'the truth about unicorns, parapsychology and other delusions'. Despite this cynical subtitle, very little in the book is concerned with conventional parapsychology at all. Most of it is devoted to such disreputable topics as 'fairy' photographs, the ancient astronaut controversy, biorhythms, and other 'scientific' borderlands.

So just what areas of parapsychology *does* Mr Randi cover in his book? Most of the coverage is devoted to what most scientifically-trained psi researchers snidely call 'pop' parapsychology or 'drug store' parapsychology. This is the world of television psychics, psychic surgery, Kirlian photography, do-it-yourself ESP development courses, and so on. These are areas towards which most orthodox parapsychologists cast a scornful as well as sceptical eye. Randi never tells his readers this, of course. But now and again he does talk about and criticize more legitimate parapsychology, and it is here where he is at his glorious worst. Time and time again he flagrantly misrepresents what parapsychologists have said about psychic phenomena. If this weren't bad enough, he goes on to woefully misquote and misdescribe their research.

This fact can no better be illustrated than by examining what Randi has to say about two well-known bodies of research:

1. The research of Dr Charles Tart of the University of California at Davis, who has been testing to see if certain people can be trained to learn ESP.
2. The highly publicized research of Russell Targ and Dr Harold Puthoff formerly of the Menlo Park, California-based Stanford Research Institute. Their investigations included a series of PK tests with Ingo Swann; some ESP experiments with Uri Geller; and considerable research into the byways of 'remote viewing'.

By examining what Randi says about this research, one sees him for what he really is — either a hopelessly confused critic who just doesn't seem capable of understanding the sophisticated way parapsychological research is designed and conducted, or a shrewd antagonist for whom debunking has become a holy war in which deliberate distortion and misrepresentation become a valid means towards a greater end.

Mr Randi's brief attack on Dr Tart's research on ESP learning is a good case in point. If you will recall, Dr Tart conducted some of his research at the University of California at Davis in the early 1970s with the use of a ten-choice trainer. The project was designed to determine if a subject's ESP scores would improve if he was given immediate feedback about his/her successes and failures. The experiments were simply run. Each subject was placed in an experimental room with a console in front of him. This console depicted ten playing cards, which were arranged in a circle. A light was located next to each one. The experimenter remained in another room in front of a similar console, where he was provided with a television monitor so that he could see the subject. The experimenter randomly chose a series of 'targets' by relying on a sequence of digits generated randomly by a device hooked to the set up. He signalled the subject after generating each target, and the subject then made his choice. After this choice was recorded, the experimenter then informed the subject of the correct target by illuminating the proper light on the subject's console. Some of Dr Tart's best subjects scored phenomenally above chance, with accumulative odds of millions to one against chance.

Randi feels confident he can explain Dr Tart's results, for he writes that:

> . . . Sherman Stein, a mathematician at the University of California at Los Angeles where the tests were done, in examining the raw data on which the book was based, came upon an anomaly. It seems that though Tart had checked out his random-number generator and found it gave a good *distribution* of digits, it did not *repeat* digits as it should. In 5000 digits produced by the machine, there should have been close to 500 'twins'. If, for example, a three comes up, there is exactly one chance in ten that another three will be produced next. There were only 193 twins — 39 per cent of the number expected. Since a subject in such tests had a tendency not to repeat a digit just used, this bias of the machine fits in nicely with the results observed.

It is remarkable how many errors and distortions crop up in just this one paragraph alone. It was, in fact, Dr Tart himself who first noticed the lack of double digits. Being a good and conscientious experimenter, this led him to seek the advice of Dr Stein (who teaches at the University of California at Davis and not at UCLA). But is it true, to quote Randi, that 'the bias of the machine fits in neatly with the results observed?'

Not on your life!

The scoring of some of Tart's subjects was so astonishingly high that the generator's slight bias does not appreciably alter the overall significance of the tests. This is true even if we adjusted the statistics to take this flaw into account. Anyone who takes the time to read Dr Tart's *Learning to Use ESP* can determine this for himself by recomputing the statistics. Despite this fact, Randi deliberately implies that Tart's work was not significant when it is re-evaluated. This misrepresentation is all the more serious since Randi surely realizes that his argument is totally ridiculous.

When Dr Tart's book was first published, it was critically reviewed in the *New York Review of Books* by Martin Gardner, one of parapsychology's most caustic critics and a long-time friend of Randi's. Gardner had learned of the bias in Tart's work from Dr Stein, so he brought up the issue in his review with seeming relish. But after a lengthy series of exchanges with Dr Tart, even Gardner had to back down on this point! Since Gardner and Randi are fellow members of CSICOP, the magician must have been aware when he wrote his book that his lame 'statistical bias' theory had been settled long ago.

Of course, Randi's criticisms of Dr Tart are really rather peripheral to *Flim-Flam*! The main crux of the book is to make a frontal attack on Russel Targ, Harold Puthoff, and the entire SRI research programme in parapsychology. This would include their remote viewing experiments, as well as their work with such 'star' psychics as Ingo Swann and Uri Geller, the famous Israeli telepath and psychic 'metal-bender'. Being that I was able to personally visit SRI to investigate Randi's claims and charges, I can only describe his chapter on their work as a shameless bit of prevarication.

Space limitations will not permit me to expose all of Randi's errors and misrepresentations. So the following pages will cover only a few of his more important criticisms.

To begin with, Randi particularly flays a series of magnetometer 'demonstrations' which Dr Puthoff conducted with Ingo Swann at Stanford University in 1972. Since these experiments were not discussed earlier in this volume, the following represents a brief summary of what occurred.

The idea behind these tests was to see if Swann could influence a magnetometer, buried under a physics building around which a decaying magnetic field was set. Since the magnetometer was protected by a super-conducting shield, the output of the decaying field should have been impervious to any random influences. These brief experiments were described by Targ and Puthoff in their book *Mind-Reach*, in which they report that Swann was asked to interfere with the magnetometer by 'remote viewing' it. When Swann began to describe the device, the output of the decay pattern suddenly doubled! (This was easy to determine since a chart recorder was constantly monitoring the decay pattern.) This curious phenomenon was witnessed not only by Dr Puthoff, but also by Dr Arthur Hebard, a young Stanford physicist. The perturbation lasted for thirty seconds and Dr Hebard was surprised by this effect, since the strange output seemed to be physically inexplicable. So he suggested that Swann *stop* the output of the device completely. Swann tried and succeeded within seconds! He produced this same result later during the test by merely thinking about the machine, and the results did not seem due to some quirk in the magnetometer. The magnetometer chart was examined for two hours after Swann left the building, but no odd perturbations were noted during this control period.

Mr Randi completely disputes this sequence of events. He reports that Dr Hebard was not happy with Swann's demonstration. The physicist was particularly annoyed that neither Russell Targ nor Dr Puthoff bothered to ask whether or not a normal explanation — such as equipment malfunction — could account for the effects.† Randi then goes on to challenge other aspects of the demonstration. Based on his personal conversations with Dr Hebard, Randi next claims that a total of fifteen minutes went by between the time Swann began focusing his attention on the magnetometer and when the perturbation really took place. It was only then, claims Randi, that Swann asked the experimenters, 'Is *that* what I'm supposed to do?' The magician further claims that Swann was never asked to stop the output of the magnetometer. The chart suddenly produced a levelling out, and then Swann opportunely asserted that he had produced the effect.

When I spoke to Dr Puthoff about these charges, the SRI physicist grew extremely annoyed. He disputed Randi's information and explained in no uncertain terms that not more than sixty seconds went by between Swann's 'remote viewing' procedure and the occurrence of the magnetometer's first perturbation. He also maintained that Dr Hebard — unimpressed by the effect — had off-handedly suggested that it would be more impressive if Swann could cause the magnetometer's output to cease.

There obviously exist several discrepencies between Dr Puthoff's views on what happened during this experiment, and what Randi claims Dr Hebard told him. So to clarify the matter, I decided to get in touch with Dr Hebard myself. I finally tracked him down at the Bell Telephone Laboratories in Murray Hill, New Jersey. He was very willing to discuss the Swann magnetometer demonstration with me, and professed to be very interested in parapsychology.

It become quite clear during our phone conversation that Dr Hebard's memory of Swann's performance differed somewhat from Puthoff's. He disagreed with the physicist primarily about the length of time that passed from when Swann *first* attempted to remote view the magnetometer and when the subsequent perturbations took place. He recalled that several minutes passed by, as Randi asserts, and not merely several seconds. Dr Hebard denied in no uncertain terms, however, Randi's claim that Swann was never asked to 'stop the field charge' being recorded from the magnetometer. He easily recalled that he had suggested that it would be a fascinating effect if Swann could produce it . . . which, of course, he actually did soon after the suggestion was made. Randi also directly quotes Dr Hebard as calling some of Targ and Puthoff's claims 'lies'. Dr Hebard was very annoyed by this claim since, as he explained to me, Randi had tried to get him to make this charge and he had refused. Dr Hebard later signed a statement to this effect for me.

So while Randi has indeed shown that there are several unanswered questions about Swann's Stanford demonstration, he has certainly not provided *the* definitive scenario of what happened that day. His portrayal of Dr Hebard as a strong critic of both Targ and Puthoff and parapsychology also seems questionable, while his summary of his conversations with the physicist is rather inaccurate as well. (I might add that several weeks after I spoke to Dr Hebard, Dr Puthoff showed me the actual graphed print-outs given by the magnetometer during the Swann demonstrations. The records supported Dr Puthoff's contention more than they did Dr Hebard's.)

Randi doesn't end his attack on SRI with his comments on Ingo Swann, though. His real focus is the research that SRI conducted with Uri Geller, which was designed to study his purported telepathic and clairvoyant powers. This research was first published in *Nature* in October 1974. Since *Nature* is a prestigious British science publication, the SRI report caused a stir in scientific circles. Their report claimed that Geller, while sequestered in a sealed isolation booth, successfully and repeatedly reproduced drawings sent to him telepathically. The SRI researchers also explained that Geller was able to 'call' the uppermost face of a single die shaken in a closed box.

Naturally, our beloved debunker plays down the importance of the *Nature* paper and states that 'as early as 1972, Russell Targ and Harold Puthoff, its authors, had submitted it to US publications as a project of the Stanford Research Institute (SRI). All had rejected it.' Now this is blatantly untrue, since Targ and Puthoff had made no prior submission. Their goal was always to submit their report to *Nature*. Randi also snidely comments that the *Nature* paper was published with an editorial explaining that the report was being issued 'so that scientists could see the kind of material that was being turned out in the field of parapsychology', and typified it as 'weak' and 'flawed'.

Randi here engages in a series of half-truths, since he seems to be implying that the paper was published in order to embarrass parapsychology. The truth of the matter was that the editors of *Nature* found many flaws in the report with which to take issue. But they clearly stated in their editorial that they had decided on publication despite some of their reservations. They simply felt that they had an obligation to bring this type of research to the attention of their readers since the experiments had been conducted by legitimate scientists. The editorial was perfectly respectful and contained none of the innuendos implied by Randi.

So let's look at the way Randi thinks Geller pulled the wool over Targ and Puthoff's eyes during *the* most critical series of experiments they ran together.

The focal point of the SRI's *Nature* report concerned a series of experiments designed to explore or expose Geller's purported telepathic powers. For this carefully conducted series of tests, the psychic was placed in an isolation booth at SRI, while the experimenters remained in an adjoining room and selected the targets from a dictionary. (They opened the dictionary randomly and then sketched the first drawable word listed on the page.) This drawing was then hung up for everyone — researchers and on-lookers alike — to see. Geller's job was to reproduce these drawings from his position inside the sealed chamber by telepathy. While there still remains some unanswered questions concerning the times Geller 'passed' on a drawing (i.e., refused to draw it), some of his successes were simply astounding. There is simply no way coincidence can explain some of them. For example, for one trial Geller drew a bunch of twenty-three grapes. The target was not only a similar drawing, but the grapes in *that* picture were even placed in the same configuration. Either this result was due to telepathy or somehow Geller managed to see the target before reproducing it.

Randi opts for the fraud theory, and he even thinks he knows how Geller carried out the shenanigans. He offers his readers a diagram of the booth and adjoining room where the tests were held. This diagram shows that a four-and-a-half inch hole (used to extend cables in and out of the booth) is situated in the booth three feet above the floor. Randi claims that Geller merely peeked through this hole for at least two of the drawing tests, and either saw the targets or was signalled by a confederate located in the adjoining room. While the magician points out that the hole is usually kept stuffed with gauze, he believes that Geller simply withdrew the material while carrying out his secret observations.

This all sounds reasonable enough until you check out the booth, which I was able to do when I visited SRI on 12 June 1981. I found, first, that the hole is not four-and-a-half inches wide at all. It is three-and-a-quarter inches and extends through a twelve-and-a-half inch wall. This scopes your vision and severely limits what you can see through it. The hole is not left open either, since it is covered by a plate through which cables are routinely run. Dr Puthoff and his colleague were, however, concerned that their subject might be ingenious enough to insert an optical probe through this hole, so they monitored the opening throughout their telepathy experiments. But the most embarrassing error Randi makes concerns the position of the hole. It isn't three feet above the floor, but is located only a little above floor level. The only thing you can see through it — even under optimal conditions — is a small bit of exterior floor and opposing wall. (The viewing radius is only about 20°, and the targets for the Geller experiments were hung on a different wall completely.) I also discovered during my trip to SRI that an equipment rack was situated in front of the hole throughout the Geller work, which obstructed any view through it even further. I ended my little investigation by talking with two people who were present during these critical experiments. They both agreed that wires were running through the hole — therefore totally blocking it — during the time of the Geller experiments.

Little more needs to be said concerning Randi's criticisms of the Geller work, since the important point is not really whether the Israeli psychic proved his psychic powers, but whether Randi can be considered a responsible critic of parapsychology. I think the answer should be obvious by now. This fact, however, doesn't keep him from making wild accusations against both Targ and Puthoff, even to the point of questioning their scientific honesty.

It is well known that the two SRI physicists issued a film which shows Geller successfully guessing the uppermost face of a die after it had been shaken in a closed box. Their *Nature* report describes these tests and Geller's phenomenal accuracy. The critical film was taken by Zev Pressman (an SRI staff photographer) and it shows Geller correctly making a guess. Randi claims that Targ and Puthoff lied when they stated that this film was taken during the actual tests. He further asserts that the film was a re-enactment. Basing his charges on information he claims came from Pressman himself, Randi maintains that the film was taken after the photographer had gone home and was merely staged. 'Pressman revealed that he was told Geller's *eight successful throws* [my emphasis] were done after he (Pressman) had gone home for the day,' writes Randi, 'and that this *film was a re-enactment* of that supposed miracle.'

Dr Puthoff was thoroughly disgusted when I read this section of *Flim-Flam!* to him. 'Not one millimetre of that film was a re-enactment,' he told me. He also claimed that he had even procured an affidavit from Pressman certifying that the footage was filmed by him during the actual SRI tests. Dr Puthoff supplied me with this affidavit and urged me to get in touch with Mr Pressman, which is exactly what I did.

I spoke directly with Mr Pressman on 5 January 1981 and he was quite interested when I told him about Randi's book. He denied that he had spoken to the magician. When I read him the section of Randi's book dealing with his alleged 'exposé' of the Targ-Puthoff film, he became very vexed. He firmly backed up the authenticity of the film, told me how he had taken it on the spot, and labelled Randi's allegation as a total fabrication. (His own descriptive language was a little more colourful!)

So just where did Randi come up with this nonsense about the SRI's Geller film? Randi does not specifically state that he personally spoke to Pressman, although he vaguely implies it. It seems instead that he procured this piece of misinformation from *another* SRI source, who was perhaps honestly mistaken about the film. Randi then repeated the error, never checked out his source, and used the error to make wild accusations against the SRI experimenters. The truly hilarious thing about this mess is that no film showing Geller *making eight hits in a row* was ever shot! Pressman only filmed one experiment, in which Geller is seen 'passing' — although guessing correctly — on the test. So Randi wasn't even able to describe the SRI film correctly, and he certainly never saw it.

So much for Randi's attacks on Geller and those who have studied him.

Finally we and Randi came to Targ and Puthoff's original 'remote viewing' research, which they pioneered at SRI, (as discussed earlier) during some informal tests conducted with Ingo Swann. These tests were refined when the physicists began conducting similar experiments with the late Pat Price, another gifted psychic and a former Burbank, California police commissioner. For these initial experiments, the subject was kept at SRI while an outbound experimenter drove to a location somewhere in the San Francisco Bay area. The subject was simply asked to visualize the outbound experimenter's location and describe it. After each session was completed, the subject was taken to the target site and a comparison was informally made between the location and the subject's description. During these early trials, each subject usually co-operated in a series of such sessions. The transcripts for *all* the sessions were then given to an independent (blind) judge, who then visited the sites or examined photographs of them. He then tried to match the sites with the descriptions. The overall success of these sets of remote viewing experiments was therefore based not only on the *quality* of the subject's responses, but by way of statistical tests calculated from the judge's correct matchings.

The only criticism that Randi can come up with is to complain that the SRI judging procedures were extremely faulty. This criticism is not an original one, for Randi bases his information on some 'findings' made by two New Zealand psychologists — the late Richard Kammann and David Marks — who visited SRI when the remote viewing research was first beginning to come to scientific attention. (They report on their visit in their own book *The Psychology of the Psychic*.) Drs Marks and Kammann discovered that the SRI researchers often forgot to edit out little 'clues' in the transcripts, clues that could have helped the independent judge to determine which target went to which description. For instance, in one test the subject was told that he already had 'three successes' behind him. The judge was thus clued to the fact that this transcript corresponded to the fourth session and target site. But this wasn't all that the psychologists claimed. For according to Randi, they also 'discovered [that] the judges had been given the locations in chronological order, and they knew it. The barest trace of experimental care would have demanded that this list be "scrambled." But it was not.' Randi then goes on to explain how the two psychologists then re-edited the transcripts for one particularly successful series of SRI tests in order to correct this fatal flaw. They then proceeded to have the entire series rejudged, but their judge couldn't make the correct matches at all.

'The Targ and Puthoff miracle is out of the window,' declares Randi.

These criticisms may seem devastating, but they really aren't. To begin with, there certainly *were* flaws in the early remote viewing work, and the issue of the faulty editing was crucial. But parapsychologists working at other laboratories were quick to point out these problems to their SRI colleagues, who immediately corrected the flaws. But the story of the SRI remote viewing work doesn't end here, by any means. Dr Charles Tart eventually came to take a special interest in these early 'flawed' experiments, and he re-edited the same remote viewing reports the New Zealand psychologists had worked with. He deleted the possible cues and then sent them to be rejudged. This time the results were still statistically significant.[8]

Nor is it true that the transcripts and/or the sites for the critical series were given to the judge in chronological order. Some time after the publication of *The Psychology of the Psychic*, I personally spoke to the psychologist in charge of judging this series. He told me that everything was properly randomized when he received the materials from SRI.

Of course, our sceptic totally ignores the fact that the remote viewing effect has been replicated both at SRI and at several other laboratories, using even more stringent controls than went into the original experiments. Successful remote viewing experiments have been reported from Mundelein College in Evanston, Illinois; from the Lawrence-Livermore

Laboratories in California; and recently from the Institute for Parapsychology in Durham, North Carolina. So the validity of the remote viewing effect no longer rests on Targ and Puthoff's experiments alone, but on a large body of experimental findings . . . findings that even Randi, with all his magical knowledge, can't make disappear.

Some Concluding Notes

So there rests the sceptic's case. Not every sceptic is this irresponsible, but the cases we've been evaluating tend to be embarrassingly typical. The simple fact remains that parapsychology's detractors have a terrible time explaining away the field's findings. If psi doesn't exist, this fact would be self-evident by now. So it is more than revealing that the field's debunkers so often fall to *manufacturing* flaws in our experiments — or even, as with the CSICOP/Gauquelin fiasco, cover up their *own* positive findings.

Where does this leave parapsychology? The field certainly seems to be in healthy shape. There is probably more fruitful research going on within parapsychology today than during any other time in its short history. It is also currently turning in even more exciting directions, and these directions promise to help convert even more scientists. We briefly examined this trend in chapters two and three, where the use of ESP for predicting the results of horse-races and financial investments was discussed.

When parapsychology first became a primarily experimental science, nobody thought that psi would ever be harnessed for any practical purpose. No one really thought that there existed a practical side to the sixth sense. Editorializing back in 1945, in fact, Dr J.B. Rhine eschewed searching for any real uses for extrasensory perception or psychokinesis. 'No practical use can be made of them with our present state of knowledge,' he wrote. 'They are not reliable enough.' Rhine didn't even think that the practical applications issue was very important to the parapsychology of his day, for he went on to write that '. . . practical application has never been the objective of the investigations. This is not because practical application is regarded as of no importance, but because the true goals of research are so incomparably greater in importance that practical application seems downright trivial in contrast.' The 'true' goal of parapsychology, believed the Duke researcher, was to disclose mankind's place in the universe.

Since Dr Rhine entered the field to resolve his personal religious conflicts, this was a reasonable view for him to take. And if we examine the research projects conducted by parapsychologists fifty years ago,

Rhine's position seems even more logical. The field had been previously preoccupied with the survival enigma and was only beginning to turn to the scientific laboratory. Rhine's pioneering research at Duke University in the 1930s certainly proved the existence of extrasensory perception and psychokinesis. But his research strategies — which were basically card-calling ESP experiments and dice-rolling explorations of PK — were extremely limited. While they demonstrated that some people possess a sixth sense, the faculty seemed to be weak and capricious. The Duke researchers came to feel that the days of the great psychics were over. These younger parapsychologists, who had been trained specifically in the lab, even began to wonder whether truly great psychics ever really existed — or whether their feats were the result of fraud clever enough to dupe their predecessors. These researchers began to see ESP and PK as incredibly elusive powers, powers that surface only rarely. In fact, they didn't even become interested in ESP and its role in day-to-day life until the 1940s.

What is so ironic is that primitive cultures, these wellsprings of the sixth sense, have never considered psychic power in this ludicrously limited way. To these peoples, ESP and PK were (and are) powerful forces that should be put to work to help their community.

This point was recently made by Dr Jule Eisenbud, a psychoanalyst from Denver, Colorado who has been studying parapsychology for years. Speaking before a conference of anthropologists in 1978, he pointed to several differences between the Western and the 'primitive' belief-systems concerning psychic phenomena. To the world of the primitive '. . . behaviours based upon the power of thought to accomplish things are reality oriented. They simply make use of processes considered to be inherent in the social order and the universe.' It was this world view that gave rise to the shamanic tradition. The shaman is supposed to employ his powers for the good of his people. It would be a pretty pathetic shaman who constantly excused himself for failing to conjure a rainstorm, couldn't find someone's lost ring, or failed to heal a member of his community. We are hardly so demanding when we work with our *own* psychics!

Luckily, though, we are seeing a real change of attitude within today's parapsychological community. Practical applications for the sixth sense is becoming *the* topic of the 1980s. This promising area of study has been christened with its own name. *Psionics* is a term originally coined by Dr Jeffrey Mishlove, who was one of the first parapsychologists to urge his colleagues to explore the world of 'applied psi' research. He employs this term to separate it from formal experimental/laboratory research.

Is there a case for psionics? There certainly seems to be. Dr Moss's research using ESP at the races constituted a good beginning, but her results weren't exceptionally strong. But the silver market research conducted by Delphi Associates was stunningly successful, to which their $100,000 in profits can testify! Research into the practical side of extrasensory perception is, in fact, currently in full swing:

1. Psionics has been especially useful in the field of archaeology. In the early 1970s the late Dr J. Norman Emerson of the University of Toronto began employing a Canadian psychic while looking for promising dig sites. He was so impressed by the psychic's success that the formal discipline of 'psychic archaeology' was soon born. This burgeoning field received a further push when Jeffrey Goodman, while working to find some early man sites in Arizona, relied on a psychic to find a productive site near Flagstaff. His colleagues were extremely sceptical, since no such sites were common to the area, but Goodman dug anyway — and he found exactly what he was looking for. Several archaeologists today consider extrasensory perception a standard tool for their research.

2. The *St Louis Business Journal* recently proved that ESP can be directed towards the stock market. Representatives from the paper contacted nineteen stock brokers and asked each of them to select five stocks. These were stocks they expected to increase in value during the following six months. These business experts were pitted against Mrs Beverly Jaegers, a St Louis psychic with no background in business or stock transactions. She, too, picked five stocks but based her choices on her sixth sense. The results? The stocks chosen by sixteen of the brokers fell in value, since the Dow Jones Industrial Average dropped during the course of the experiment. But the psychic's stocks increased by 17.4 per cent. When psychics start making better investments than stock brokers, potential investors better take notice!

3. The use of the sixth sense in police work is currently becoming widely known. Several newspapers in California ran feature stories in 1979 when a psychic helped sheriffs in Calavaras County solve a difficult case. The case concerned an elderly gentleman who had disappeared during a camping trip. The man's wife contacted Mrs Kathlyn Rhea who proceeded to describe the exact location where the body could be found. Her description was so precise that the county sheriff knew the exact spot she was describing. He drove

directly there, and retrieved the man's body. (He had died from a heart attack.) Several similar cases have recently come to light, since more and more police departments in the United States are currently relying on the services of psychics.

4. The world of medicine has been infiltrated by parapsychology and psionics, too. Some pioneering experiments in psychic healing conducted by the Institute for Applied Biology in 1977 were stunningly successful. Researchers there proved that a psychic healer could extend the life spans of cancer-ridden mice by close to 50 per cent.

Police work, investment counselling, archaeology, medicine — these represent but a few of the fields to which parapsychology is fruitfully contributing. It should be obvious by now that ESP can serve as a valuable tool for both science and industry. The sixth sense is currently benefiting the needs of society in ways never dreamed of by the first experimental parapsychologists.

Putting the sixth sense to work will also finally silence the sceptic's ultimate gripe. More than a few of them like to challenge parapsychologists with an extremely barbed, but valid, point: Even *if* ESP and PK exist in the world, they demand to know what *good* these faculties represent. Parapsychologists have never really known what response to make to this charge. Their only recourse has been to say that psychic phenomena are probably telling us something extremely important about mankind's place in the physical world. But such an abstract point doesn't seem to impress the sceptic. But today the parapsychologist *can* respond to the sceptic's gripe: for ESP can be used to find missing people, help the sick, and locate lost civilizations. When all else fails, it can be used to make money!

But perhaps Dr Mishlove, today's chief exponent of psionic science, should be given the final word on the subject. He spoke on the importance and promise of psionics in 1984 at a private parapsychology conference which convened in New Orleans, Louisiana. There he stated that '. . . after one hundred years of research, our experimental researches and our theoretical progress have still been insufficient to establish a mainstream position in society for parapsychology. It may be that the demonstration of psi's practical influence will speak more directly and forcefully to a world in search of solutions.'

Society today still has important problems to solve — both social and scientific, not to mention spiritual. Parapsychology is a unique science since it can potentially contribute to each of these concerns. If the scientific establishment turns its back on the field, it turns its back on mankind in general.

End-Notes for Chapter Seventeen

* Evidence has recently come to light that Dr Pfungst conducted similar experiments to which the horses responded successfully. The eminent psychologist could not explain these results so he covered them up when he wrote his official report. See Remy Chauvin, *Parapsychology — When the Irrational Joins Science* (Jefferson, N. Carolina: McFarland, (1985).

† This isn't true since Targ and Puthoff do mention in *Mind-Reach* that Dr Hebard suggested that equipment failure could explain Swann's initial success.

§ This still, leaves us with a bit of a puzzle. Why was the Marks/ Kammann rejudging a failure, while Dr Tart — using the same design and procedures — came out positive? My guess is that Dr Tart's judge was probably more sympathetic to parapsychology. He therefore probably spent more time and care while making his evaluations. Judging remote viewing transcripts can be very time consuming, and the process simply can't be rushed or taken lightly.

References

The following abbreviations are used throughout the references:

AJN   *American Journal of Nursing*
AP   *Applied Psi*
BMJ   *British Medical Journal*
IJN   *International Journal of Neuropsychiatry*
IJP   *International Journal of Parapsychology*
JASPR   *Journal of the American Society for Psychical Research*
JCD   *Journal of Chronic Disease*
JP   *Journal of Parapsychology*
JSPR   *Journal of the Society for Psychical Research*
NR   *Nursing Research*
PASPR   *Proceedings of the American Society for Psychical Research*
PMS   *Perceptual and Motor Skills*
PR   *Parapsychology Review*
PSPR   *Proceedings of the Society for Psychical Research*
RIP   *Research in Parapsychology* [followed by year]

1. The Case for Parapsychology

Krippner, Stanley; Honorton, Charles and Montague Ullman. 'A second precognitive dream study with Malcolm Bessent.' *JASPR*, 1972, 66, 269–79.

Nicol, J. Fraser. 'Some difficulties in the way of scientific recognition of extrasensory perception.' In *Extrasensory Perception*, edited by G.E.W. Wolstenhome and Elaine C.P. Miller. New York: Citadel, 1965.

Palmer, John. 'Scoring in ESP tests as a function of belief in ESP.' *JASPR*, 1971, 65, 373–408/ 1972, 66, 1–26.

Ransom, Champe. 'Recent criticisms of parapsychology: A review.' *JASPR*, 1971, 65, 289–307.

Schmeidler, Gertrude and R.A. McConnell. *ESP and Personality Patterns*. New Haven, Conn.: Yale University Press, 1958.

Schmidt, Helmut. 'Precognition of a quantum process.' *JP*, 1969, 33, 99–108.

Schmidt, Helmut. 'A PK test with electronic equipment.' *JP*, 1970, 34, 175–81.

Tart, Charles. *The Application of Learning Theory to Extrasensory Perception*. New York: Parapsychology Foundation, 1975.

West, D. J. 'Reasons for continuing doubts about the existence of psychic phenomena.' In *A Century of Psychical Research — the continuing doubts and affirmations*, edited by Allan Angoff and Betty Shapin. New York: Parapsychology Foundation, 1971.

2. Isolating the Sixth Sense

Braud, Lendell and William Braud. 'Further studies of relaxation as a psi-conducive state.' *JASPR*, 1974, *68*, 229–45.

Braud, William and Lendell Braud. 'Preliminary explorations of psi-conducive states: progressive muscular relaxation.' *JASPR*, 1973, *67*, 26–46.

Braud, William; R. Wood; and Lendell Braud. 'Free-response GESP performance during an experimental state induced by visual and acoustic ganzfeld techniques: a replication and extension.' *JASPR*, 1975, *69*, 105–114.

Charlesworth, Edward. 'Psi and the imaginary dream.' *RIP 1974,* Metuchen, New Jersey: Scarecrow Press, 1975.

Dean, E. Douglas. 'Plethysmograph recordings as ESP responses' *IJN*, 1966, *2*, 439–47.

Green, Elmer and Alyce Green. *Beyond Biofeedback*. New York: Delacorte, 1977.

Honorton, Charles and Sharon Harper. 'Psi-mediated imagery and ideation in an experimental procedure for regulating perceptual input.' *JASPR*, 1974, *68*, 156–68.

Parker, Adrian. 'Some findings relevant to the change of state hypothesis.' *RIP 1974*, Metuchen, N.J.: Scarecrow Press, 1975.

Ullman, Montague and Stanley Krippner (with Alan Vaughan). *Dream Telepathy*. New York: Macmillan, 1973.

3. ESP Goes to the Races

Godley, John. *Tell Me the Next One*. London: 1950.

Lyttelton, Edith. *Some Cases of Prediction*. London: Bell, 1937.

Moss, Thelma and Harry Sands. 'Why did I flunk the horse test?' *PR*, 1970, *1* (No. 5), 10–12.

4. The Psychic and the Stock Market

Targ, Russell and Keith Harary. *The Mind Race*. New York: Villard, 1984.

5. A Workshop for Psychic Development

Targ, Russell and Harold Puthoff. *Mind-Reach*, New York: Delacorte, 1977.

Targ, Russell and Keith Harary. *The Mind Race*. New York: Villard, 1984.

6. Psychic Phenomena and the Brain

Broughton, Richard. 'Possible brain hemispheric laterality effects in ESP performance.' *JSPR*, 1976, *48*, 384–99.

Maher, Michaeleen. 'Correlated hemispheric assymetry in the sensory and ESP processing of continuous multiplex stimuli.' *RIP 1983*, Metuchen, N.J.: Scarecrow Press, 1984.

McHarg, James. 'An uncanny temporal lobe epilepsy apparition.' *RIP 1976,* Metuchen, N.J.: Scarecrow Press, 1977.

Neppe, Vernon. 'The relevance of the temporal lobe to anomalous subjective experience.' *RIP 1983.* Metuchen, N.J: Scarecrow Press, 1984.

Persinger, Michael. 'Propensity to report paranormal experiences is correlated with temporal lobe signs.' *PMS,* 1984, *59,* 583–86.

Persinger, Michael and P.M. Valliant. 'Temporal lobe signs and reports of subjective paranormal experiences in a normal population: A replication.' *PMS,* 1985, *60,* 903–909.

Roll, W.G. and Elson de A. Montagno. 'Neurophysiological aspects of psi.' *RIP 1984.* Metuchen, N.J.: Scarecrow Press, 1985.

Roll, W.G. and Elson de A. Montagno. 'Psi and the brain.' *RIP 1983.* Metuchen, N.J.: Scarecrow Press, 1984.

Rose, Steven. *The Conscious Brain.* New York: Vintage, 1976.

Solfvin, Gerald and W.G. Roll. 'A case of RSPK with an epileptic agent.' *RIP 1975.* Metuchen, N.J.: Scarecrow Press, 1976.

7. Can the Weather Make You Psychic?

Adams, Marsha. 'Variability in remote viewing performance: possible relationship to the geomagnetic field.' *RIP 1985,* Metuchen, N.J.: Scarecrow Press, 1986.

Persinger, Michael. 'Intense subjective telepathic experiences occur during days of quiet global geomagnetic activity.' *RIP 1985.* Metuchen, N.J.: Scarecrow Press, 1986.

Roney-Dougal, Serena. 'Some speculations on a possible psychic effect of harmaline.' *RIP 1985.* Metuchen, N.J.: Scarecrow Press, 1986.

Tromp, Solco. 'Effects of weather and climate on mental processes in man.' In *Parapsychology and the Sciences* edited by Allan Angoff and Betty Shapin. New York: Parapsychology Foundation, 1974.

8. The Search for ESP in Animals

Braud, William. 'Psychokinesis in aggressive and non-aggressive fish with mirror presenting feedback for hits: Some preliminary experiments.' *JP,* 1976, *40,* 296–307.

Duval, Pierre and Evelyn Montredon. 'Precognition in mice.' *JP,* 1968, *32,* 153–66.

Esser, Aristede, et. al. 'Preliminary report: Physiological concomitants of "communication" between isolated subjects.' *IJP,* 1967, *9,* 53–56.

Morris, Robert. 'Psi and animal behaviour: A survey.' *JASPR,* 1970, *64,* 242–60

Osis, Karlis and E.B. Foster. 'A test of ESP in cats.' *JP,* 1953, *17,* 168–86.

Randall, John. 'Experiments to detect a psi effect with small animals.' *JSPR,* 1975, *46,* 31–39.

Rhine, J.B. 'Location of hidden objects by a man-dog team.' *JP,* 1971, *35,* 18–33.

Rhine, J.B. and Sarah Feather. 'The study of cases of "psi-trailing" in animals.' *JP,* 1962, *26,* 1–22.

Richmond, Nigel. 'Two series of PK tests with paramecia.' *JSPR,* 1952, *36,* 577–88.

Rogo, D. Scott. 'J.B. Rhine and the Levy scandal.' In *The Skeptic's Handbook of*

Parapsychology, edited by Paul Kurtz. Buffalo, N.Y.: Prometheus Books, 1986.

Schmidt, Helmut. 'PK experiments with animals as subjects.' *JP*, 1970, *34*, 255–61.

Schouten, Sybo. 'Psi in mice: positive reinforcement.' *JP*, 1972, *36*, 261–82.

Terry, James and Susan Harris. 'Precognition in water-deprived rats.' *RIP 1974*, Metuchen, N.J.: Scarecrow Press, 1975.

9. The World's Greatest Psychics

Barker, David. 'Psi information and culture.' In *Communication and Parapsychology*, edited by Betty Shapin and Lisette Coly. New York: Parapsychology Foundation, 1980.

Barker, David. 'Psi phenomena in Tibetan culture.' *RIP 1978*. Metuchen, N.J.: Scarecrow Press, 1979.

Bogoras, Vladimir. *The Chukchee*. New York: Memoires of the American Museum of Natural History, 1904–1909.

Boshier, Adrian. 'African apprenticeship.' *PR*, 1974, *5* (No. 4), 1–3.

Eliade, Mircea. *Shamanism*. Princeton, N.J.: Princeton University Press, 1964.

Halifax, Joan. *Shamanic Voices*. New York: Dutton, 1979.

Lewis, I.M. *Ecstatic Religion*. New York: Penguin, 1971.

Neihardt, John. *Black Elk Speaks*. New York: Pocket Books, 1972.

Rose, Ronald. *Living Magic*. New York: Rand McNally, 1956.

10. The Threat of Psychic Warfare

Ebon, Martin. *Psychic Warfare — Threat or Illusion?* New York: McGraw Hill, 1984.

Gris, Henry and William Dick. *The New Soviet Psychic Discoveries*. Englewood Cliffs; N.J.: Prentice-Hall, 1978.

Honneger, Barbara. 'Encouraging and containing government involvement in psi research.' *RIP 1979*, Metuchen, N.J.: Scarecrow Press, 1980.

McRae, Ron. *Mind Wars*. New York: St. Martin's Press, 1984.

Roosevelt, Edith. 'Will ESP be the weapon of the future?' *New American*, 9 December 1985.

Targ, Russell and Keith Harary. *The Mind Race*. New York: Villard, 1984.

Targ, Russell, and Harold Puthoff, *Mind-Reach*. New York: Delacorte, 1977.

Swann, Ingo. *To Kiss Earth Good-bye*. New York: Hawthorn, 1975.

Swann, Ingo. *Star Fire*. New York: Dell, 1978.

11. The Psychic Power of Prayer

Breecher, Maury. 'Three cardiologists report prayers for their patients are answered.' *Medical Tribune*, 8 January 1986.

Collipp, Platon. 'The efficacy of prayers: A triple blind study.' *Medical Times*, 1969, *97*, 201–204.

Gardner, Rex. 'Miracles of healing in Anglo-Celtic Northumbria as recorded by the Venerable Bede and his contemporaries: A reappraisal in the light of twentieth century experience.' *BMJ*, 1983, *287*, 1927–33.

Joyce, C.R.B. and R.M.C. Welldon. 'The objective efficacy of prayer.' *JCD*, 1965, *18*, 367–77.

Loehr, Franklin. *The Power of Prayer on Plants*. New York: Doubleday, 1959.
Spraggett, Allen. *The Unexplained*. New York: New American Library, 1967.

12. Psychic Healing by Touch

Clark, Philip and Mary Jo Clark. 'Therapeutic touch: Is there a scientific basis for the practice.' *NR*, 1984, *33*, 37–41.
Heidt, Patricia. 'Effect of therapeutic touch on anxiety level of hospitalized patients.' *NR*, 1981, *30*, 33–37.
Krieger, Dolores. 'Healing by the laying-on-of-hands as a facilitator of bioenergetic change: The response of in-vivo human hemoglobin.' *Psychoenergetic Systems*, 1974, *1*, 121–29.
Krieger, Dolores. *Therapeutic Touch*, Englewood Cliffs, N.J.: Prentice-Hall, 1979.
Krieger, Dolores; Peper, Erick; and Sonia Ancoli. 'Therapeutic touch — searching for evidence of physiological change.' *AJN*, 1979 (April), 660–661.
Macrae, Janet. 'Therapeutic touch in practice.' *AJN*, 1979 (April), 664–65.
Quinn, Janet F. 'One nurse's evolution as a healer.' *AJN*, 1979, (April), 662–64.
Quinn, Janet F. 'Therapeutic touch as energy exchange: Testing the theory.' *Advances in Nursing Science*, January 1984.

13. Science Investigates the 'Flight of the Soul'

Crookall, Robert. *More Astral Projections*. London: Aquarian, 1964.
Crookall, Robert. *The Study and Practice of Astral Projection*. London: Aquarian, 1960.
Crookall, Robert. *A Case Book of Astral Projection*. Secaucus, N.J.: University Books, 1972.
Crookall, Robert. *Out-of-Body Experiences — A Fourth Analysis*. Secaucus, N.J.: University Books, 1974.
Fox, Oliver. *Astral Projection*. New Hyde Park, N.Y.: University Books, 1962.
Gabbard, Glenn and Stuart Twemlow. *With the Eyes of the Mind*. New York: Praeger, 1984.
Green, Celia. *Out-of-the-body Experiences*. London: Hamish Hamilton, 1968.
Greenhouse, Herbert. *The Astral Journey*. Garden City, N.Y.: Doubleday, 1975.
Gurney, Edmund; Myers, F.W.H.; and Frank Podmore. *Phantasms of the Living*, London: Trubner's, 1886.
Mitchell, Janet. 'Out-of-body vision.' In *Mind Beyond the Body* edited by D. Scott Rogo. New York: Penguin, 1978.
Muldoon, Sylvan and Hereward Carrington. *The Projection of the Astral Body*. London, Rider, 1929.
Osis, Karlis. 'Out-of-body research at the American Society for Psychical Research.' In *Mind Beyond the Body* edited by D. Scott Rogo. New York: Penguin, 1978, 162–69.
Osis, Karlis. 'New ASPR research on out-of-the-body experiences.' *Newsletter* of the American Society for Psychical Research, 1972, No. 14.
Osis, Karlis. 'Perceptual experiments on out-of-body experiences.' *RIP 1974*, Metuchen, N.J.: Scarecrow Press, 1975.

Palmer, John. 'ESP and out-of-body experiences: An experimental approach.' In *Mind Beyond the Body* edited by D. Scott Rogo, New York: Penguin, 1978.

Palmer, John. 'ESP and out-of-body experiences: EEG correlates.' *RIP 1978*, Metuchen, N.J.: Scarecrow Press, 1979.

Rogo, D. Scott. 'Experiments with Blue Harary.' In *Mind Beyond the Body*, New York: Penguin, 1978.

Tanous, Alex. *Beyond Coincidence*. Garden City, N.Y.: Doubleday, 1976.

Tart, Charles. 'A psychophysiological study of out-of-the-body experiences in a selected subject.' *JASPR*, 1968, 62, 3–27.

Tart, Charles. 'A second psychophysiological study of out-of-the-body experiences in a gifted subject.' *IJP*, 1967, 9, 251–58.

Yram. *Practical Astral Projection*. London: Rider, n.d.

14. New Evidence for Life After Death

Clark, Kimberly. 'Clinical interventions with near-death experiencers.' In *The Near-Death Experience* edited by Bruce Greyson and Charles Flynn. Springfield, IL.: Charles C. Thomas, 1984.

Gauld, Alan. 'A series of "drop-in" communicators.' *PSPR*, 1971, 55, 273-340.

Jay, Carroll. *Gretchen, I Am*. New York: Wyden, 1977.

Moody, Raymond. *Life after Life*. Atlanta, Georgia: Mockingbird Books, 1975.

Osis, Karlis. *Deathbed Observations by Physicians and Nurses*. New York: Parapsychology Foundation, 1961.

Osis, Karlis and Erlendur Haruldsson. *At the Hour of Death*. New York: Avon, 1977.

Ring, Kenneth. *Life at Death*. New York: Coward, McCann, Geoghegan, 1980.

Sabom, Michael. *Recollections of Death*. New York: Harper and Row, 1982.

Skutch, Judith and Tamara Cohen. *Double Vision*. Berkeley, CA: Celestial Arts, 1985.

Soal, S.G. 'A report of some communications received through Mrs Blanche Cooper.' *PSPR*, 1924, 46, 471–592.

Stevenson, Ian. 'Xenoglossy: A review and report of a case.' *PASPR*, 1974, 31, 1–268.

Stevenson, Ian. *Unlearned Language*. Charlottesville, VA: University of Virginia Press, 1984.

Stevenson, Ian. 'The combination lock test for survival.' *JASPR*, 1968, 62, 246–54.

Thouless, Robert. 'A test of survival.' *PSPR*, 1948, 48, 253–63.

15. Searching for Proof of Reincarnation

Jussek, Eugene. 'The puzzle of Charles: Many lives?' Unpublished ms.

Lenz, Frederick. *Lifetimes*. New York: Bobs-Merrill, 1979.

Rogo, D. Scott. *The Search for Yesterday*. Englewood Cliffs, N.J.: Prentice-Hall, 1985.

Stevenson, Ian. 'Reincarnation: field studies and theoretical issues.' In *The Handbook of Parapsychology* edited by Benjamin Wolman. New York: Van Nostrand Reinhold, 1977.

Stevenson, Ian. 'Twenty cases suggestive of reincarnation.' New York: American Society for Psychical Research, 1966.

Tarazi, Linda. 'The reincarnation of Antonia.' *Fate*, 1984, 37 (4), 50–56.

16. Do the Planets Influence Us?

Gauquelin, Michel. *Birthtimes*. New York: Hill and Wang, 1983.

Palmer, John. 'Parapsychology as a probabilistic science: Facing the implications.' *RIP 1979*, Metuchen, N.J.: Scarecrow Press, 1980.

Rawlins, Dennis. 'STarbaby.' *Fate*, 1981, 34 (10), 67–98.

17. The Failure of Scepticism

Carrington, Hereward. *Modern Psychical Phenomena*. New York: American Universities Publishing Co., 1920.

Eisenbud, Jule. 'Differing adaptives roles of psi in primitive and non-primitive societies.' *Psychoanalytic Review*, 1982, 69, 367–77.

Gardner, Martin. '*Science — good, bad and bogus.*' Buffalo, N.Y.: Prometheus, 1981.

Goodman, Jeffrey. *Psychic Archaeology*, New York: Berkely, 1977.

Gurney, Edmund; Myers, F.W.H. and Frank Podmore. *Phantasms of the Living*. London. Trubner's, 1886.

Maeterlinck, Maurice. *The Unknown Guest*. Secaucus, N.J.: University Books, 1975 (reprint).

Marks, David and Richard Kammann. *The Psychology of the Psychic*. Buffalo, N.Y.: Prometheus, 1980.

Mishlove, Jeffrey. 'Psionics: The practical application of psi abilities.' *AP*, 1984, 3, (fall issue), 10–14.

Puthoff, Harold and Russell Targ. 'Information transmission under conditions of sensory shielding.' *Nature*, 1974, 252, 602–607.

Randi, James. *Flim-Flam!* New York: Lippincott/Crowell, 1980.

Rhine, J.B. 'The question of practical application of parapsychical abilities.' *JP*, 1945, 9, 77–79.

Sagan, Carl. *Broca's Brain*. New York: Random House, 1978.

Sidgwick, Henry, et. al. 'Report on the Census of Hallucinations.' *PSPR*, 1894, 10, 25–422.

Targ, Russell and Harold Puthoff. *Mind-Reach*. New York: Delacorte, 1977.

Tart, Charles. *Learning to Use ESP.* Chicago: University of Chicago Press, 1976.

Index